THE
PLATEAU

THE
PLATEAU

MAGGIE PAXSON

RIVERHEAD BOOKS

New York

2019

RIVERHEAD BOOKS
An imprint of Penguin Random House LLC
penguinrandomhouse.com

Library of Congress Cataloging-in-Publication Data

Names: Paxson, Margaret, author.
Title: The plateau / Maggie Paxson.
Description: New York : Riverhead Books, 2019
Identifiers: LCCN 2018050747 (print) | LCCN 2019012889 (ebook) |
ISBN 9780698408739 (ebook) | ISBN 9781594634758 (hardcover)
Subjects: LCSH: Le Chambon-sur-Lignon (France)—Emigration and
immigration. | Refugees—France—Le Chambon-sur-Lignon—History—
20th century. | Refugees—France—Le Chambon-sur-Lignon—History—
21st century. | World War, 1939–1945—Refugees—France—Le Chambon-
sur-Lignon. | Refugee children—France—Le Chambon-sur-Lignon. |
Le Chambon-sur-Lignon (France) | Anthropologists—Biography. |
Paxson, Margaret.
Classification: LCC JV7990.C43 (ebook) | LCC JV7990.C43 P39 2019 (print) |
DDC 362.870944/595—dc23
LC record available at https://lccn.loc.gov/2018050747

Printed in the United States of America
1   3   5   7   9   10   8   6   4   2

BOOK DESIGN BY AMANDA DEWEY

So much is in a name, but for the sake of their privacy and safety—now
and in the future—I have changed the names (and certain identifying features)
of the people who appear in the present day in *The Plateau*, with the exception of
public figures and published historians. To mitigate the loss, I have renamed
each person with a name, attribute, color, or sound that I love. I've also tried to
preserve in the spelling something of the languages of the names' origins. For
example, in Chechen, a language with a complex sound system, the consonant
transcribed as *kh* comes in a few forms, but if you hear the Hebrew *chai* in
your head, as in Hanukkah (or even the *ch* as in the Scottish Gaelic *loch*),
it's close enough; *dzh* is more or less an English *j*; and so on.

For Charles and, in memoriam, for Daniel.
Bright angels.

CONTENTS

Chapter 1. UNANSWERED   *1*

Chapter 2. DAYS OF AWE   *17*

Chapter 3. EXODUS   *29*

Chapter 4. FIRST ON THE ROPE   *49*

Chapter 5. ALL THE LITTLE CRICKETS   *70*

Chapter 6. HANDS AND FEET   *97*

Chapter 7. THE HUNT   *122*

Chapter 8. HYMN TO SPRING   *151*

Chapter 9. LA BURLE   *169*

Chapter 10. ELSEWHERE   *188*

Chapter 11. SUFFER THE CHILDREN   *208*

Chapter 12. SONG OF THE *CHEREMSHA*   *232*

Chapter 13. ALONG CAME A SPIDER   *258*

Chapter 14. MASHALLAH   *290*

Chapter 15. THE FRUIT OF THE TREE   *319*

Acknowledgments 351

A Note on Sources 355

*Il y avait, sur une étoile, une planète, la mienne,
la Terre, un petit prince à consoler!*

—ANTOINE DE SAINT-EXUPÉRY, *Le Petit Prince*

Chapter 1

UNANSWERED

I Daniel was grieved in my spirit in the midst of my
body, and the visions of my head troubled me.

—DANIEL 7:15

L ET'S JUST SAY THAT suddenly you are a social scientist and you want
to study peace. That is, you want to understand what makes for a
peaceful society. Let's say that, for years in your work in various parts of
the world, you've been surrounded by evidence of violence and war.
From individual people, you've heard about beatings and arrests and
murders and rapes; you've heard about deportations and black-masked
men demanding people's food or their lives. You've heard about family
violence and village violence and state violence. You've heard these stories from old women with loose, liquid tears; from young men with arms
full of prison tattoos.

There were men on horseback calling the boys to war, and long black
cars arriving to steal people away in the dead of night; girls who'd wandered the landscape, insane after sexual violations; there was the survival of the fittest in concentration camps; there were pregnant women
beaten until their children were lost, and bodies piled up in times of
famine; there was arrest and exile for the theft of a turnip; there were

those who were battered for being a Jew or a Christian or a Muslim or a Bahá'í.

Let's say that, in the world of ideas that swirled around you, approximations were made of how to make sense of this mess: the presence of certain kinds of states; the presence of certain kinds of social diversity; the presence of certain kinds of religion. And let's say that the shattering stories had piled on over the years until, at some point, you just snapped. You wanted to study war no more.

As it turns out, it's harder to study peace than you might think.

Or it has been for me. I'm an anthropologist who spent years living among country people—mostly in a couple of tiny villages in Russia—asking basic questions about how memory works in groups. I had some ideas about how I might start a search for peace. After all, even though the stories of violence were many, for the most part people seemed occupied with other things: They worked in kitchens or fields, hauled water, made decisions about what to do based on the weather, ate with guests, cleaned up after livestock. Even if they bristled sometimes, people generally faced each other day to day with working problems and working solutions. There was love and there were revelries and heartbreaks. And in spite of what they'd seen in life, or what their very own hands might have wrought on their worst days, people saw themselves as basically decent, and expected basic decency back from the world.

Surely, there had to be ways of looking for that kind of eye-to-eye decency. Surely, there were ways to study its power and its limits, particularly when people were faced with tempestuous times. Were there communities out there that were good at being good when things got bad? In my research on memory, I'd studied practices of resistance and persistence. Could there be communities that were somehow resistant to violence, persistent in decency? I didn't know exactly what I was on to, but I knew I wanted to study it. In shorthand, I called it peace.

But peace was hard to find. I dug into contemporary scholarship in anthropology, sociology, and political science; I went through databases and bibliographies and talked to colleagues who had been in the trenches with me in the study of a tumultuous Eurasia, and to other colleagues in peace studies programs or peace institutes. What I found was this: There is vastly more contemporary social science on violence than there is on peace. And most contemporary empirical research that says it is about peace is really about conflict. About resolving conflict, cleaning up after conflict, about programs to bring aid to people in conflict settings. About law and justice within the context of conflict. On the whole, these literatures are about peace only insofar as they point to the suffering of millions, and lament.

This kind of work is important, but it wasn't what I was looking for. I wanted social science that landed smack on the inside of peaceful societies and studied human interactions at ground level there, distilling something about how peace works in its tight mechanics. I wanted empirical research that regarded the social body up close and asked about its long-term health and stability; research that asked how, in hard times, regular decency can sometimes translate into extraordinary kindness. Here and there I found brilliant examples of work like this, but strikingly few of them.

Why, I began to wonder, is peace so hard to think about? Or conversely, why is violence so easy?

When writers and academics talk about violence, it can seem to have a "thingness," to stand out from the background. It can be counted (a shot, an explosion, a bullet, a death), or so we believe. It can be added up and placed into data sets. In the aggregate, and with a measure of confidence, political scientists can fit violent acts into models, which they use to make statements about the world. Violence happens: a gun goes off; a person is killed; a neighborhood is raided; a border is breached. The n is large here; the data take shape. We can decide that more violence happens, say, when there are more young men than usual, or when there is a weak state, or mountains, or too much petrol in an economy. Violence happens, and it is awful, and it is counted; and from that counting, the contours of probable outcomes are given a local habitation and a name.

But can peace be counted? Where is it located? When does it

happen? Peace lacks this analyzable "thingness": It seems like a non-event, a null set. Characterizations of peace and peaceful societies—from the Eden of the Bible to the "radiant future" of Lenin—look dull and flat, or else gauzy and kitsch. As a child, I would leaf through *The Children's Illustrated Bible* in the dentist's waiting room. In the Eden of those illustrations, religious peace looks like the beatific expressions of light-skinned people gazing heavenward. Perhaps a lamb sits there, too, legs folded, under a tree. Peace is bland and blond, utterly lacking the dark ring of truth.

The political peace of Marx and other visionaries of the nineteenth century is not much easier to make out. In the end, at any rate in Marx's version, it looks like getting to hunt and fish when you want and passing around the milk can so everyone gets a fair share. It's the end of history there, in the land of peace at the end of time, after the wars have all been fought and all the blood is shed. On the subject of capitalism, Marx was keen-eyed, detail-oriented, and extremely voluble. But when it came to imagining communism in practice, he, too, reverted, in effect, to lambs, legs folded, under a tree.

In these visions, peace is a thing only to the extent that it is an impenetrable, immovable, unchanging thing. There is a long philosophical history to this line of thinking, but the gist—with a nod to Descartes and his venerable method—is this: Some stuff (the physical world) is amenable to science and scientific law, while other stuff (poetry, theology, the matter of emotion) just isn't. Peace—a place where nothing ever happens—can't, in our easy thinking, be divided up at all. And if it can't be divided, it can't be studied; only felt. That's a terrible shame. After all, what could be more important than the actual content of peace? What could be more useful, when you look into the eyes of individual people who have faced violence right up close, than to have some understanding of what kind of effort peace might take? Of what ingenious (or even banal) habits it depends upon?

It's worth trying, no?

What if we began by regarding peace not as timeless, but as dynamic; not located in the beginning or the end, but in the unfolding; something not of the ether, but of lived grounds and interactions; something not perfect but flawed and rough-grained? Social science can handle that. It can handle dynamics, can look toward the *longue durée*, settling happily into the study of actual, imperfect behavior. That kind of research requires no calls to the angels or to Elysium. You just look into the faces of real people and the connections they make or don't make with each other, the stories they tell or don't tell, and the ways they decide or don't decide to treat a stranger as one of their own.

If peace can be this—defined within a regular, real kind of social world—how, then, would you know a peaceful community when you saw one?

A lack of violence would be a good start, of course—though this is a definition in the negative, like defining health in terms of the absence of illness, and not as the brilliant sum of systems that preserve the spark of life. Still, it's useful. Some recent research on social networks seems to show that violence is less likely when there are deep and common contacts between communities. It also seems that societies where girls are educated are less likely to be violent. In some warring parts of the world, it is possible to identify—and count and describe—specific communities that somehow manage to avoid the scourge of war and become, in effect, "peace enclaves." Little by little, with the help of data, we can begin to pinpoint places in the world where violence goes down and down—perhaps, someday, all the way to zero. And this is an excellent start.

Still, for me, the close-up is necessary. What is peace, face-to-face, even as war rages all around? You should be able to find it, in how a community solves even its small problems; how it handles inequality and sharing; how it defines and deals with diversities; how it makes a habit of protecting the vulnerable in troubled times; how some behaviors become, in effect, unthinkable within it.

If you want to study peace, face-to-face, you need to find peaceful faces. And you need to have a plan. And you need to start counting things, maybe, but the right things.

Above all, you need an example.

I HAVE AN AUNT, Barbara, who sends me things—mostly little family keepsakes and her own artwork. Years ago, she sent me a book that arrived smelling of old wood and tin. That book, *Lest Innocent Blood Be Shed*, by Philip Hallie, seemed special—and my aunt said that our family was somehow connected to its story—but I didn't read it right away.

Then one day—after many travels and many adventures, and many hours contemplating the meaning of violence I had learned of up close—I did.

It was a remarkable story, set on a tiny plateau in south-central France called Vivarais-Lignon. From 1939 to 1945, the people of Vivarais-Lignon took in hundreds if not thousands of strangers who had been doomed by the Nazi occupation of the Second World War. They were farmers, tradesmen, clergy, teachers, and politicians—and despite terrifying conditions all around, they fed the strangers, hid them, schooled them, and eventually ferried them off to safety in Switzerland. The rescuers were in constant mortal danger. And indeed, some villagers were punished by the German occupiers and the collaborating French police. Some were killed.

How many people—as a collective, no less—would do this? How many would gird themselves for the mortal haul? And how many, in the face of the daily pressure to go with the forces of the blood-dimmed tide, would resist? These people, tested by fire, landed far on the end of the bell curve drawn by "rational choice." So rare was their shared effort during the Holocaust that the community of Vivarais-Lignon is one of only two to be singled out by Israel's Yad Vashem for memorialization in its Garden of the Righteous Among the Nations.

Was their effort during the Holocaust a brilliant fluke—or something more, some deeper reflection of their social practice? Hard to say, but there is this: It turns out that for hundreds of years—from the time of the first religious wars in France, through revolutions, colonial wars, and the fascist and nationalist conflagrations of broader Europe—the community of Vivarais-Lignon has been, on and off, actively sheltering vulnerable peoples in violent times. So perhaps the people living in this high plateau do know things that we don't. Perhaps we can learn them.

And so, having found an example of a place on the end of the bell curve, a place where common decency seemed to have become *un*common decency, I began to hold this example up like a precious stone, its structure a crystalline mystery.

ONE DAY, I decided to hitch a ride with friends to Washington, D.C., to visit the United States Holocaust Memorial Museum, which promised to take me down into the depths of the story that was drawing me forward.

The museum's interior is a marvel of evocation: You enter into the rust-gray walls of an elevator. As the doors open, the story begins, as it will end, in darkness. Right away, there are images of skeletal human beings looking straight into the camera—one man, bald and in rags, holding a metal bowl—and corpses on train tracks, in Buchenwald and Dachau. Then you walk, in the dark, toward the story of the rise of Nazism. Photographs of men with swastika armbands; of muzzled dogs, eye-high and ready for attack. Songs that, even if you don't know German, sound like the melody of a nation careening toward its moral end. Down the hall, you see posters from the 1930s that explain the Nuremberg Laws, using little stick silhouettes in white (for Aryan), black (for Jew), and gray (for somewhere in between). And then, artifacts of that era's hair samples, and eye-color testers, and metal instruments invented to assess the size of a forehead, a nose, or a skull—all to determine the hidden presence of a Jew. Here, up close, is the science of race in all its Weimar glory—early anthropology's poisoned fruit.

I wound my own way through the exhibit, feeling my hand brush up against the railing from time to time in the dark. The war years passed like the ticking of a great, unstoppable clock. *Tick.* 1938: Kristallnacht. Jews race over borders, smuggle themselves onto ships, fleeing as they can. *Tick.* 1939: The German army—eager to increase the *Lebensraum* for the Aryans of the Third Reich—gobbles portions of the Czech lands and Poland, and Jews are sent to ghettos. *Tick.* Spring of 1940: France falls. *Tick.* 1941: Germany advances its armies eastward toward Russia, Ukraine, Belarus, followed quickly by elite mobile killing units called Einsatzgruppen. Village by village, SS soldiers aim guns at locals together with the question, "Where are your Jews?" and the goal: to gather, shoot, and kill them all. *Tick. Tick.* Babi Yar.

I paused here. Babi Yar, Ukraine. This was the site where, on September 29 and 30, 1941, more than thirty-three thousand Jews were collected in downtown Kiev, marched past throngs of onlookers, led to the edge of a forest, up to the precipitous edge of a ravine. There, those more than thirty-three thousand people were shot and killed and sent tumbling into the depths below. The Babi Yar massacre in Kiev has been called the largest single massacre in the history of the Holocaust, and one of the deadliest episodes of mass killing in the entire history of human conflict.

Once, I visited Babi Yar myself, alone on a dark December day. The massive site was trash-strewn, its memorials adorned with frozen sputum. I saw, in nature itself, signs of dreadful return: Trees had grown up everywhere, their branches like skeleton fingers grasping at the mud-gray skies; a pack of dogs barked madly around a single dog, piteously alone; a vast murder of crows hunkered in a tree-lined allée, turning over rotting leaves one by one, as if working at some great silent enterprise—grounded, earthly, wing-clipped.

Tick. Tick. Tick.

From there, in the museum, the depths grew deeper, darker. Hidden from the gaze of children, but not from me, were a series of grainy black-and-white films showing scenes of violence erupting toward Jews: women, clothes torn from their bodies, taunted by onlookers in the gray bitter chill in the air; men, safe in their prickly woolen suits, laughing as the women, soft and pale, caved into themselves and wept. There were taunting onlookers, laughing onlookers, onlookers who covered their mouths or closed their eyes as frail Jewish bodies tangled themselves together, inert now and forever more.

As I stood in front of these grim artifacts, a terrible thought came rushing toward me in the dark: Anyone, at some point, might be asked— with a gun, eye-high, pointed right at his face—"Where are your Jews?"

And what if this anyone has been himself starving? What if he has been reduced to eating grass and sawdust? What if he has watched his neighbor sent to exile for the theft of a turnip? How do you know who you will be?

I want to be good, I thought to myself. But how do I know—how do any of us know—what we will be when the army advances and the guns are waved?

Maybe we like to think there's a kind of trumpet blast that sounds through history, that tells us when it is time to be on the side of the angels. But what if the trumpet doesn't blast? What if the moments are so small— say, a neighbor who asks to come in even as I pretend not to be at home— that they pass without notice? And what if I am left, then, in terrible times, with my own frailties? Would I be good? Would I be good, after all?

But the museum pulls you ever forward. You keep walking with your questions. There is no choice.

1942: The Final Solution. *Tick*, the Ghettos and the Work Camps and the Killing Centers and the great metal sign, ARBEIT MACHT FREI—work makes you free—and *Tick*, the medical experiments and the models of gas chambers.

Beyond, in the dark, you see a hall filled to the ceiling with family photographs from shtetls destroyed; whole rooms full of shoes; a metal table from one extermination camp, Majdanek, where corpses were ransacked for their gold teeth before heading to the ovens. It is worse and worse down there, in the depths. Closer to some essential barbarity. Deeper and deeper; worse and worse.

After the shoes and the ovens, after the images of tattooed arms, the room of photographs that might as well rise all the way up to the sky . . . there is, finally, one last floor to the museum. This one is dedicated to rescue and resistance during the Holocaust. Here are different kinds of things: a photograph of Oskar Schindler, and the story of his famous list; the story of the Danish boat that transported thousands of Jews to safety in Sweden in October 1943; the stories of Jewish fighters who lived in forests and the youthful anti-Nazi groups like the White Rose.

On a far wall, an exhibit shows blurry images of houses on the edge of piney hills; of young people in groups, playing in the snow, carrying pails of milk, sitting in the window frames of great stone buildings, legs dangling down. Framing the whole of the exhibit are photographs of individual children—dark-eyed children, light-haired children, smiling children, knit-browed children; each face a mustard seed containing, up close, an entire world.

This was the story of that cluster of villages on the Plateau Vivarais-Lignon, whose community had collectively rescued hundreds, thousands of people—most of them children—from near-certain death at the hands of the Nazis.

And that's where I saw a name I knew: Trocmé.

In my mind's eye, I called up an image: my great-grandfather Dr. Henry Sweany. He is bent and ash-white with age, stern, sitting on a couch bathed in sunlight, wearing a bow tie. Next to him is his second wife, Suzie. She is small, smiling, kind, with a tidy black bob. Suzie, who once told my Jewish mother that her own family had been part of the French Resistance during the Second World War. Suzie Trocmé.

Once, Suzie had sent me a letter, and I never answered her.

———

I grew up in Rochester, New York, in a small wooden house in a row of other small wooden houses on Salisbury Street. Kids would careen around on bikes all summer long in the neighborhood—down streets of the twiggy new trees that replaced the elms felled in the blight of the 1960s, through overgrown back lots, then maybe up to Calabrese's bakery, where the older boys smoked pot on the roof. At five o'clock the mothers, cigarettes hanging from their mouths, would start screaming to get their piles of kids home for dinner, and sooner or later, the kids would oblige.

My family were, in a way, immigrants to Salisbury Street. My dad, Dana, an artist by training and by lineage, goateed and high-browed, spoke with the straight-spine precision of a midwesterner. In college, he made wooden sculptures splashed with gobs of paint, destroyed them, and took pictures of the rubble. *Click.* Now, every evening, the number 9 Bay/Webster bus would drop him off after a long day at the Xerox offices in downtown Rochester—he'd learned computer programming on the fly after my sister was born—and he'd pace his way down the street toward home in his spongy suit and wide striped tie. My mother, Flo, a New Yorker, a corker, a pip, was little and dark and Jewish. She knew how to argue. She knew how to dance, how to pitch a baseball, how to elbow her way in with a hug.

We were immigrants in the sense that in the Salisbury Street land of the cracked-open Genny cream ale, and the well-earned weekend, and the wide-open nasal *aaaaaaaaaaaa*, my family was mostly pretty earnest and eggheaded. And because nobody else quite looked like us ("Ha-ha-ha-ha, she's got a witchy noooooose," kids would yell as I zoomed by on my bike). And because, in an inner city of intricate and rigid patchworks of white and black and brown folks, my little brother happened to be a ravishing mix of all three. And maybe also because of religion: While other kids were rehearsing their sins for confession on Sunday, we were heading to Hebrew school out in the suburbs, where I learned how to dress up like Queen Esther and say *sheket bevakashah*; and then crosstown to Bahá'í classes, where we would sing, together black and white and brown, "We are drops (—we are drops—) of one ocean (—of one ocean—), we are pearls (—we are pearls—) of one sea (—of one sea—) . . ."

Still, like everyone, we would careen through that small world that we knew, block by added block, and have pizza nights, and go to Seabreeze Amusement Park, and have some extras in life, but not so many. And we would share anxieties in the long wake of the race riots of the 1960s, when anger periodically exploded and then hardened, so all the children of all the colors had to wonder, periodically, on their long walks home from school, "Is that kid going to throw a rock at my head?"

Together, we would swim, eyes wide open, in the murky brown waters of Lake Ontario and, when chance permitted, grab one of a mass of thousands of poisoned silver fish as they floated toward the shore and toss them at one another. And scream.

Together, we would panic over the Alphabet Murders, where a series of little girls were stalked, snatched, raped, and murdered. One of the girls—Michelle Maenza—lived just a few blocks over, and was in a class with my big sister; now, when we drove around town on both sides of the Genesee River, great rusty billboards with her looming little face, and guileless little eyes, and pigtails bowed with yarn were a lesson to us all about the penalty for talking to strangers.

And together, we would trudge below the milk-and-water gray skies of the long winters; wobble around and around the skating rink at the corner rec center, swirling through the sweet smell of wet wood and sweat. And, when walking alone late at night in those winters, the streetlamps would light the whole of the broad cottony sky. And, then, it was as though you could feel the turning of the earth beneath your feet right there on Salisbury Street—so quiet it was in the night, and so warm and monumental and bright it was, in the darkness.

From time to time I, with my long stringy hair and my long witchy nose, would sneak off into someone's yard, and scramble up into one of Salisbury Street's few remaining climbable trees, and perch for a while—twisting the stems of fire-red maple leaves as I did—and think. And imagine worlds beyond.

The summer I was fifteen years old, a friend of mine from the trimmer, tonier side of Rochester invited me to go with her family on a trip to

Austria. I would board a plane alone, meet them all in Frankfurt, and then, after a week in Europe, take a train to a village on the Tyrolean border with Italy, and I would stay a month with the family of a girl named Karin.

It was amazing that my parents let me go. In our family, money generally went toward essentials or, if not that, then for college funds, or trips where we'd pile, all five of us, into the orange Plymouth Volaré to stay in motels with outdoor pools. *Marco! Polo!* It was dearly paid for, you could say, in foreign currency. But it was well worth it. That Austrian village was where I first learned to let the music of foreign languages wash over me; where I first heard Gershwin's "Rhapsody in Blue"; where I first heard someone say, as she pointed out of a window on a train, "That's where Hitler was born."

It was while I was in Austria that Suzie—Suzanne Trocmé—wrote to me. At the time, I could barely place who Suzie was. I knew she was part of the feminine swirl that surrounded my paternal grandmother, Dorothy. Dorothy had once been a ballerina with the San Carlo Opera Company, clacking along on trains all across America during the Depression. But in 1954, her husband was killed in a plane crash, leaving her to transform from ballerina into junior high school art teacher, and raise my dad and my aunts Barbara and Elizabeth, in genteel poverty, alone. Suzie was my grandmother's stepmother, as it were, and my own mother had gushed about her warmth and kindness.

On thin blue paper, Suzie Trocmé wrote to invite me to come visit her in Montpellier, near France's Mediterranean coast. She even drew a little map of where Montpellier was, relative to my village in the mountains. Of course I wanted to go. I had been dreaming about France as only a fifteen-year-old can: I saw myself walking, gauzily clad, through the very same fields of Arles where Vincent van Gogh had lost his mind. But I was only a teenager, and graceless. I didn't know how I could even ask my mother about seeing Suzie in France; it wasn't like it was easy to call home from abroad back then. How would I get there? How could I pay for it? I choked. I left the letter unanswered. There would be no visit.

Now, in an exhibit on the final floor of the Holocaust Museum, I again encounter Suzie's name.

The exhibit tells how a pastor, André Trocmé, and his wife, Magda, were among those who figured prominently in the rescue effort on the Plateau. An image of André shows a tall man in glasses, standing next to a striking woman with dark braids folded at her temples, surrounded by four children. Born in Saint-Quentin, France, the pastor was a fierce charismatic, a proponent of the philosophy of nonviolence; in the 1920s, he was reading Thoreau and Gandhi at Union Theological Seminary in New York; by the late 1930s, he was posted to the faraway town of Le Chambon-sur-Lignon, on the Plateau Vivarais-Lignon. Magda, it was said, never turned away from her door a person in need. Both were part of the French Resistance, but this was resistance of a nonviolent—if no less perilous—kind: retrieving Jews from concentration camps, finding homes for them, finding work and schools for them, helping them move on toward Switzerland.

I let my eyes float over the rest of the exhibit, taking in a sea of children's faces. Children who, in the days before the war, must have barreled through their own worlds—steering their bikes through streets, block by added block, discovering the fire-red leaves of their own trees, knowing the clocked rhythms of their own waking and studying and sleeping, and the crunching rhythm of their own snow-walks on moonlit nights; falling in love with some boy or girl, or in hate with some kid from the other street. These were children who once had, surely, arms to hold them in the fearsome night. Who belonged to someone.

I looked at those faces, one by one. I thought about what their singularity meant, in this pitch-black place. The text to the exhibit said: "Nobody asked who was Jewish and who was not. Nobody asked where you were from. Nobody asked who your father was or if you could pay. . . ."

Who was this André Trocmé to Suzie? I had no idea.

But that's when I saw that there was another Trocmé mentioned in the exhibit. This was André's cousin—a lanky young man with thick darkish hair, swept back, with full lips and dark eyes behind spectacles, and ears that stuck out.

This Trocmé, I would come to learn, was Suzie's little brother. He'd arrived on the Plateau Vivarais-Lignon in the late summer of 1942. *Tick.* There, he directed first one and then two homes for refugee children and young people on the hilly outskirts of Le Chambon-sur-Lignon. By the summer of 1943, he was arrested in a raid, and spent the next several months in concentration camps in France, then Germany, and then Poland. He died in Majdanek in the spring of 1944. *Tick.*

A light switched on in the darkness for me. His name was Daniel.

And so, a new journey began for me—a journey toward a place called Vivarais-Lignon, a journey to reconcile things-as-they-are with things-as-they-might-be.

One day, I woke up a social scientist. Then, I snapped. I wanted to study war no more. And I started thinking about how I might do that, started looking at stories that might help me learn.

"It is connected to our family," my aunt Barbara said, her melodic voice trailing in my head for years, as I held up that single gem, inside that book that even today smells like old wood and tin. I know my Durkheim and *le social*. Social science doesn't need my family. It doesn't need—from Salisbury Street—me. When it comes to the story of the large-scale *n*, and the brilliant end of the bell curve, it doesn't even want me.

But it seemed there was nothing I could do.

Somewhere, between the lines of that book from my aunt—and then elsewhere, and again, elsewhere—stood a figure . . . a figure connected to my family. And that figure, who was long dead, long gone, began to haunt my own journey. And to steer it.

Taped to my wall is Daniel's photograph, printed on tea-stained paper. He is in three-quarter profile. He is young. He is wearing glasses and a tie, his dark hair carefully combed back. Next to his face, in my own handwriting, are penciled the following words: *Arrest, June 29, 1943. Moulin Prison. Compiègne. 1943. Buchenwald. Dora. (Heart problem.) 1944. Majdanek.*

I look at his face. His gaze reaches into the indefinite distance. His expression is inscrutable.

There is such a thing as good science, properly applied. There is the question of how things work. But then there is also the question of how, as plans are mislaid and theories crumble, we might just be claimed, ourselves, by a larger purpose than we imagine.

I am a social scientist; I want to study war no more. But it turns out, I can't do it alone.

Chapter 2

DAYS OF AWE

Blessed are You, Lord our God,
King of the universe,
Who creates the fruit of the tree.

—ROSH HASHANAH BLESSING
FOR THE APPLES AND HONEY

Y OU OPEN THE BOOK OF LIFE and the story begins. And what do you first see?

"Good night, darling," the nanny would whisper to him, in some of the few English words she knew. "Sleep well . . ."

Daniel was a boy with wavy light brown hair and ears that stuck out in magnificent curves. He had a soft, round mouth, and eyes that could lock into the distance. They say he was a smiling child. A laughing child. *Un enfant délicieux*—a delicious child. Surely he loved his nanny, who lived with his family in their home outside Verneuil-sur-Avre, in Normandy, and who called him, softly, darling. One day she was sick with a cold and he thought she was crying. "'Zelle"—mademoiselle, he said, rushing to her—"you shouldn't cry! Dani is here!"

Daniel's parents, Henri Trocmé and Eve, née Rist, were both from old and influential families. The ancestral tree was solid as an oak, its history written in the annals of great French lineages. From the seventeenth century forward, Trocmés settled in a cluster of villages in the northeast region of Picardy, France, where many of the local noble families—Trocmés included—had converted to the dangerous new religion of Protestantism. In the centuries that followed, with religious wars and then the antireligious aftermath of the French Revolution, the Trocmés and their neighbors lived, on and off, in fear, worshipping in hiding, at night, in a chalky quarry known as the Boîte à Cailloux, the Box of Stones. As Protestantism became more and more normal in France—and as Protestants were able to come out of hiding and into broader society—the Trocmé family flourished. Soon, along with the landowners and ministers of Daniel's line, there was a noted sculptor, a *médecin aliéniste*—a nineteenth-century proto-psychologist—and even a Knight in the Legion of Honor.

Daniel's father was one of the founders and directors of the elite boarding school École des Roches. The school was leafy, orderly, Apollonian; the core of the campus included large lawns, tall trees, and the ribbon of a river, all surrounded by hundreds of acres of fields and woods. Everywhere were signs of dewy wealth: the stables, the outdoor pool, the tennis courts, the elegant residences where staff and students lived together in cozy homelike environments with huge hearths and pianos in the foyers. But while the school was patently intended for the rich, it was founded, too, on a kind of modern get-up-and-go principle called active learning, where, along with classical subjects, students were exposed to down-to-earth problem solving. The study of science required actual lab work in the classroom; out in the fields and waters and stables beyond the classroom, students would figure out how things grew by growing them, or how things flew by flying them. It was a real innovation at the time, that you could aim to create, among the nation's most fortunate sons, an uncoddled generation of problem solvers who, as the school's motto read, would be *bien armé pour la vie*. Well armed for life.

Still, there was much at Roches that reinforced the school's ties to that elite wider world where class and continuity ruled. The director would smoke a pipe with children sitting in a circle around him, heads tilted back, looking up at him, rapt. Religious education and worship—in both Catholic and Protestant chapels—were crucial. The older students wore ties and jackets with fashionable pointy collars; the younger ones wore knickers that puffed out below the knees. At the beginning of the school year, parents dropped off their children in great shiny motorcars, or—just years after the Wright Brothers figured out how—on an airstrip a couple of kilometers away. The children of Roches would lead France someday, from the fields and from the skies.

Henri and Eve had nine children: Marianne, Charles, Elisabeth, Michel, François, Suzanne (Suzie), Daniel, Geneviève, and Robert. When Daniel was born, the mayor sent out a birth notice for him. It was late April 1912, and just weeks earlier the *Titanic* had set out from the nearby port city of Cherbourg toward the unconquerable seas. It was the end of the age of unself-conscious empire; the beginning of the age of great world wars; and the time of the full ascent of those gods of modernity—the nation, the race, the ethnically pure. Daniel was born into a world, then, at the edge of a great precipice. And that April, clouds were darkening in the distance.

At Roches, young Daniel—with his owl glasses, and his magnificent ears, and his curly hair, and his smile that appears more wistful in photographs than the notes of his brothers might lead you to believe—was beloved, if not, in any outward measure, extraordinary. He was a child who possessed some curiosity, yes, and a certain talent in mathematics and physics—in those subjects he was at the top of his class—but otherwise, he was an unremarkable student. Notes from his teachers would say things like "evident goodwill" but "a chatterbox [*bavard*] . . . and inattentive," or "has difficulty singing on the right notes," or "a good little man—a little childish (that's a compliment)—but already so serious, so grave."

Childish, childlike, alternatively chatty and grave, singing out loud but wrong, Daniel also suffered crippling bouts of pericarditis, a condition where fluid collects around the heart and can lead to terrifying pain in breathing. Suzie and Daniel, closest in age, "loved each other tenderly," wrote their eldest brother, Charles, many years later, but Daniel, along with his brothers, also jumped into the animated debates that would arise in the heady evenings of their childhood. The older brothers, and Suzie herself, studied well: Charles would become a prominent physician; Michel, a banker; François, a factory director. Suzie, too, would become a physician, specializing in work with tubercular patients. Daniel's ambitions were comparatively unformed. Once he confided in Suzie, *"Je veux rayonner."* I want to shine.

In photographs of the family, Henri is erect, mustachioed, bespectacled; Eve is next to him, with sad, kind eyes and straight hair pulled back in a bun; the older brothers stand with hips cocked assuredly in woolen suits; the sisters are sitting, hands folded, hair in fashionable bobs and headbands. The walls look velvet. Chandelier light falls, liquid, in lush Edwardian rooms. Daniel stands on the edge of things; Daniel looks right into the camera. There is warmth in his eyes. And distance.

And so: The Book of Life opens. A child toddles out into the world, with tenderness and gravity. He grows, well-armed for life. Or so it seems. He wants to shine.

At some point near Daniel's adolescence, the Trocmé family seemed to have made some kind of collective decision for him: Daniel would follow in his father's footsteps, to become an educator, and then one day to take over the directorship of École des Roches. What did the family see in Daniel, to make this choice for him? He had finished school solidly; after École des Roches, he'd gone on to study physics and math at the prestigious Paris lycées of Louis Le Grand and Henri IV, whose alumni included Voltaire, the Marquis de Sade, Victor Hugo, Molière, Émile Durkheim, and Edgar Degas; and where Daniel's contemporaries included Simone Veil, Jean-Paul Sartre, and Georges Pompidou. Philosopher Maurice Merleau-Ponty, who dazzled with his "primacy of perception," and Aimé Césaire, a poet founder of the Négritude movement, might have passed Daniel in the venerable hallways.

From the salon at École des Roches, everything was set up for a young Frenchman with a future. The velvet, the chandelier light. The good name. The solid tree, planted by the water. Father, mother, brothers, and sisters: They all wanted the good life for Daniel, saw themselves in his face. But then something happened. The Victrola skipped; the music shifted. Daniel, the delicious child, began to search.

WHO KNOWS WHAT WILL BE? Who knows, when the Book of Life is opened, what names will appear there, in the end? No one knows. Things can look just right, of course, only to prove all wrong.

Daniel was certainly poised, at birth, for a good life, and a right life. But as he moved out of childhood, it is clear from letters and from family recollections that he began to wrestle with himself and the terms of his oak-solid life. What would he do? Who would he be? Decisions had to be made.

I see him in my mind's eye, already in young adulthood, walking down the waterlogged fields of the far stretches of the École des Roches, along the train tracks leading out from that velveteen haven to the world beyond. I see him on the spot where trees give way to silver-green fields, alone, slightly bent to the sound of light rain. I imagine him lost in his thoughts—the forceful voice of his father, and the soft appeals of his mother, a background music that almost never ceases. One foot, and then the next, he's walking alone, wondering what will be. He hears a bird, maybe. A single bird cry once, then twice. He knows something is wrong, where he is, but he doesn't know why. The train station is ahead. The rain comes down. He's leaving, but he's not sure where he's going.

On Daniel's twenty-first birthday—April 28, 1933—the *Deutsche Allgemeine Zeitung* published its last article criticizing the Nazi Party in Germany; Chancellor Hitler was now officially, fully, on the rise to power. But what did that mean? All these years later, it seems crystal clear where 1933 was going. But what did that mean, then, to a young man of twenty-one? Someone with plans already made for him? What did it mean if he had curiosity and some talent and some means? What did it mean if he still didn't know who he was?

That year, Daniel was in Paris, at the Sorbonne, studying for his teaching license, and living in the lively Latin Quarter. He had friends, according to his brother Charles, "from all the races," and they would argue about the world. Politics were growing denser and stranger and angrier as one day followed the next. In the winter of 1933–1934, Daniel witnessed great riots in the city; an extreme right-wing group rose up against a leftist parliament. Absorbing the constant clamor of the crowds, Daniel watched as the orderliness of the grand boulevards gave way to chaos; he wrote home describing how iron grates were pulled up from around trees and strewn all over the streets, and the "sinister din" created when the grates were then crushed by passing trucks.

Daniel also wrote about the electric political environment of the city and the talks he'd attend for alumni of École des Roches: There was the great reformist writer on Islam, Father Henri Sanson, who spoke about "The Eternal Scandal," and the journalist and sometime anti-Semite Wickham Steed asking, "Can England Remain Neutral?" He wrote his parents about his new friends who had names that sounded Jewish, and names that sounded Middle Eastern, and he told them—with some firmness—that they should understand that now it was his friendships that mattered most to him. And the conversations that blazed, day after day, among them all.

Then, in 1934, Daniel took his first job. It was in Beirut, at the American University. In the 1930s, Beirut was a still-great cosmopolitan metropolis, recently of the Ottoman Empire, now under the French mandate, with a brilliant mixture of migrants living together as Muslims, Christians, Jews, and Bahá'ís. Traveling whenever he could, through Lebanon, up into the mountains toward Syria, then visiting the family of a close friend, Chafik, at his family home in Cairo—Daniel was actively wondering if he'd chosen the right field in life. He wrote home that maybe, after all, he ought to have studied modern history instead of the sciences. He was excited, in letters, that the poet Rabindranath

Tagore would be coming to Beirut to speak—that same Tagore who only a few years earlier had saved Gandhi from one of his fasts-to-the-death. Beirut was so small as a place, but so magnificent in its traffic across languages, religions, arts, and ideas. The doors were opening for Daniel, it seemed. The doors to all of it.

Daniel's parents chafed at what they saw in their son's progress. Their message: Daniel needed to keep studying, if he was to earn his proper teaching qualifications. He was already twenty-three; what was he doing with his life? Daniel wrote back that, yes, maybe it was a kind of adolescent crisis he was having, "fed by contestation and dreams." His parents fretted about these new political obsessions and the far-flung travel that seemed aimless, if not pointless. Already, he was venturing out of the cozy fold of country and class and profession. This much was clear.

Mostly, though, I think, his parents worried about their son's relationship to religion—about his relationship to Christianity, specifically; and to God. Daniel, now in the sun, now in the land of the orange blossoms, wrote to them:

> The loosest frameworks are still too narrow for me. I want to be
> absolutely free to say and to do, what I think and what I wish. And
> that seems almost impossible in most of the classic bourgeois
> careers. . . . I have not finished evolving, certainly. Nevertheless,
> the trip this year to Lebanon was long enough for me to judge
> with a completely new eye, our European society, our French
> society. . . . I see [that society] with a certain recoil, now . . . and
> from time to time with the eyes of the Oriental, who understand it
> poorly. I see the French administration of Syria. If I told you some
> things, you wouldn't believe them to be true, the extent to which
> they are monstrous. . . . Don't believe that I am so much of the
> extreme left. But I am detaching myself from western civilization.
> If you will, for me, it represents not the Civilization, but a
> civilization, which I place not only in space next to others, but also
> in time. . . . I see that [Christianity] contains the beautiful and the

true, but also the false and the ugly. So, in conclusion, I want to continue to travel, to see new things, and to liberate myself.

Who knows what will be when the Book of Life is opened? But how could Daniel not dream there, in his new city on the dazzling sea, in the biblical land of Canaan, just up the coast from Palestine itself, the sight of cedars on craggy soils, the perfume of orange blossoms, the ancient questions lingering there, still? In the single photograph of Daniel that exists from that time, he is on a boat, turned toward the camera and away from the sea, his cheeks brushed dark, his glasses reflecting a brilliant sun, obscuring the sight of his eyes. How could he not contest, and dream?

From Beirut, Daniel returned to Europe and found himself in Paris again, finalizing his teaching qualifications. Then, in 1937, he got a job at the Lycée Chateaubriand in Rome. The Eternal City was astir, everyone rushing toward the left or the right as Mussolini's power grew. Daniel met a woman in Rome—though never naming her in letters—and it's clear his family didn't approve of her. He wrote to them not to worry, that she was like a "pretty little box, hermetically sealed, where you can never see inside." But he clearly thought of her again and again. They would break up and reconcile, then break up again, and he would rush long distances to see her when he could—wondering out loud if his parents' fears, advice, and admonitions hadn't somehow undermined his discussions with her about their future: "Am I being demanding and perceptive, or just prideful and pretentious?"

He didn't know. Nothing felt right. The pressures of the world were mounting, and everywhere, everyone was looking for answers. What did it mean to be part of a community? Part of a religion? Part of the order as it stood?

"Money," he wrote home, "makes people mean." And that was a nice way to put it. Europe was reeling, full of seekers of the left, of the right, of the kind who wrote poems and saved Gandhi from his starvation protests. It was full of raised fists and marching, and more and more filled with great black swastikas splattered on flags, and ever newer forms of the sinister din.

In 1937, Daniel traveled to Potsdam and sat in on lectures on National Socialism; he wondered out loud if, in the future, he would be a bourgeois or an extremist. The left pulled at him, the right, the nation. Religion called, and pacifism, secularism, history, poetry . . . even the pretty little boxes that hid their insides from men. Daniel now wrote home: "I live in this moment very intensively, and a little on all points of view: socially, sentimentally, intellectually. If to live intensively is the cause of happiness, well, then I'm very happy. If happiness consists, on the contrary, in a calm and simple life, then I am the most unhappy of men."

Soon, of course, everything would change. The war itself would come to France. Because of his pericarditis, Daniel was exempt from military service. He was still teaching in Rome in May 1940, when the Germans rolled into Verneuil-sur-Avre. Clearly sobered, Daniel wrote home that he was sure, *chers parents*, that they must now be part of the Resistance. The Germans immediately took over the École des Roches, turning the orderly complex into the hub of a concentration camp, Front-stalag 200A. Barracks went up in the fields beyond the school; barbed wire was braided along the periphery; a watchtower perched above.

In what appeared to be a kind of last mad dash, Daniel tried to get out of Europe. He sped south on the train to Toulouse, then borrowed his brother François's car and raced toward Marseille, where he hoped to catch a ship to North Africa. But the last ship out left without Daniel. And without thousands upon thousands of others, all hoping for that last chance to escape a narrowing continent.

With his parents remaining in Verneuil, Daniel then headed to Maslacq, where École des Roches had set up a second campus for the time of the war. He went back to work there, but he was unhappy, arguing with other staff members, some of whom would eventually become part of the Vichy regime. "I'm suffocating here," he wrote, "and I don't know at all if I'll stay another year." He started desperately looking for something else. There was a job in Barcelona, a city still roiling in the aftermath of the Spanish Civil War. There was also the possibility of finally getting his doctorate, back in Paris. And the possibility, which he couldn't yet bear to finally toss out, of fully conceding to his parents' wishes to make his whole life career at Roches—forever leaving behind his own dreams and contestations.

Then, in the summer of 1942, Daniel got a letter. His cousin, Pastor André Trocmé, invited him to a village in the French backwoods to help with a far-reaching rescue effort. André needed help quite urgently. He'd been traveling back and forth to French-run concentration camps in Gurs and Rivesaltes, helping to identify and then do paperwork for children to come to the Plateau in safety. André couldn't pay a salary, but he needed someone who could run a home for young children in the outskirts of Le Chambon-sur-Lignon. The children in residence at the home were from many different countries, and they desperately needed help. This would be practical work, yes, but it would also have some academic sides to it.

André's work in the rescue effort was already gaining some attention. It was a risky business, for sure. Daniel's parents weren't thrilled at the prospect of him going. They sent François to see Daniel and plead their case to him in person.

There was a chapel on the grounds of the École des Roches of Daniel's childhood. It was spare and white-walled, made of plaster and wood. How many hours had Daniel spent there as a boy, alone in his thoughts, reading the simple words over the altar: *Faire Christ Roi*, Make Christ King. Maybe Daniel was like me, and his thoughts would have lingered anxiously on the paintings that stood out against the bare white walls: one of the Parable of the Prodigal Son—"This thy brother was dead, and is alive again; and was lost, and is found"; and a second of the Parable of the Vine—"Every branch in me that beareth not fruit he taketh away"; and a third, of the Parable of the Lost Coin—"Rejoice with me; for I have found the piece which I had lost." A son; a vine; a coin. What would

Daniel have dreamed of there? Of prodigality? Lostness? Of what it might mean to bear no fruit?

Daniel opened the book of his own life and he thought and thought. Surely, he thought about André over in that backwoods—a place that was no Paris, no Beirut, no Barcelona, and where there was no woman, like a pretty box. Maybe he thought about how money makes you mean. And maybe he thought about the left and the right and the fists he had seen raised up, all over Europe. Maybe Daniel reread a last letter his mother sent him. Maybe he put that letter in a pocket for safekeeping.

Daniel made up his mind.

He picked up a pen to write to his parents. It was September 11, 1942. In the world outside, it was the day a train called Convoy 31 left the Drancy camp just north of Paris, with a thousand souls heading for Auschwitz-Birkenau. And, in the world outside, it was nearly one year since 33,400 Jews had been gathered in the streets of Kiev and led to the ragged ravine at the edge of the city, where they were shot and killed, falling to unseen depths.

And in the world outside, it was the eve of Rosh Hashanah and those ten Days of Awe, when the shofar sounds: "Awake, sleepers from your sleep, and slumberers arise from your slumber! Search your deeds, repent, and remember your Creator!"

I hold a copy of Daniel's letter in my hands. It reads:

> As of this morning, the die is cast. . . . Le Chambon represents for me, first of all, an education. . . . Then a kind of contribution to the reconstruction of the world. . . . On the other hand, Le Chambon represents for me an affirmative response to a vocation, a rather intimate call, almost religious, or even completely religious in some respects. I will honestly be myself there, the future will tell me if I am equal to the task or not—and, what's more, will only tell me—because it's not a question here of success in the eyes of the world. Worldly wisdom directed me to the

doctorate, or at least to Barcelona, or in any event to public teaching. Le Chambon means adventure. . . . I have chosen adventure not because it's an adventure, but so that I would not be ashamed of myself.

I, too, want to be part of the reconstruction of the world. I, too, wish not to be ashamed of myself.

And so, I go.

Chapter 3

EXODUS

Are thy wings plumed indeed for such far flights?

—WALT WHITMAN, "PASSAGE TO INDIA"

I'T'S MARCH NOW, and damp and cold outside as I board the train. I find my seat at the window and look out into the steel-gray light of the platform. My brand-new husband, Charles—it still feels a little funny calling him that, but so nice—waves good-bye, one more time, and the doors all close. Then, finally, I feel that first pull of gravity against my back as the train leaves the station.

The journey from Paris to the Plateau Vivarais-Lignon will take many hours and include three full legs. First, I'll catch the SNCF train to Lyon, then switch to a commuter TER to Saint-Étienne. After that, it's bus number 37—Saint-Étienne–Montfaucon–Saint-Agrève—which should leave me off in the center of Le Chambon-sur-Lignon. I'll be traveling roughly six hundred kilometers, from city to countryside, lowland to highland, center to periphery, cacophony to—perhaps?—consonance.

I close my eyes with the first even lull of the train.

Up until now, Russia has been my whole career, the sole focus of my work for more than fifteen years. As a doctoral student of anthropology at the University of Montreal, I went to Russia to learn something about how communities far from the center of power grapple with their past—particularly when the state is making big, obvious, and sometimes violent efforts to shape how people think. The Soviet Union had already collapsed; in the chaos that followed, mine was a pretty good question. For my research, I spent around a year and a half living in a tiny Russian village—in a little wooden house that smelled of sour milk and hay—learning about every manner of life: the production of sustenance with the help of scythes and rakes and no running water; the makeshift, almost moneyless economy; the ways of maintaining social cohesion in times of trouble; the orientations toward all manner of powerful figures in the past and present, from Stalin to Yeltsin to the guy who runs the collective farm, and even toward the invisible creatures of the home or barn or forest. I, the girl from Salisbury Street, learned how to live under one roof with a middle-aged couple, along with their cows and sheep and chickens. To be warm when they were warm, and cold when they were cold.

I wrote a doctoral dissertation about "social memory" in that village, concluding that rural people did a pretty impressive job of resisting (or ignoring) the will of the state when it came to things that really mattered to them—and then turned that dissertation into a book, and then started a new fieldwork project in one of the Muslim regions of Russia's North Caucasus Mountains: Kabardino-Balkaria.

It was a strange and beautiful place, with immense mountains in the distance, appearing and disappearing with the moods of the sky. But with brutal wars spanning into two decades, especially in the nearby Republic of Chechnya, it was also ever more dangerous and sad. There were arrests, public denunciations, murders. There were showdowns in the streets between police and religious or ethnic or mafioso clans. Friends began having trouble; the trouble inched closer and closer to me.

It was time to go.

So here I am: on a train on the way to the Plateau Vivarais-Lignon, with no more Russia for me, and with no storehouse of knowledge that took years to accumulate. Instead of feeling bereft, though, I feel somehow free.

And—as foolish as this new journey might seem to my academic friends, who have learned to be exceedingly cautious when new questions come around the bend—I am not going empty-handed. So what do I have?

First of all, I have the idea, from my own up-close research, that even powerless-seeming people can find ways to resist the will of a violent state. There is such a thing as collective power, even for the least of us.

Then, I have the three months I spent at the Center for Advanced Holocaust Studies, as a research fellow, where the archivists and librarians and researchers treated me like a fellow traveler and not some reckless adventurer. In those three months, I plunged into Holocaust history to absorb its basic contours. I learned how to talk about the culpability of perpetrators (those who create the architecture of mass murder, or write up the orders, or pull the trigger, or open the valves in the gas chambers), collaborators (those who, as states or groups or individuals, make deals with perpetrators, to their own benefit), and bystanders (those who stand and watch and do nothing). I learned about specific modes of resistance during the Holocaust—violent kinds and nonviolent kinds. And I learned what political scientists say about the structural factors that encourage resistance. One arresting example: being a highlander.

I read everything I could get my hands on about the Plateau and its own (highland) brands of wartime resistance, and—more generally—about the social psychology of heroic altruism. Then, I spent weeks watching interviews of Jewish survivors who had passed through the Plateau Vivarais-Lignon. Sitting there with my headphones on, day after day, I would blink; I would cry. I read and read; and watched and watched; and walked through the museum again and again to sear those images of fire and light into my mind's eye.

So I have that now.

What else do I have? French. I speak French—the vowel-bending Quebec version—which I learned in Montreal. For years, in fact, I lived my whole life in that language: I studied in it, I dreamed in it, I argued in it. I had a graduate school husband and then a divorce in it. The French—like the Russian that came after it—was hard-earned. When you learn a new language, especially in our parochial Western world, you have to be stupid for years before you start getting to be a little bit smart again. People treat you like a child—which, in a way, you are. And if you grew up thinking that, of all the things you might be in life, you are smart, mostly, then . . . you have lots to give up along the way, lots to lose. Some never manage it. In my case, the years of stupidity paid off. My French, like my Russian, is the kind that puts people at ease. I love the music of both. And so, on this train, I carry a twangy, provincial French. And the ability to be a person in it.

And—I open my eyes and check my notebook at the bottom of my bag—I also carry one, two, three phone numbers: one for my hotel; one for a local historian, Monsieur Bollon, whose work I've gobbled up; and one for a lovely woman from the tourist office, Muriel, who has been helping me with logistics. In recent weeks, Muriel has been sending me messages with liberal use of the exclamation point: We will be delighted to give you a good welcome!! Bring a warm coat, it will be cold!

And so I carry a warm coat.

But most of all, I carry with me this: the sense that what might have looked, in my own life, like an alarming break away from a known path, is instead a new moment where, who knows, I might be able to learn something about what most matters to me. And whatever this moment will reveal, right now it feels fresh and green and bright. Or, perhaps, like the kind of snow that barrels through the sky at night, like ever-shooting stars.

Two eyes, two ears, three phone numbers, a coat, a fluent tongue. Some knowledge and some questions, barreling through the sky.

That's not nothing. And anyway, the readiness is all.

. . .

THE TRAIN PUSHES FORWARD to the rusty edges of Paris—mottled with their graffiti conversations—and then out past the gray, rowdy *banlieues*.

What was it like, out my window of the train, when the story I am seeking began?

After the devastation of the First World War—fought over the airy nothing of nascent nationalisms—there was no clear pathway forward to the time of war-no-more, no clear way to bind the collective wounds of the continent. There were shattered families, destroyed economies, political ravings in chilling new forms. In the decades that followed Versailles, more and more people abandoned their homelands, seeking something better, or brighter.

By the 1930s in France, this very rail line I travel on now was freighted with so many outsiders, so many strangers to the country. There were thousands upon thousands of souls who had fled the Spanish Civil War. There were political activists trying to create communism, or run from it, or crush it. There were economic refugees—poor, jobless strangers filling the nooks and crannies of cities with their indecipherable languages and foods and ways of worship. And added to that were layer upon layer of still-new migrants from earlier waves—from the Russian and Ottoman Empires, from North Africa, from the remnants of Austria-Hungary. Pressures were mounting in the country. Resources were scarce. Provisions were getting harder and harder to acquire. People were hungrier and hungrier, inside and out.

Among the desperate people traveling on these tracks, looking out through windows pitched exactly as mine is now, were a great many Jews. Hitler's rise itself was, of course, responsible for a good portion of the Jewish refugees in the 1930s. But it was also the simple, terrifying tenor of hatred throughout the German lands that led people to flee their homes: the caricatures, blown up to gargantuan sizes, of sallow-skinned Jews with huge beakish noses, cradling the world; the smashing of temples by neighbors or teachers; the beatings by police. Jews arrived not only from Germany and Austria, but—trickling in for years—from Eastern Europe's Pale of Settlement, with its own fraught history of pogroms and mounting political instabilities. By the last days of the 1930s, there were 350,000 or so Jews in France, more than half of them foreign-born.

For those Jews in flight, Paris—now teetering anyway, with its own ragged poor, and its own leftist parliament, and its rightist riots, and its trucks rolling over the detritus of violence in the streets and their "sinister din"—made for a tense new home. There were so many of them, and despite the urge to catalog them as a heterogeneous and ugly other, they made for a very diverse crowd. On the twisty streets of Montparnasse, or the Marais, or the Left Bank, you could expect to see any kind of Jew walking by. There were fancy Viennese Jews who might speak French already, and whose menfolk might wear shiny top hats and white gloves when they went out at night. The Jews from Eastern Europe—having escaped pogroms a decade or two earlier—might be businessmen from Odessa, or artisans from Warsaw. They might speak Russian or Hungarian, if they were of a certain class—the class of the shiny top hat—or only Yiddish, if they had never been much exposed to the world outside the shtetl. The men might walk the Parisian streets in long black coats, bearded, covered, strange. The very religious and the very political among the new arrivals could embarrass those who had preceded them.

Depending on class and language and background, these different Jews might also have very different ways of dealing with authority. French-born Jews and upper-class Jews from German lands tended to believe in the Law, and to refer to authorities when asked; the Central and Eastern Europeans, however, having lived through periods where no state would protect them, possessed life-preserving instincts to keep bureaucracies and police officers at bay. This would have very real implications for their survival in the years ahead.

In 1938 and 1939, Germany began its expansion into Austria, the Czech lands, and Poland, changing the equation yet again. Aggression mounted, and who knew where it would land next. By the spring of

1940, Hitler was strolling down the Champs-Élysées; soon the German army would occupy the whole of northern France. It was then, under occupation, that France began its twin response of resistance and collaboration. Jews rushed south to Vichy—nominally still under French control—in what was known as *l'exode*, the Exodus of 1940. They jammed the roads for hundreds of miles, carrying their possessions in cars and on bikes and in covered wagons. Thousands of Jews were captured and sent to French-administered concentration camps with names like Gurs, Rivesaltes, Compiègne, and the transport camp of Drancy. What had once been a general atmosphere of pressure and anxiety and dispossession became one of mortal danger. In the summer of 1942, thirteen thousand Jews—already wearing their yellow stars—were rounded up in Montmartre and other neighborhoods, and jammed into a bike-racing arena. Several days later, those Jews were sent to Drancy, and from there, to Auschwitz. By November of that year, Germany had invaded the South of France, too, and it became impossible to be both Jewish and safe. Native and immigrant Jews alike would all, very soon, be tempest-tossed.

Desperation looked like that: a tempest. Crowds of strangers; a fallen Tower of Babel with no common tongue, with no consensus on the meaning of a good society. It looked like a freighted train careening forward into the unknown, a covered wagon with all your possessions crammed in, with planes overhead and a parent lost somewhere down the road.

My own train speeds farther and farther from Paris, and as I look out the window again, the landscape has begun to roll.

By the 1930s, my mother's ancestors, from Vilna and Kraków, were all in the United States; my mother's few brushes with anti-Semitism, the usual: getting blamed, personally, on the playgrounds of Brooklyn, for the murder of Jesus Christ. Years later, in Russia, I realized that having Jewish ancestors from Vilna who spoke Russian by no means meant I would be welcomed there as some kind of long-lost compatriot. During the Soviet period, "Jewish" was something that got stamped on your passport, something that could bar you from getting into a university; that could keep you from jobs, or—during the worst of things—get you purged.

I was in Russia when *Schindler's List* came out, and I watched it with a friend in a theater, sitting in the dark on rickety wooden seats, bundled into our winter coats and hats as the terrible story unfurled in blinking black-and-white and that one spot of rose-red. Outside, right on Nevsky Prospekt, neo-Nazis were protesting in the snow. Afterward, I noted that nobody seemed impressed by the film: "You Jews lost six million in the war? Russia lost twenty-five."

Later, in work trips to Ukraine that followed, I came to realize that the war stories were told differently from how I'd expected there, with no sense of regret or shame, and with maybe even the sense that, to some Ukrainians there was something rotten about being Jewish. Jews were, in their minds, the same as communists. Communists were the same as Stalin. Stalin was the same as Hitler, or worse. Or worse. So, in Ukraine there was and perhaps still is a sense that the Jews got what was coming to them. More or less.

As for me, I didn't have much formal Jewish education—we left our synagogue when I was around six years old after my mother had a fight with our brand-new rabbi over matters of principle (according to this rabbi, my brother, who came into our family when he was eleven months old, wasn't allowed to be a Jew). From then on, most of our religious education came from my father, a Bahá'í. But there were vivid moments in my early Jewish life.

There was the time when I was on a walk with a small group of kids from my Hebrew school, out in the leafy suburbs. One of the kids stooped down on the sidewalk and, rock in hand, started smashing at small black dots on the ground. Seeing this, our teacher stopped everything: "Hey! You! Why are you hurting that ant? Don't hurt that ant! It never did anything to you!" In that moment, for me, ants became beings—animated, precious, deserving of protection. And the world woke up in that way.

Then, there was the Shavuot, when I was little and lifted over the Torah by our wonderful first rabbi, unbound by gravity, the taste of honey candy in my mouth; and there was, sweet to my memory, the sound of my grandfather's chanting, and the smoky smell of his skin as he wrapped me in hugs; and the voice of my mother, correcting my irreverent moments: "God doesn't want to hear you like that."

I look out the window again, as great trucks lose the race with my train. How many ghoulish caricatures do we make of each other? Of ourselves? How much hiding is there, in the black of night? How many raised fists; how much cheering for the nation or the kin or the kind? Academia has been like a soft padding, protecting me from the sound of the hardest questions. I can't help but wonder: What does God want to hear?

At the Lyon-Perrache station, I transfer to a double-decker commuter train. I pick a seat on the top deck, in front of two young guys who are loudly joking, using little bits of English in their speech in a point/counterpoint—"It looks like a bird! It is not a bird! . . . It looks like a bird! It's not a bird!"—and laughing hysterically. Soon, there are small farms in the landscape beyond. Geese wander in people's yards. A man makes a fire with sticks on the far bank of a creek. Farms grow farther and farther apart; in between them, it's all rust and rickety gray. And then mountains appear in the distance.

When the train stops at the industrial city of Saint-Étienne, I find a café where I can sit and wait for my bus to Le Chambon-sur-Lignon. The young man who serves me has bright eyes and a dark brow; he speaks French with a little bit of an accent, and he looks confident, at ease. Halal kebabs are on the menu. And a creamy puffy pastry called *la religieuse*. All over Paris, there were signs of a full and diverse Muslim community, and signs of the city being now—as it has been for a very long time—a cosmopolitan haven for the peoples of the world, stuffed together in metro cars, hollering over one another's heads in musical foreign tongues, lighting up the streets with the colorful swirls of their *grands boubous*, the smell of their varied spices, a handshake where one brown hand covers another brown hand and presses, a beautifully draped headscarf, the sale of some delicacy, some foreign song.

Finally, the bus arrives for the last leg of my journey. I ask for "one ticket to Le Chambon-sur-Lignon" and feel my throat tighten a little as I pay, and my change clangs musically in a tin dish next to the driver. I find a seat next to a window and the bus begins to wind its way out of the gray city, and soon there are hills in the distance ahead, and then forests and mountains. As the bus creaks ever upward, the palette outside begins to change, too, with dark green pines out the window, and craggy stones, and light white snow on the ground. The bus swings up, down, then over, higher and higher. Here and there are fields and cows and horses.

IT'S HIGH UP, the Plateau where I'm headed: three thousand feet in the air. High up and hard to get to. For centuries, its people were poor and isolated, their patois singular, the weather harsh. Centuries ago, Protestantism found a home on the Plateau, and to this day, the region is not only more religious than most of France, but more heavily Protestant—in forms that secular outsiders might consider quaint or even vaguely unsettling. The most religious of its people—*les purs et durs* (the pure and hard ones)—are known for their long skirts and dour faces and their habit of avoiding talk with strangers. There are winds in the winter so fierce and so familiar that they are given names, like La Burle or Le Mistral. Politically, too, the Plateau is an outlier. For centuries, it was—and still is—an island of political liberalism in a sea of the French Right. It is a quirk of a place, a geographic afterthought.

If you lived on the Plateau Vivarais-Lignon in the late 1930s, you would have been one of around twenty-five thousand people. You probably would have been Christian, though if you were a refugee you could easily have been Jewish or nonreligious. If you were, in fact, Christian, you were a bit more likely to be Catholic than Protestant, though

Protestants made up a hefty 38 percent of the population on the Plateau (and over 90 percent in the villages of Le Chambon-sur-Lignon and its neighbor, Le Mazet-Saint-Voy). You would have grown up living in a cold and difficult place. You would have lived your days near the land, far from the ease and anonymity of big cities, speaking a dialect that outsiders called quaint. You and your parents and grandparents would have lived through an economic decline spanning many decades. You already knew what it meant to be hungry, when nature failed you.

More than that, you would have understood something about suffering. For centuries, on and off, the Protestants of the Plateau Vivarais-Lignon—most, but not all, of the Reformed Protestant Church—had been subject to bloody persecution. At the same time, over those same centuries, the people of the Plateau developed a kind of habit of sheltering vulnerable outsiders from violence—hiding them, feeding them, shuttling them out of the country. They protected Protestants during France's religious wars of the sixteenth century; then, during the French Revolution and the Reign of Terror that followed, they protected Catholic priests. In the nineteenth century, they took in poor children from industrial cities in early versions of fresh-air programs; then children from Algeria; then, during the Spanish Civil War, mothers and children from Spain, and political undesirables from all over Europe. During the Second World War they sheltered Jews, yes, but also all kinds of other refugees from the Nazi occupations. Accustomed to suffering themselves, they sheltered the sufferer. It was, you could say, a kind of intimate moral roundelay.

On June 23, 1940, just a month after Hitler invaded France, and a single day after Vichy was established in the south, Pastor André Trocmé delivered a bold sermon in the Protestant church of Le Chambon-sur-Lignon. "The duty of Christians," he said, "is to use the weapons of the spirit to resist the violence brought to bear on their consciences. . . . We will resist whenever our adversaries try to force us to act against the commands of the Gospel. We will do so without fear, but also without pride and without hatred." On July 17, just three short weeks later, Vichy signed its first homegrown anti-Semitic legislation. The time was nigh for resisting; or not.

If you were on the Plateau, then, that summer of 1940, you had some thinking to do. You knew what suffering meant. You knew what a hard life was like. Your ancestors understood something about how to shelter people in need. Would you decide, all things considered, to choose the path of your own mortal danger? To protect people you didn't know, people you had never met; who were unrelated to you; who spoke foreign languages; who didn't share your religion; who had no real means?

Later in 1940, Tante Soly, a first home for refugee children, was opened in Le Chambon. The children there were mostly Jewish. Several more homes would open in the months that followed: La Guespy, L'Arbric, La Maison des Roches, Les Grillons, and others. The police presence mounted. The numbers of refugees—and the diversity of their backgrounds—increased. The mayor, Charles Guillon, quit his post in protest of the collaborating regime and began a massive effort to help the displaced. By August 1941, some open defiance was beginning to be seen on the Plateau: a religious woman refused to ring the church bells in honor of Marshal Pétain's army during a high-profile visit to Le Chambon. Local pastors, including Trocmé, started taking children directly out of French concentration camps. Trocmé's actions, in particular, began to cause some consternation in the Reformed Protestant Church hierarchy. In the summer of 1942, police authorities tried, unsuccessfully, to round up Jewish children at one of the homes. A month later, the BBC broadcast a story about how children were being welcomed in Le Chambon; under Vichy, the rescue was not yet a secret.

In this context, if you were, in fact, moved—as most of those on the Plateau were—to choose the path of your own mortal danger and protect perfect strangers, there were any number of ways that you could act. Those from larger towns like Le Chambon-sur-Lignon, Le Mazet-Saint-Voy, Tence, and Saint-Agrève—about five thousand of the twenty-five thousand in all—could greet newcomers, find them homes, offer them a place to stay. They could give away some of their own scarce food or clothing, or the traditional wooden clogs they wore, called sabots. They could volunteer to teach—anything at all that they knew—at a local school; with wave upon wave of refugee children of different ages, everything from philosophy and theology to higher mathematics and farming techniques was needed, so there was plenty to sign up for. People might also volunteer to cook in one of the local residences for refugees, or to be in charge of forging documents. For the young and daring, there was the possibility to become a *passeur*, clandestinely leading refugees through the mountains to the relative safety of Switzerland.

The townsfolk had infrastructure on their side. With access to train stations and telegraph stations and even telephones sometimes, they could communicate with a plethora of organizations that brought aid and succor to refugees; notably, there was the Protestant Comité Inter-Mouvements Auprès des Évacués (CIMADE); the Jewish Œuvre de Secours aux Enfants (OSE); the American Friends Service Committee; and the Cartel Suisse Secours aux Enfants. They also had contacts with Resistance organizations large and small, like the Éclaireurs Israélites de France, and networks of Le Combat, based in Lyon. In towns, as in the countryside, big, active churches were able to do heavy lifting in the rescue: not only were priests and pastors sources of inspiration, but they also dispersed crucial information through Bible study groups, which—in their clandestine functioning—operated much like the secret cells of the communists in their formative pre-Soviet years.

These townsfolk, many of whom would have had networks far beyond the Plateau itself, were not the only kind of rescuers. Whether catalyzed by the thunder of a pastor or the call of their own hearts, it was the country folk—the farmers and shepherds and milkmaids—who made up the bulk of the twenty-five thousand on the Plateau in the late 1930s and, in everyday ways, lived at the heartbeat of the rescue. It was they who would secretly take in families, sometimes long-term. I had been able to learn their brilliant, varied stories—as recounted by survivors—at the Holocaust Museum. Often, it was women farmers who bore the brunt of the risk in helping the strangers, since their husbands had been forced to take up arms elsewhere. These women were the ones who answered the door in the middle of the night, who learned to bark at the police and then lie right to their faces. These farmers and shepherds and milkmaids would get information about what was needed from their Bible circles, often taking long walks through field and forest to get there. Information was slow to travel, but it traveled.

The Plateau is so small, so far away; France is so large. And yet, people found their way there. Somehow or other—whether through friends or aid organizations, at a stopover or mid-flight—they got word that this place was taking people in. They'd get word, and then somehow aim their exodus to this higher ground. They traveled on the great French railways, in trains and cars, in bikes or on foot. The roads south, toward nominal safety, were full and chaotic. On them, children might see dead bodies for the first time, after bombardments; people would hide among the roots of trees in the forests by the sides of roads; police were everywhere.

By 1940 and 1941, the first Jewish children had begun to arrive on the Plateau with regularity, mostly under the protection of the Swiss Red Cross. Pastors in the Plateau, like André Trocmé and Édouard Theis, and aid workers, like Friedel and August Bohny-Reiter from the Swiss Red Cross, and heroes of the OSE like Madeleine Dreyfus, were instrumental in identifying the children in Gurs and Rivesaltes near the Spanish border, and then bringing them up to the Plateau for safety. Once identified, most of the children would have to leave their parents behind in the camps, facing this next new chapter of flight alone.

The interviews I had watched at the Holocaust Museum gave me the illusion of intimacy with the people who journeyed to the Plateau during the war. They were boys and girls. They had French names and Yiddish names; Polish names and German ones. They spoke English with *r*'s rolled in the back of their throat; or French. Watching the people in those interviews—now aged and gray and lined—I imagined their faces as children, small and tender and full of longing. And full of fear.

There was Elizabeth, a teenager from Vienna, who got separated from her parents and brother after their exodus south from Paris, and who rode her bike for hundreds of kilometers, weaving among the cars and covered wagons that jammed the highways. Elizabeth kept meeting soldiers and other strangers along the way, who could have robbed her or raped her or fatally turned her in to the police. But somehow, she managed to find her mother in Toulouse, and one day she got a letter from her former teacher from Vienna, urging her to come to the Plateau. So, she went.

And there was Jacob, a tough and handsome kid from Kleinlangheim, Germany, who saw his mother's teeth fly out of her mouth when a policeman punched her during Kristallnacht. Jacob was living in the lice-and-mud barracks of the Gurs concentration camp, near the Spanish border, when a member of the Swiss Red Cross came to the camp offering to find homes on the Plateau for a group of children. So, he went.

Then there was Étienne, who, even with his last name of Weil, was fiercely proud of his family's French origins: "We'd been in France for one thousand years!" Étienne, fine of feature, was hiding with his mother right there in Saint-Étienne during the early years of the war. They were in constant, immediate danger, their names surely on the careful lists made by the regional authorities. His mother, trying desperately to inure her little boy to their false new identities, would cradle him every night before bed, incanting: "You are not a Weil, you are not a Jew, you are not a Weil, you are not a Jew," like a lullaby of erasure.

And there was Paulina—with the Yiddish nickname Feigelah, like my mother, Flo—whose own mother would steal cherries and an extra glass of milk for her in the Rivesaltes concentration camp, also in the south. Paulina found her way to the Plateau with her sister, at just about the time when her mother was gassed at Auschwitz.

Up they went, all of them. Up into a brand-new place, where, perhaps, they would be safe for a time.

WE'VE LEFT BEHIND the cities now, left behind the din; one by one, the passengers leave until there are only a handful of us remaining. The bus strains with effort on its ascent, the temperature drops down and down. Soon, there are pine forests, and the smells of horses and hay; and soon massive stone houses dot the landscape; and cows, donkeys, and chickens nuzzle the ground for food. The greens grow deeper, the mosses richer, the air cleaner, the snow heavier, whiter.

And now: Night falls. I can see my thoughts better, in the dark.

WHY AM I HERE?

If ideas are shapes—as they are to me—then the idea that brought me here is surely the circle: the circle of a social group. I draw one in my head, now. To be honest, I seem to draw them in my head all the time—it comes from being trained as a social anthropologist, probably, but one with just a little excess of math in her background. Something about the circles comforts me—they have a way of cutting through the swirl.

So, here's my circle: Black border around it. Nice and clean and clear.

Now, I can populate the inside of my circle with people. So I do. Hello, people. Who are you?

You could say that I am here on this bus, climbing up toward the Plateau right now, because I learned from Émile Durkheim, the great French father of sociology, that it is not only individuals who act—individuals like me, or a king, or a Nazi, or a charismatic—but groups act, too. Groups like the circle now in my head. The idea that groups act—that they can be the very unit of action—means straightforward things like how, if it's an individual that lifts a pen, it's a group that lifts a coffin; an individual that makes a loaf of bread, a group that makes a vat of wine. But as you push the idea further, the philosophical nooks and crannies come into view, and soon things get more complicated: An individual thinks up the theories of relativity (Einstein!); but a group also thinks up the theories of relativity (as ideas conceptually ripen broadly over time). An individual prays with private, desperate longings; a group prays with deep and social longings. An individual feels sad at the death of a loved one; a group feels trauma after a war. An individual remembers the tree she climbed in the neighbor's yard when she was a girl, or how to ride a bike; a group remembers what it was like under Stalin, or how to behave with outsiders, or how to be kind to guests.

Okay.

Inside the circle in my head, I have now placed the villagers of the Plateau Vivarais-Lignon. I don't know these people yet, so I'll imagine them. I'll like them already. *Bonjour, tout le monde!* Some are digging up gardens, some are struggling with a plow, some of them are working in little stores. Now, I'll add a dimension: Let's say the times are terrible and there is mortal danger everywhere around. Outside my circle, I now draw big fat arrows, in red, pressures from the outside, bearing down on the boundaries. What would you expect a circle like this to do under such circumstances? You would expect—let's just say—for the black border of the circle to thicken, harden, make it more difficult to come inside. You would expect the group to look out for itself, to bar the vulnerable outsiders from entry.

Why would you expect that? Because in the world of social science there is an almost religious belief in something called rational choice, which refers to the pretty good bet that we will, in the aggregate, act in such a way as to maximize the best outcomes for ourselves. That is, every man for himself—with a nope and a sorry and the close of a door to others in need. And indeed, that's what most people seem to do in terrible times. Certainly, it is what most people did during the Holocaust.

But lo and behold: The villagers populating the inside of my circle do something else. During these terrible times, they actually open the borders of the circle, change it to dotted lines, now permeable. As a group, they let rough-looking wayfarers inside. As a group, they give up their own food, their own sustenance, to those strangers. As a group, they repel the exigencies of a powerful state. As a group, they invite danger and death to themselves and their families, just as they share culpability when things go wrong. As a group, they absorb the sorrow that invariably ensues. They do all of this together, intertwined, collectively, sharing risk. Furthermore, they do it not once in some heroic dash, but day in and day out, for years on end. They do it during the Holocaust, that is, as they have done it for centuries, on and off. Taking in the stranger.

What a nice circle. What a rare circle. There's resistance for you. There's your subversive irrational choice.

The bus groans higher and higher. Why am I here? I'm here because this circle in my head is nearly singular. Because it's an illogical thing of great beauty.

And because maybe, if I can learn its contours—its ins and outs and rules and habits and flows of resources and power—something might be done about the story that my own book of life will tell, someday.

THE DRIVER CLEARLY KNOWS the road so well that he doesn't fear the hairpin turns up here among the snows and stones and deep green trees. Towns come into view: Dunières, Montfaucon-en-Velay, then Tence— where we barrel over a stone bridge across the Lignon River—then Les Barandons. These are names that I have read about in the Holocaust Museum, places that now have, for me, the whiff of the familiar. After one more breakneck turn, we arrive at a stop called Collège Cévenol—I recognize it from my reading of these past several months—and two messy-pretty teenagers are let off the bus.

The streets are now fully lined with snow as the bus takes a last left turn onto Route de Saint-Agrève, into the center of Le Chambon-sur-Lignon. The door opens, and I scramble to get my bags. A rush of cold, wet wind hits my face as I step out onto the street. Here, in my first moments in the land of peace, I am alone, with no one to greet me.

I pull my coat closer and set out to find the hotel where I'll be staying for the next few days, the Hôtel du Velay. I have to ring the bell and then ring again before a boy finally answers and calls his father over. A few moments later, I am in my room, square and small and gray.

I look out the window at the main crossroads of the town of Le Chambon-sur-Lignon. There is a bank across the street, with the faded words CENTRAL HOTEL. On the other corner, there is the Office de Tourisme, and a bar, La Mandarine. I notice that the shutters in all the great stone buildings of the town are shut tight, to let no light in or out. Everything seems closed, and there is almost no one on the streets. I realize I'm hungry, and I don't know how to get food.

The wind blows; the snow falls sideways; I'm a stranger here. Alone with my stories and the pictures and in my head. Breathe it in. The readiness is all.

In the small gray room, my own shutters are closed tight now. I'm cold; I use my coat as an extra blanket. Thank you, Muriel, for warning me about the cold. Thank you for each one of the exclamation points. I close my eyes. Images swirl in my head of pastoral beauty and of crowded roads. It's the early 1940s, and children are arriving, one by one. I see the snows of a late winter. And a train . . .

AND THERE HE IS. A boy from the past. A boy of around twelve. Peter is his name. His hair is straight and dark, parted on one side. It's winter, and he is alone on a train. He carries a little bag his mother sewed, and his father gave to him. He has seen many cities already in his young life: Berlin, Vienna, Brussels. He's seen the fires of Dunkirk, and the raids of Paris. There are the memories he carries, too, of his mother being paraded through Vienna with a sign around her neck, Pig Woman; and of his father's face, covered in black soot from being smuggled on a coal train; and of people dying right next to him on the road; and of his time in Gurs, where his mother slapped a nun, saying, "We don't live to eat— we eat to live!" and the time his father gave him that little sewn bag before riding off on a bicycle, getting smaller and smaller in the distance; and the time when nuns prayed for nine days but still couldn't keep his parents from the convoy to Auschwitz.

And the memory he carries, too, of the moment he lost his faith.

I see Peter on a train, traveling up the hills on this snowy night, holding the little bag. In it is a bit of French money, his father's gold pocket watch, a small silver horseshoe, a large ring that his mother always wore, and a miniature sparkplug, for luck.

Peter is alone as the train churns up to its final station of Saint-Agrève, right at the edge of the Plateau. It is the very middle of the night and snow is everywhere when he arrives. Peter gets off the train, and standing there in the quiet of the station is a lanky man with glasses and dark hair and big ears. The man greets him and tells him his name is Daniel. Together, the two set out for a long walk up through the forest, toward the stone house that Peter will call home. Les Grillons. The Crickets.

Now. I imagine how the trees looked that night, heavy, aching with snow. And how the sky looked, lit up from a brilliant moon behind the clouds. And how there were two solitary figures, one long and one small, walking through those forest paths. And how, in the hush of snow and night, there was just the syncopated sound of footfall: one tread, and the next; one tread and the next. . . .

Now: Sleep.

Chapter 4

FIRST
ON THE
ROPE

Say what you like and do what you like—
and I'm not forgetting what you *have* done for me—
I can't breathe down here. It's just too low down. . . .

—R. FRISON-ROCHE, *PREMIER DE CORDÉE*

IT WAS LATE AUTUMN OF 1942, and Daniel had been reading to the children in the evenings.

Things were finally settling down a bit. Les Grillons was only a few months old, one of several homes for children that had sprung up on the Plateau since the start of the war. Back in May, just days before Jews in France were ordered to wear Stars of David, André Trocmé had written to the American Friends Service Committee, requesting funds for a home that would "readapt young refugees and victims of war to their new conditions of life in France, especially boys and girls . . . whose studies have been interrupted by an arbitrary incarceration in a concentration camp, at the age of adolescence, when opinions and convictions on life and men develop in their minds." In his proposal to the Quakers, Pastor Trocmé suggested candidates for the directorship of the home that would be called Les Grillons—The Crickets—but by the time the funds came through in the summer, there was still no one to run the place.

Consequently, André had found himself writing to his young cousin with a proposition. Daniel was a logical choice. He already had several years of experience as a teacher and working at homes for children— and, of course, he'd grown up at one. Plus, he was a Trocmé, of the same solid oak family tree—and that, too, must have meant something.

And so, Daniel weighed André's proposition against all the others— the doctorate, the job in Barcelona, the pretty little box of a woman his parents disapproved of, getting out of France altogether. He wrestled with his fate. Finally, he decided that the die would be cast. He would come up to the Plateau, after quick stops in Lannemezan and Toulouse in the south. He would choose adventure; he would choose some hope for the reconstruction of the world.

But first, the final construction of Les Grillons itself.

Months earlier, space for the school had been located in the hamlet of Les Barandons, three kilometers up from the center of Le Chambon-sur-Lignon, in what had once been a *pension de famille*—a kind of vacation guesthouse where families could rent rooms inexpensively and from there enjoy the surrounding nature. It was in this long stone house on the edge of a woods that Daniel would make physical and emotional space for refugee children to engage in the puzzling task of "developing their minds" in these strange and awful times.

Daniel wrote home:

I arrived here Thursday the first [of October], and right away got myself set up at Les Grillons, which really is a bit of a distance from the town of Le Chambon. Aided by a Mr. Munch and his wife, who are handling the material issues, I still have a lot to do. . . . I think there will be more than twenty [children], and I'm afraid of that, because there will hardly be enough space. But the work is looking very promising, and although we are still on holiday, the house is not too bad, I think. Three young Czechs have already arrived, two boys and a girl, brought here by their parents. . . .

In the business of sheltering children, there were many jobs to be done, and many on the Plateau were already engaged with the endeavor. There were those who retrieved children from the train stations; those who took care of their daily needs; those who passed on messages or forged documents. There were those who inspired at the pulpit—not just André Trocmé but a dozen other pastors—and others who inspired in the classroom or the town square; and those assigned to the psychological well-being of the kinds of children who were so seized by fear and sorrow that they had night terrors and wet their beds.

As the director of Les Grillons, Daniel would have to do all these things, and more. *Il faut tout faire,* he wrote home. Everything must be done. There were accounts to be figured out, special releases to write up to get children out of the concentration camps. And then, the children's immediate, physical needs had to be dealt with: "We must clothe the children, head to foot," he wrote home, "get their measurements, find sabots for them, and practically become cobblers ourselves." Whenever possible, Daniel had to be in contact with parents—those who were not already dead or disappeared. Many of the children had been in flight for months or even years, and were often in terrible shape. Of them, Daniel wrote: "We have to take care of their health in large and small ways (lungs and boo-boos)." He had to travel—meeting with aid organizations and bureaucrats. He had to deal with problems he'd never imagined before—how to procure big batches of hot water bottles, or how to get a vat of soup up a steep hill on a wheelbarrow in the snow.

Les Grillons was no École des Roches. Daniel reported that temperatures regularly fell to minus five or minus ten Celsius, well below freezing, even inside the house, with its walls of thick stone. There was barely enough to eat. The children had to walk twelve kilometers a day—first down to Le Chambon-sur-Lignon for classes, then over to a cafeteria building for food, and then back up the hill in the evenings. Here, nighttime smelled of wood burning in the great hearth, and the wet wool of the children's cloaks and socks and scarves, drying after a long day soaked in snow. These children were not future rulers and politicians and industrialists, like the children at École des Roches. They were, at that moment, the cast-offs of the world.

For them, Daniel learned to lope down the hills and clamber back up, over and over again, his glasses fogging up in the cold. For them, he would start to figure out the documents and the rooms and the space and the boo-boos, large and small. Some things were easy enough—the practice of reading to the children, for instance, as Daniel himself had been read to as a boy. Evenings, once the school day was over and dinner was done, everyone would gather together, a fire crackling nearby. Daniel would open a book and begin—chapter by chapter, adventure by adventure, carrying the children to different places and peoples and worlds of love and bravery, suffering and inspiration.

There were very few books to choose from at Les Grillons—Daniel hoped more would arrive after Christmas—but one was a bestselling adventure novel called *Premier de cordée—First on the Rope*—by R. Frison-Roche. In it, young Pierre, the son of a famous mountain guide in the Mont Blanc region of the Alps, wants to become a guide himself. His family is dead set against it, particularly because Pierre's father has recently been killed—struck by lightning—up on the needle peaks of Les Drus. The book describes, in dizzying detail, a series of climbs and the resulting loss of life and limb. Pierre bears the burden of his father's death, from that bolt out of the blue over which there is never any control—and then, after an abysmal fall of his own, the curse of vertigo.

The children who sat together to listen to the story of brave young Pierre and the cracking ice, and the daring jumps, and the near misses in the lofty heights, ranged from six to sixteen. With names like Kurt and Juan, Sarah and Simone, Stanislas and Antyma, they had come from Spain and Germany, from Czechoslovakia and Poland and Austria. Some were Jewish, and some were not. When they laid themselves down to sleep, all of them had dark pictures in their mind's eye; they all had sorrows. And so, when they crammed into a circle each evening to hear Daniel's voice narrating the story of young Pierre, the children surely pictured something vivid and large—the image of vast yet somehow attainable heights; the feel of bounding upward; the music of a well-purposed pace; pictures of stars at night in the highest places; the dizzying pull of vertigo; even the brilliant, incandescent look of death itself. . . .

"The guide had been struck by lightning," Daniel read from chapter nine, "at the very instant when he was preparing to straddle the rappel line. He had been struck while standing upright, with his right hand grasping a hold, his left flat against his body, feeling for the rope, and his head bent slightly forward. . . . The fingers of his right hand still gripped the rock. . . ."

Did Daniel close the book and end there? Was it time for bed?

Clearly, the story had had some effect on the children. "The other day," Daniel wrote home, "seven of the girls left the house to do some mountain climbing." You can read his smile between the lines. "When you know the country here well, you see how funny this is. In the end, the girls found a rock and managed to struggle up it with the help of their rope. . . ."

Now that I am in Le Chambon-sur-Lignon myself, I can't stop thinking about those seven cast-off girls, and how they woke up one day on the edge of a towering forest, on a perch in the dazzling hills. Looking for a rock to climb.

On my first morning here, I keep trying to get the attention of an old black dog. He's been wandering around the café on the ground floor of the Hôtel du Velay, sniffing methodically under tables for food, and I am sitting alone at a long window, light pouring in, feeling the March chill through my wool sweater and scarf. A cast of characters surrounds: the handsome older men with flowing gray hair, drinking coffee; the owner, making saucy remarks to a disheveled man in the corner; some guys with cameras, laughing. People are greeting each other, and kissing, and gossiping as the old black dog shuffles from person to person, hand to hand. But not to me.

I'm nervous, of course, to begin.

But soon, my coat is on and I am outside in the fresh light of day. Everyone else is bundled up, too; they wear good thick boots and sensible fleece. Locals look slim and strong, with mild, attractive faces. The men are wiry and many of the women have their hair cropped prettily short.

The streets in the center of town are narrow; the buildings, of stone-gray brick, come right up to the sidewalk. Here is a *tabac*, where you can buy pens and lottery tickets and phone cards. Here is a bookstore; here are two pharmacies, a couple of bakeries, a couple of banks, a chocolate store. Across the way from my hotel, a little square with a stone fountain, dry for the winter months. Then, turning a corner, I get a first look at the Protestant church that figures so famously in the histories of the Plateau. A simple square form in grayish stone, it has one rounded stained-glass window above the door, and a bell on top. Etched on its front face is the single phrase: AIMEZ-VOUS LES UNS LES AUTRES. Love one another.

Here André Trocmé delivered, during the thirties and forties, sermons of great, galvanizing power: "Loving, forgiving, and doing good to our adversaries is our duty. . . . We shall resist whenever our adversaries demand of us obedience contrary to the orders of the gospel." Religion, I've learned over many years, is a complicated social form. But there is no doubt that—against the horrible backdrop of the emerging Holocaust—resist his listeners did.

Beyond the church flows the great winding Le Lignon. Beyond that, there are craggy hills with pine trees anchored up the sides, towering higher and higher overhead, and swallows that dip and dart through the skies. Then, a highway ribbons off toward ever darker patches of green. They say that on the clearest days, from the highest spots around, you can see the lazy hump of Mont Mézenc and the isosceles point of Le Lizieux, and maybe, even, the crystal outlines of Mont Blanc itself, hundreds of miles away.

The Plateau Vivarais-Lignon really does inspire raptures in those who have seen it, and all the more so in those who have sought to understand it. If I am honest, I must admit I've been in a bit of a swoon myself these many months since I first opened Hallie's *Lest Innocent Blood Be Shed*. Because if there is a Babi Yar—with its abysmal depths—there is also the great reciprocal longing for height. And here I am, now, walking in the fresh air, my head tilted up and back, taking in these streets and these stones, and these fresh-faced people going by.

One thing is clear: It's beautiful here. So beautiful, in fact, that I could almost stop in my tracks right now, and decide that beauty *is* truth, and truth is beauty, and be done with it.

Ha. Well. I do know how symbolic logics go, and I know how to parse them. The equation—ludicrous on the surface, but bearing a real emotional force—would go like this: It is *fitting* that (morally) beautiful people live here in this stunning place. And it would have a corollary: This physically beautiful place has somehow produced a morally beautiful people. And it would have another corollary, now in much more familiar terms: To be born here *makes* you good. This whole line of logic would be an outrage to real social science, of course, but stranger outrages have wedged their way into influential views of the world. People become, say, nationalists—and then write books about their nation, or sing about their nation, or scream about their nation with raised fists—because on some level they think their mountains are more divine, their women more stunning, their blood redder, their beards more manly, their customs more gracious. And even, while we're at it: their skulls more perfected than any other skulls. How different is it to say, *ah!*—there's something in the water here, something in the air, something in the heights, some magical something that bestows goodness? How is that logic so different?

It's a kind of magical thinking from the deepest places, in the oldest fairy tales: The sun dazzles, the mountain streams are crystal clear, the waters, the mosses, so vivid against the rocks; it's easy to believe that they heal the world, all by themselves. It's easy to believe that to be born here makes you beautiful on the inside, makes you good.

I might as well go ahead and say it out loud. It's what I'm thinking, anyway.

BUT STILL. *Il faut tout faire.* There is much to do, and nothing can be done without people. Real people. The ones who don't live in the history books or on walls of museums.

Muriel, for starters, who turns out to be as lovely as her messages to me these past several months, dotted with encouraging exclamation points. She has big blue eyes and a pixie haircut, and the first time we meet she hugs me like an old friend, before bringing me a perfect cup of hot sweet tea at the tourist office where she works. Muriel grew up on the Plateau, in a little farming hamlet down the road. She's not a historian, but it's dawning on me that she probably knows every single one of the old people around here who remember the war. In her work, she gathers testimony, carefully preserving letters and names and addresses and dates. She also leads small groups of schoolchildren and tourists around Le Chambon to tell them about the many sites of rescue. When survivors come through—as they do from time to time—she is the one who hears their stories and, if they allow, records them.

Muriel takes me around town, telling me stories of the war. In her voice, it all sounds like a song. She shows me the train station, now painted a peach pink, where the refugees arrived by the scores. She shows me some of the buildings in town that have special meaning to the story of the war; even my hotel, where the old black dog now roams, was once a first stop for the refugees. And then she points out two houses down the street. The first was Tante Soly—Aunt Soly—one of the early homes for refugee children during the war. The second, right next door, was—from 1943 onward—a home for German soldiers who had been wounded on the Eastern Front. They would lie in their beds, alone with their thoughts there, even as the foreign accents of child refugees wafted up into their windows. As it happened, Muriel tells me, pointing up at the building's second story, these war-weary Germans never denounced the refugee children, or the locals who protected them. No one ever came to harm because of them.

Then, I meet Monsieur Bollon, the scholar from whom I first learned about the Plateau's long history of shelter. Monsieur Bollon's face is rugged, handsome, his hair a shock of white, his voice soft. He takes me around to the sites that served as homes for children during the war, pointing out the places where the children ran into the forest to hide or where barking dogs alerted people to danger.

I meet other people, briefly, at the pizza place, at the mayor's office, in the library. Once in a while, I say a couple of words to these bright new faces about my family connection to the place, my grandmother's house, the book my aunt Barbara sent. I begin, then I trail off, embarrassed. How could these things matter? They don't.

I gird myself, and gird myself again. There is so much to do, and I am dazzled and I am shy and, as always, a little scared. I make phone calls, despite being shy. I spend hours in my tiny hotel room, looking out the windows, looking beyond the windows, taking notes.

Il faut tout faire. This is the beginning.

———

On my second full day in Le Chambon, I decide that I need to see Les Grillons with my own eyes. And I need to walk there, as Daniel and the children walked there all those years ago. I have a map of the area—provided by Muriel—and I have a few hours. So I bundle into my coat, my hat, my mittens, and, map in hand, I start past the town square, past the post office, and then past the train station again. As far as I can tell—looking now at the long and winding road ahead, puffing forward with longer and stronger strides—the entire walk will be uphill.

I've been here before. That is, I've been in this moment before—the one when you arrive in a place you've thought about and dreamed about and imagined and, in my case, drawn little circle-schemes for in journals, or on the empty back pages of books, or the reverse side of envelopes. And so now I begin, as I have begun before—trying to figure out the lay of a brand-new land.

How to be good? The question looks as large and embraceable as the nighttime sky. But it isn't. Not for social scientists, anyway. With a question like that—or any large question, really—each of the disciplines lives in its own little inquiry neighborhood, with its own rites and habits, where "goodness" comes in smaller packages, each with its own animating logic. Political science is the study of the assertion of power, asking: Who gets to decide? When? And who's got an army to make that happen? Economics is the study of exchange—of money and goods, yes, but also of all things deemed valuable in a given place and time. With political science and economics, we take goodness where we can find it: in the lack of wars, perhaps, or the means of distributing or sharing necessities.

Sociology and anthropology share the domain of social groups—their formation and boundaries and maintenance. But they are also quite different, in ways that actually matter very much in my work here. Sociology, as it developed in North America, has focused on "our society"—our cities, farms, neighborhoods, and enclaves—and tends to ask the kinds of questions about groups that are socially meaningful to us: Who has wealth, health, income, access? And how do, say, race, gender, religion, age, ethnicity matter to those? Sociology has the great advantage of knowing what it's about before research is even conducted. Its sense is literally common, agreed on, right here at home. Because of that, it can embrace methods that thrive when there are a smaller number of meaningful things, or variables: surveys, statistics, fixed questions about known institutions, with nice big data sets that can be crunched this way and that. So in sociology, if you wanted to know about goodness, you might jump straight to things that common sense tells us are related to morality: churches, charities, stated beliefs. You might then conduct surveys about how often people show up on Saturdays or Sundays to their temple of choice, how they vote, how much they give away. Fair enough.

Because of the peculiarities of its own history, though, anthropology has long looked farther afield for its social groups—literally to faraway islands, and jungles, and deserts, and hollows. You can blame colonialism for that. As missionaries and explorers first descended onto new landscapes hundreds of years ago looking for markets and souls, and as they first spied brand-new peoples going about their business in life—eating, drinking, working, worshipping—they were clearly struck with both wonder and terror at the strangeness of it all. They wrestled with the meaning of this strangeness and—with their own meager conceptual tools—tried to figure out if they were beholding madmen in these new worlds, or grown children, or demons, or not-quite-humans at all.

Eventually, anthropology emerged as a social science that at a baseline accepted the rationality (and, finally, the dignity) of all peoples, in all their diversities. And anthropology came up with methods that were flexible enough to describe ways of being in the world that have their very own sense and coherence: worlds where you can gain prestige by having little, say; where a family isn't nuclear; where the beings you worship look like trees or men or nothing at all; where gender comes in many splendid forms; where healing depends, too, on a social body. Or where goodness itself doesn't look only like a blond man and a white lamb, legs folded, under a tree—but like a million other vivid things.

With anthropology, the doors are flung open wide to sense. And common sense, far from being the amiable pal that guides you aright in life, becomes the quiet tyrant that ruins everything—as it actually prevents you from seeing other senses, other logics, other ways of being. Common sense makes you think that church attendance might have something to do with goodness; but anthropology takes you to places where that might be the furthest thing from the truth. Because of all this, when you start out in anthropology—innocent as you are—you have to kill common sense in yourself. And that long process of the murder of common sense—and creating space for new senses, in their own terms—is called fieldwork.

Fieldwork is like walking into a big dark room with no light switch.

Lost, you need to figure out with all your senses what makes sense (Who's in charge of what, where? What's a family here? What is a saint? How do you show gratitude or give a gift?). All of the social sciences are, or should be, empirical; they all take their questions and smack, let them butt up against the world. But unlike the cool-and-collected data sets of the other social sciences, with anthropology's fieldwork, you spend every day guessing, sometimes wildly; every day getting things wrong, breaking rules, hurting. But it is only by crashing into things that you learn what goes where. With each crash, another hypothesis is falsified. Hooray, you say—or try to say.

Fieldwork is always hard at the beginning. It's always about taking your map and going someplace strange. You arrive, and almost immediately, you're lost. Nothing is as you expect; but what you do see is peculiar, luminous, indelible.

There were those first moments in the Russian village that became my home for over a year. I had traveled from Saint Petersburg a day and a night and a day, before a rusted old bus finally left me off at the very last stop on the line. I found a spot in front of a grassy knoll at the edge of the village. After I'd waited for hours, a small group of farmers appeared above the knoll, dressed all in white. They were walking home from a long day of work in the fields, rough-hewn rakes and scythes in hand, a quiet ballet of return.

Or later, in the Caucasus, I'd landed near green mountains ravaged by war, passed long tangles of police and guards at the airport, and driven twisting roads under pounding rain to arrive at last in the village where I would be living. Power was down. Inside the compound that was to be my home, three girls—daughters of the family, all laughing and pretty—led me to my room by the blue glow of their cell phones, under the electric staccato of the storm.

These first moments, they dislodge expectations. They scrawl all over the precious schemas and equations. They make them strange. They make everything possible.

Naturally, inside those moments, nothing is ever quite as it appears.

I look down at my map now. It seems I'm supposed to go past this roundabout and then up toward what looks like the beginnings of a forest. I pass the sign I saw from the bus the other day, for the Collège Cévenol. I pass more houses, some of them looking very old, of stone, and some of them looking quite modern. I imagine the people inside, talking to each other or eating; watching television or chatting on the phone.

Now, from force of habit, I draw a circle in my head. And fill it with the people in that house right there. I don't know them yet, but I figure they are wearing fleece; they are attractive and wiry and mild. I picture them about to open their door.

To answer my questions—how to be good when it's hard to be good—I need to know these people in my circle. I need to learn from them. I need to be the kind of person they can be themselves around, rather than one they elaborately perform for. That means I need to earn their trust, to be worthy of real entry. There are no shortcuts for that. It was hard to live inside that one-room log cabin with the Russian villagers, and to become the kind of person who could witness their mornings and nights, their work, their states of health—good and bad—their crabby moments, their pain and their tears. And to share my own. It takes time, even if the clock is ticking, the meter running on your limited research funding. It was months before I did any formal interviews with villagers in Russia. Before that, I spent days and even weeks going out into the fields and forests with the farmers, hauling logs onto a sleigh, cooking, helping with the cows, carrying water, pail by pail, from the nearby lake for cleaning and drinking. People watched me. Got used to me.

It will take that here, too, I know—before I get to be the kind of person who gets to come inside.

In fieldwork, soon enough, you see how people have their very own common sense. And one of the things that means is that they will interpret what they think you are up to in your research, according to things that matter to them. So, for example, they will decide—out of kindness or expediency—to take you to their leader. In Russia, folks kept wanting me to talk with the head of some ethnographic institute, or with the head of some local collective farm, or with a group of ladies at the police station. In the Caucasus, it was this member of parliament or that clan leader, or some other person who represented one of the many ethnic minorities. People want you to talk with their experts. And so you talk with their experts—you meet the guy who keeps all the sepia photographs of the local soldiers who fought in the Second World War; you meet the woman who casts the spells; you talk with the mayor; you write a polite message to the head of the institute. You are grateful to have someone to meet with when no one else seems inclined.

But if my real need is to understand the whole social lay of the land in a new place, meeting with leaders and experts—powerful and compelling though they may be—is never as important as getting to know, well, folks. Folks who aren't practiced at telling big stories with formal logics that happen to line up with broader systems of power; folks who, in fact, live mostly outside the swirl. Here on the Plateau, I'm already aware that there will be a particular hurdle to that end. From the earliest mentions of their rescue effort during the Second World War, it is clear that people here mostly really don't like talking about what they or their kinfolk did back then. "We're not heroes," they would say. "We just did what was natural." And that was it. So, I have on my hands a methodological puzzle: the folks I most need to learn from are likely to be silent.

That's fine with me. I like it better in that quieter world. I just do.

There are fewer and fewer houses on the road now. The trees are growing darker, taller. I keep walking, up and up. I'm sweating and my feet are starting to get wet. I realize, after a time, that I have no idea if I'm even on the right road.

I press on, toward the darkest patch of trees in the distance.

In the Plateau, the question of *how to be good* also gets wrapped up almost immediately with the problem of religion, where religion is seen—at least by some—as the *cause* of the goodness. That logic goes like this:

The Plateau is the place where extraordinary rescue happened during the Second World War. The Plateau is a region with a high number of Protestants. Therefore, Protestantism is the cause of the extraordinary rescue. Well, sadly that does not parse, any more than it parses that all men are Romans, just because Caesar happened to have been one, once. Goodness and religion might be intertwined, or they might not.

Religion is always complicated, always hard to meaningfully fit into discrete social science boxes, with causal arrows pointing this way or that. Not only do people have very strong and often very sincere ideas and feelings about their own religions—religion is itself, socially speaking, so much more complex than just the set of authoritative texts that experts hold forth on. It can't be understood by holy books alone. It is, as practiced everywhere, a deep and moving target. In Russia and the North Caucasus, it was full of surprises for me—communist sorcerers, Orthodox priests with elaborate demonologies, affable Soviet-era Muslims, fashion-forward *adyghe-khabze* girls—each of which, I learned, possessed its own uncommon sense.

It's easy to understand why you might want to just go ahead and knit the Protestantism and goodness together here: You think about the ghettos and Babi Yar and the mobile killing units and Auschwitz, and then you go by that beautiful church, with its simple words of love, and you think of brave and fiery sermons and all the stories of rescue. And you get out your survey questions, and you find the Protestants, and you correlate them with the rescue and, depending on who you are, you see some grace in that.

But despite the beauty of the little church in Le Chambon, I can say this with full assurance already: to claim that Protestants (or Protestant-ness) caused the magnificent rescue here doesn't work. All you need to do is show a little bit of what other Protestants, worldwide, got up to during that war—say, the 66 percent of Germany's population—to reveal that hypothesis as falsified. And, of course, claiming heroism for Protestants also ignores the fact that it wasn't only Protestants doing the rescuing. There were also Catholics, Jews, people of no religious affiliation, or people who had religious affiliations but doubted and wrestled with their beliefs, just the same.

All this to say: Just because the church is lovely, and the people here are mild-faced, does not mean that the Protestant religion is the cause of the rescue here. Yet still—in the privacy of my being—the words on that little church, "Love one another," hold a newly wrenching and revelatory power over my heart. Daniel Trocmé, in faraway Beirut, saw in Christianity "both the beautiful and the true, and the false and the ugly." And who is to say his cri de coeur from the sun-drenched land of many religions was not moral and analytical, both?

Sometimes religion makes you better than you might have been without it; sometimes it makes you worse. To me, this is what counts here: Did a person open the door to a stranger when it was hard to open the door? Did they do it once; twice; ten times? Did they teach their children so well about opening doors that those children learned to do it themselves, as a matter of habit?

It's true, institutional religion is important. But what people really do is more important, more real. After all, Jesus said, "Ye shall know them by their fruits." And why shouldn't that also be a methodological caution?

I'm LOST. I've been walking uphill for almost an hour, but no sign of Les Grillons. Big scary trucks keep zooming by, so I've found a spot in a snow pile on the side of the road where I can stop and take off my gloves and think a minute. The map said to go right at the crossroads, and so I went right. But as far as I walked, there was nothing but a great corridor of pine trees. Then I tried going left instead, and still I saw nothing resembling the long stone house in the pictures I'd studied.

My map is sweaty now, and crumpled. Between cars and trucks, I can hear the sound of melted snow trickling down the road. That, and my own breathing. And the singing of some stray birds.

It's such a simple set of roads and turns—how can I have lost my way?

It's absurd. I scan the edge of the woods at the highway. Could it be that Les Grillons is simply hidden from view, tucked in somewhere among the trees? Or is it possible that the house no longer exists?

I go down one road, then another. Then I follow a snow-lined creek into the forest, down this path and that. Still nothing. I pause for a moment. The towering pines are heavy with snow. I fold my neck back toward the sky. I close my eyes and breathe. Then, just as I am about to leave the woods again, I see, as if it had emerged from behind some cloak of invisibility, a long stone house, divided into many sections, just down the road. Les Grillons.

A woman is going in and out of it, with something in her hands. From the distance, I strain to imagine outlines of children from deep in the past. Some are running or playing or carrying water—or a rope. I try to imagine the inside of that house: its hearth; its small cold rooms; Daniel, finally settled in himself, reading to the newly arrived children. His glasses are flickering by the light of the hearth, his voice rising and lowering dramatically.

And because of his voice, I imagine now a small group of girls, listening, rapt, longing to climb.

It strikes me: Sure, it was a little absurd, the image that Daniel conjured for his parents of the rope, the rock, the earthbound girls. You imagine the girls' shoes, you hear the sound of them slipping in the cold. You imagine them miscalculating and falling, and then running back to Les Grillons when—as Daniel reported to his parents—a pack of stray dogs that roamed the forest paths got too terrifying.

But it makes sense to me what the girls were thinking, even if it made Daniel laugh at the time. To be a mountain climber, all you need is a rope and a rock, right? To find yourself in the cleanest air, the purest sky, higher than the jackdaws can circle—higher even than this Plateau—all you need is to find your rope and go.

I'm for science. I really am. But I understand those girls, I think. I know what it is to have improbable longings for the crystal heights.

BACK AT THE HÔTEL DU VELAY that night, after hours of walking and searching, I am tired. And, despite the pleasant faces, the deepening story, the beauty of the endeavor I get to be part of, I am, I admit, feeling overwhelmed. *Il faut tout faire.* And so much of what there is to do is just waiting, being quiet, and waiting some more.

I went to graduate school thinking that my shiny mind was my best asset—a shiny mind that could take in some dazzling theories (Bakhtin and Foucault; Althusser and Vygotsky; Sperber and Halbwachs!), apply them to a difficult puzzle, and—*poof!*—come up with some clever new thing to say about the world. But by now, that idea seems practically ridiculous, not least because my mind doesn't feel so shiny anymore.

The hardest part of fieldwork—and the most important thing to be good at—is gathering what you need to gather in order to answer the questions that matter to you. Things could have gone differently in my life. I could have gathered fossils. Or bird scat. Or whale talk. Or numbers, in their glorious aggregate. This I know: It helps if you love the stuff you gather. An anthropologist who doesn't love people will find it hard to listen, to wait, to watch. An anthropologist who does love people may crave affection more than is good for science or for herself, maybe, but she might also be inclined, by love, to pay extra attention; she might even swoon a little at the marvelous human theater of it all.

Beyond the obvious barriers here—the seventy years that have elapsed from the time of the war, and the fact that those who still remember are known for not wanting to talk about it—lie the methodological limitations: If the question is how people are good when it's time to be good, what exactly counts as a goodness? You can't just sit down with a pen and paper and count goodnesses or nicenesses. Or hugs. Or invitations. Or gifts. You have to figure out about habits. You have to learn them, like you'd learn a map, like how you learn the difference between a pathway in the forest and a road, or a stream. You have to learn them so that the habits of being are visible to you when you close your eyes.

You learn them like you learn how water is likely to flow in a storm. You aren't sure, but you have some assurance when it comes to the lay of the land. You can anticipate.

In my work, I get to ask the best questions. My research on memory let me cast an immense net, where I got to learn, over time, about how people dreamed and loved, and incanted and cursed, how they wandered in forests to breathe in the healing air, or how they were lost, in their soul, in a war—I am grateful for that, as I am grateful for the great big questions now. But in messy, informal Russia, you had only to show up at someone's house in the village and bang on their heavy wooden door before the flurry of welcome, the argument about taking off shoes or not, the tea, the candy, the offering of stories, a first time, a second time, a tenth time. Even when you'd return to the village after years of absence, the old women would throw their big strong arms around you—giggling and patting you, petting you like a cat.

The Plateau is going to be different, I can tell. You call people *vous* here, and Monsieur and Madame and the like. They give you a wide berth. You give them the same. Even as I was walking up the hill toward Les Grillons, they crossed the street rather than share the sidewalk with me. Here the shutters close; then they open; then they close again.

Monsieur Bollon has told me wonderful stories about André Trocmé's life. Trocmé was, he said, a great man, a larger-than-life man once called *un violent vaincu par Dieu*—a violent man, conquered by God. But he was a man. He made a point of warning me not to put Trocmé or anyone else up on a pedestal. I know I'm not inclined to linger too long on singular personalities, but the advice is not lost on me. I know the dangers in idolizing a person, or a people. Fieldwork is hard. If you do it right, it can be perilous, as you undermine your own common sense and try to merge it with another one. One minute you are arriving on a grassy knoll with farmers coming home in white, and the next thing you know, you are getting cures for curses, hands waving over your bare stomach, and you start wondering if maybe there really is something to fear alone in the cemetery at night. Or you, who considered yourself a feminist from age twelve, are suddenly wondering if maybe, as people say, you really are selfish, as a woman, for not having children. Are you?

Something can break inside, as you work for those moments when you get an idea right or a word right, the moments when you finally master the liquid gestures of these other folk. All in the quiet hope that you might, one day, say, be mistaken for a kolkhoz worker on a train. It all feels so lonely, then, and beautiful and right. And then lonely again.

Something can break at the pedestal of the new common sense.

I collect the moments as best I can; I listen and watch and wait. It's a tricky business, yes, the meeting of the lofty equation and the childlike swoon. And, one foot after the next, it's a tricky business to labor up a hill when everything you are seeking—home, hearth, family, love—is still invisible to the eye.

There was a girl, among the girls at Les Grillons, who was older than the rest. Her name was Fanny, and she was born in Lodz, Poland, in 1925. By the early 1930s, Fanny had learned many things that other children didn't know how to do. When she heard *"Hep, hep, Jude!"* chanted by mobs on the streets, she learned how to crawl up into a space above her kitchen door. She learned what the face of her father looked like when the police arrived and he threatened to kill her with his own hands if she didn't run *now*. Later, in France, she learned how to wear a yellow star, and then how to hide in a slaughterhouse, and then among the roots of trees. And once, she learned how even their family dog could stop moving, and then stop breathing, when police finally nabbed them all.

As a child, Fanny knew very little of the religion that would drive her life onto this dangerous course. She remembered how her parents didn't eat during Yom Kippur. She remembered how a rat once showed up under their sukkah in the courtyard, and how all the ladies stood on chairs, screaming. She remembered, too, how scared she'd always been of that extra glass of wine poured at the end of the Passover Seder, because, she'd been told, the Messiah was supposed to come and drink from it when the time came. Every year she would watch the wine, as the men opened the front door and recited, "Pour out thy wrath upon the heathen that have not known thee, and upon the kingdoms that have not called upon thy name," waiting for evidence, in the wine's diminishing, of the coming of the end of days.

So maybe it wasn't surprising that when Fanny was eventually hidden away in a convent—far from her parents and her brother, who had all been arrested and sent to prisons and camps—she began to have nightmares of angels and cathedrals. Terrified, she went to speak with the bishop himself, saying maybe, maybe she was in the wrong religion? Maybe this was a sign? But the bishop responded, with words that would stay with her for the rest of her life: "This is not the way to gain souls to God."

And that's how Fanny got sent to Les Grillons, where she was the oldest of all the children; La Maison des Roches, the only other place where there was room for her, had too many "big boys." She was so far from her home in Lodz, where 160,000 Jews now lived, crammed in a world wrapped in barbed wire. But she was safe, for the time being at least. By day, she went to the Cévenol School. In the evenings, she returned for roll call, and Daniel's stories—*Heidi, Toilers of the Sea, The Swiss Family Robinson, The Sea-Wolf, Les Misérables, First on the Rope.*

I wonder: On that one December morning in 1942, did Fanny join the little band of girls, with their rope—a rope I picture somehow floating alongside them, erect in the air, as if with a will of its own, with its own sense of direction, looking for its own mountain to climb? Or did she go out into the forest—as I have done—away from the road, away from the gorgeous vistas and valleys, lost, for the moment, to her old home and her new home, too?

Or did she stay inside that cold day—near the fireplace, near Daniel, as he wrote letters about hot water bottles and vats of soup and wooden shoes—and did she think again about the terrors of angels, such as they are, or might be?

Chapter 5

ALL THE LITTLE CRICKETS

O what a voice it was, for making household music
at the fireside of an honest man!

—CHARLES DICKENS, *THE CRICKET ON THE HEARTH*

U P IN LES GRILLONS, Christmas was coming, and Daniel was far from home. But what was home to him now, anyway, in the seventh month of his thirty-second year? The world outside was at war, France was under occupation, and Daniel had made his move, up into the Plateau. What was home to him, after all of his seeking and all of his wandering?

Was home a place?

Was it somehow still Verneuil-sur-Avre, in the north of France, where Daniel was raised under those luminous gray skies, and where his elderly parents—having watched École des Roches turn into Frontstalag 200A—were now holed up, running a small and weakened version of the once great boarding school? Or was home Maslacq, where Daniel had grumbled that he was suffocating, and that money made men mean; where he fought with the director of his school, and periodically dashed down to Marseille to go see the "pretty little box" he just couldn't get out of his mind?

Home. Two clicks of Dorothy's ruby slippers send us, eternally, back there, to that place, full of grace; the place unlike any other. Home, that locus of coziness and common sense, where we know the cracks in all the sidewalks, the knots in all the trees, the water stains on all the walls; where we know how to intuit our way through cordiality and conflict, the whole lay of the social land; where our kith and kin surround us; where our language and symbols and stories resonate. Home in a warring world should be the place to exhale, the shelter from the storms. But where was home to a young man full of great centrifugal longing?

All of Daniel's brothers and sisters were now struggling to figure out how to live their own lives under siege. On November 8, 1942, François received a German delegation at the magnesium factory he directed in the southern French town of Lannemezan, in the Pyrenees. François had a beautiful American wife, small children, a cozy home, a cadre of close friends that included some Jews and some refugees from the Spanish Civil War; and now, in addition to a factory full of workers to direct and protect, he had an unsettling group of Germans at his door.

Daniel's eldest brother, Charles, was a doctor in nearby Saint-Étienne—a city buzzing with refugees and ever-heightening police activity. His sister Elizabeth was clear across the ocean with her husband, Robert. Daniel's sister Suzie—still ten years from meeting her American husband—was a doctor in a tuberculosis sanatorium about two hours east of Verneuil-sur-Avre. There, at the once-glorious Château de Franconville—graced with vast gardens, and marble lions to either side of the front door, and great staircases leading to ballrooms—Suzie pumped oxygen into dying patients' lungs, day after day after day.

Affable, boyish Daniel was the closest thing the Trocmé family had to a black sheep. Just two years earlier, François had written that Daniel's spirit was "nothing but ardor, contestation and generosity"—an uncomfortable mix, if you were a Trocmé. Indeed, his parents had fussed and worried—not without reason—that his political and emotional ardors would lead him down dangerous paths. By now, though, the entire family had been forced to confront their own dark nights of the soul. Their friends and cohorts among the French elite were wavering, some even casting their lot with the Vichy regime. No longer did the Trocmé world feel uniquely wholesome, grounded, and rock solid. Their lives were unsettled, barbed, strange. Would they, as in the Parable of the Vine, bear fruit in the end?

So perhaps home had moved, for Daniel, farther afield, beyond the now wobbling world of the France where he'd been raised. Under the brilliant sun and bright waters of Beirut, perhaps, or up in the mountains of Syria, or in the Egyptian deserts where he'd seen how the Pharaohs were entombed. Perhaps home was the aggregate of every one of the places he'd wandered those years of his early youth, where the cryptic music of foreign languages wafted through the air. Where he'd learned about how there were really many civilizations, not just one. Where he'd learned that religion—even his own Christian religion—could be at once beautiful and foul.

In the winter of 1942, in any event, home would be right here, in a great long stone house in a cold place with fierce winds, surrounded by pine trees and rocky escarpments. Home was a hearth, surrounded by twenty children who had come from all over Europe.

And home was lonesome now, in some ways—Daniel wrote to his parents that he was *"vraiment bien seul,"* truly very lonely. But the children around him, like the twittering crickets in the old legends—*les grillons*—distracted Daniel from his solitude. They went to school again—the best students to Cévenol—and at the end of the day they gathered to do their homework, chattering and debating and sometimes even singing with their improbable leader. Referring to his famously poor sense of pitch, Daniel wrote his parents, "I'm the one who has to direct songs and teach the children!! Imagine the scene!"

Imagine the scene.

The winter had been bearing down on the residents of Les Grillons.

The rules of life in the cold season were hard, and if they were broken or forgotten, disaster was likely. By no means could you leave any water in the faucet, or anywhere else in the pipes, since it would freeze and explode them. By no means could you leave skin exposed to the elements. Fire was not to be taken lightly, either. One night in mid-December, during a brutal patch of weather, the children left their wet clothes to dry too close to the embers. At one o'clock in the morning, they awoke to unruly flames engulfing "two brand-new cloaks, one cloak in good shape, a coat, a pair of pants, two berets, two scarves, and two chairs." "The result," wrote Daniel to his parents: "the children will be cold." And, he added, "when you know what it took to procure these items"—up the hill, down the hill, over to Lyon, over to Saint-Étienne, down to Le Puy-en-Velay—"you could almost cry." Daniel was given a stove for his own room, but he lit it only twice in as many months. Dry wood was too rare, too precious, and his own comfort not worth the expense of it. The cloaks, the mittens, the scarves, the fire. The sweater his mother offered to send but which he needed not for himself but for a child.

What was home?

Maybe home wasn't exactly a place at all.

Home was warmth, in the cold.

What else?

When Daniel had taken the job, the understanding was that he would be in charge of "moral, intellectual, and spiritual life" at Les Grillons. A couple—the Munchs, with small children of their own—was in charge of the material and logistical duties. But, in these cold and difficult times, even that burden proved too much for them. The young wife would repair to her room at night, alone with her fireplace and her baby. Daniel, who had grown up in the orderly École des Roches, found this situation less and less tolerable. Wash was piling up. The children were ill clothed. The menu—Daniel was still French, after all—was "ridiculously monotonous." Meanwhile, his own duties were also piling up. He wrote to his parents:

There are administrative issues to be settled . . . social insurance, taxes, family allowances to be regulated. There are reports for funding, photos that must be taken, identity papers, math review for some of the kids (and on this subject, following two hours of substituting in math, I was asked to teach descriptive geometry). I've been also trying, as much as possible, to get in touch with the parents of those children who still have them.

Daniel was staying up late, barely getting sleep some nights. There were endless trips to town to meet with authorities and aid organizations. He wrote anxiously that he had no time for his own work—doctoral research must have still been on his mind—so weighed down was he with every little thing. Before long, he realized that it would be best for him to let the young couple tend to their own lives; and so it was decided, with the help of André Trocmé, that he take over the administrative duties and find a cook and a housemother of his own. One of the children in his care at Les Grillons—a little girl named Odette—had a marvelous mother who just might fit the bill, and Daniel was clearly excited by the idea of bringing her in to help. This woman, Hermine Orsi, herself a Protestant refugee from Italy, was "hardworking, cheerful," Daniel wrote to his parents, and that "filled him with joy."

And so, home was now, well, homely. And homeliness was somehow a source of happiness.

What else was home?

Soon, it was the holidays: School was out; a few of the children joined their families; most, though, remained at Les Grillons. Packages arrived, from Daniel's parents, but also from a hodgepodge of well-wishers: A local woman named Aimé Guibert presented the children with nice leather mittens. The "Americans"—Quakers, most likely—and the Secours National, a Vichy aid organization, completely "spoiled the children." The holidays and these small presents brought a kind of relief to Daniel and the children, as did the distractions of games and reading and songs. There were plenty of parties and classes and comings and goings, ones that reminded him of the holidays of his childhood:

> We had a very nice Christmas, with plenty of gifts: books, galoshes, cloaks, sleeping bags, a toboggan, little flutes. . . . The children were truly very happy. (I forgot the society games and the card games—especially the Yellow Dwarf!) Otherwise our Christmas was, in almost all the details, very much like the Christmases at Les Sablons [at École des Roches]. More songs, though, and readings, big meals and gifts. . . .

The Cévenol School was closed until January 18, so at Les Grillons, where new children kept arriving, there was plenty of time to play. Daniel was getting into a rhythm of his duties, the rhythm of bringing new children in. And this, perhaps, was the greatest unexpected gift of all: the children themselves. Daniel had a sneaking feeling, even by November, that he was falling in love with them. "You imagine I forgot them?" he wrote to his parents. "I love them very much, and besides, now, in a fully global manner. But I look forward to knowing them better individually, and that shouldn't wait."

You can imagine the *grillons* in their aggregate: these small and bright beings, with dark and light hair, round and oval faces, broad smiles and faraway, worried looks. It was a busy, buzzing entity in its wholeness. But for Daniel, at thirty-two, the Little Crickets were coming to life as unique persons, too. Right before his eyes.

Peter was coming to life. Peter of the pleasant face and the brown hair swept across his forehead. Peter, born in Berlin, whom Daniel had picked up at the train station just after the new year and who had carried his father's sparkplug, for luck, as Daniel walked him for kilometers through the moonlit forest. Before coming to Le Chambon, Peter had lived at a home for children in Marseille, which he described, many years later, as being like a prison. Once, Peter had gotten himself in big trouble there for asking some SS soldiers on the street for chocolate—brazenly, as if he were any other child. When a friend from Marseille was sent on to Les Grillons, Peter wrote to his father—in the pages of his diary, since he had no way to reach him by post—that if he went to Les Grillons, too, he would have "food fit for kings," which meant, he added parenthetically, "butter, potatoes, etc." Now, settled in the Plateau, Peter played with his new friends, like Amedée, a frail orphaned boy from Paris with light gray eyes and dark hair swept away from his face; and with Kurt, from Austria, with whom he could speak German. Perhaps he was in love with his friend from Marseille, Simone, of the curly black hair; or the Czech girl, Tatiana. Certainly, he was in love with the Spanish girl Rosario, with her black hair tied with a bow on the top of her head. No, none of them ever held hands, he later said. No, they never kissed. Peter had that big smile, but many years later he described himself as a loner. He drew hearts next to the photographs of his parents in his diary.

Peter was becoming a person to Daniel.

And Suzanne, one of the older girls at Les Grillons, from Strasbourg, was becoming a person. After the wartime years of displacement and worry, Suzanne sometimes needed help with her schoolwork, particularly in math. Daniel would sit down and work with her, always with clear and simple explanations. Soon, she would excel in that subject. Suzanne remembered, too, how Daniel would pull vats of soup on a wagon all those kilometers down to the center of town, for the children at public school. And how he would fix shoes at night, while the little ones slept. And how, once he realized it was important to them, he made sure they were dressed well, and in good taste.

And a couple of brothers were becoming people to Daniel—brothers who had been causing him no small measure of trouble. One of them was quite "intelligent, and without egoism," Daniel noted, but full of behavior problems. "No matter how much I upbraid him or punish him . . . he's the most insufferable of children, an exaggerated specimen at an ungrateful age." On a short trip to Lyon, he'd tried to talk with the boy's father—the mother was already gone and there had been a string of new women in the father's life—but the man seemed more interested in his own social life than in the trouble with his children. "What will become of these children, uprooted since their birth?" Daniel fretted.

And there was a little girl who was coming to life, too. Daniel never named her in his letters home, so there is no way to know exactly who she was, but I have a guess. I think she was a girl named Régine, who—in a photograph saved by Peter himself—had dark fuzzy hair pulled back with barrettes, a soft grin, and a sad, deep gaze. Next to her name in a document from Les Grillons is the notation "a good student, literary."

"One of our girls . . ." Daniel wrote,

> not pretty at all, has lost the cousin who was acting as her
> guardian. Not even a year ago, she also lost her father and her
> mother. She was much comforted by an evening bulletin where I
> thanked her, in the name of her sweetness, and her beauty, and
> her indulgence for her comrades. Everyone applauded
> spontaneously.

This girl, whoever she was, was becoming a person to Daniel: her homeliness turning to loveliness here in her new home, her aloneness, out of the blue, turning to belonging.

Some of the children were good students. Some were kind, but slower to learn. Some had the qualities of leaders. All of them, though, were encouraged to express themselves, to show generosity.

"And again . . ." Daniel wrote,

> and again, there are joys. Truly, they make me happy. The other
> day, we had a very animated debate: Say a young girl lives with her
> aged mother. Should she accept to marry a young man whom she
> loves, but who would oblige her to leave for Tonkin? There were
> eight against, and nine for.

Collectively, these little individuals were up to all kinds of things. Another ongoing debate Daniel mentioned to his parents was the question of what the motto of Les Grillons should be. Entirely on their own, the children had pretty much decided on *Agir pour tous!* Act for all!—the same motto as the one at École des Roches. The only serious objection to *Agir pour tous*, the children argued, was that it failed to mention *l'amour du prochaine*: loving your neighbor. This debate delighted Daniel. The next task, he wrote, would be for them to find themselves a proper coat of arms.

Oh, little *grillons*! You head down into the village in the day, off to school with your books. You play in the snow until the tips of your fingers and toes are frostbitten. You are thin as little rails, and some of you are very strong, and others of you are very weak. In the evening, you gather around the fire, you do your homework, and there is a lanky man with dark hair and big ears who runs the games and directs the songs, helps you with homework, and sets the rhythms of the day. He is standing guard, making the rules. Who is he to you, as you grab a rope and look for a mountain to climb?

This is what I see, here in the late fall of 1942, before the war would change again, and things would become newly terrible: Daniel's home was this new beginning. These were the first building blocks of his reconstruction of the world. Ambitions and vanities slid away here, as by the hearth, the young ones—and Daniel himself—learned their ABCs.

"Never have I seen such an easy group of children," Daniel wrote to his parents. But maybe it was more that, here finally at home, his eyes had changed, too.

———

What if you became sure that—regardless of how terrible everything got—returning blows for blows would never fix the world? And you wanted to fix the world.

What if it was the 1930s, and you were a pastor charged with the spiritual lives of a community of villagers way up on an isolated plateau? And what if this community was growing poorer by the year, as its young people left to find prospects—good education and paying work—elsewhere? And what if, even as remote as you were in that plateau, first a trickle and then a stream of refugees—escaping the tumult of the age—began arriving into your world, changing the fluid dynamics of the place?

And what if you had, for good measure, been reading a lot of Gandhi and Thoreau?

You might have thought a lot about what you were going to teach children, for a start.

The Cévenol School was founded in 1938 by pastors André Trocmé and Édouard Theis. As conceived, the school would be of general service to this relatively poor and isolated plateau community—to stave off rural depopulation with quality education—but it would also become a place where a philosophy of nonviolent resistance could be taught to young people. At the heart of the philosophy was this core idea: to fix the world you need to count on the fundamental humanity of every person, you need to see that humanity, and you need to act in such a way to encourage it to emerge, even when people's actions are at their bestial worst.

Like, for example, when they become Nazis.

In 1942 this was still a radical idea-in-progress—that the essential humanity in all of us could lead, in the aggregate, to history bending its long arc toward justice. It was just in August of that very year, after all, that Gandhi launched the Quit India movement, calling for "an orderly British withdrawal" from the subcontinent. And Gandhi, despite the bloody massacres of his followers and the utter incredulity of observers, would win that withdrawal. Twenty years later, Martin Luther King, Jr., would win, too, despite the hoses and nooses and attack dogs. You can say nonviolent resistance is a naive idea, or an impractical one, and you can say that it fails at protecting every individual who wields it. You can have midnight fights about the Manichaean nature, or not, of existence, and argue—really argue, because it matters and it isn't easy—about what the resistance to evil means or doesn't mean. But you can't say that this weapon of the spirit, as Trocmé famously called it, is of no consequence. Nor that it is for the faint of heart. Not in Ku Klux Klan America. Not in the Raj. And not in the Reich.

Trocmé and Theis decided that they would cast their lots, even in this worst of times, with nonviolence. And the Cévenol School they founded would live that solution: it would be part of the Resistance by teaching children to regard life as precious, to help them look for peaceful resolutions to problems, to warmly welcome—and not fear—internationalism. The school would take in those who suffered; it would co-opt the sufferers into the cause of peace; it would teach that even one's enemies were creatures of God.

The Cévenol School sheltered and educated hundreds of children during the war. Every month during those dangerous years, its enrollment went up, and its student body and faculty diversified anew. Teachers came from France, Italy, England, Scotland, the Netherlands, and elsewhere; several were Jewish refugees. Students from every corner of Europe—a great number of them also refugees—could learn languages, classics, mathematics, natural sciences, philosophy, and letters. And they would also study peace.

Cévenol was an elite school: Only the strongest students could attend, even during the war. At that time, the facilities were makeshift, with classes held in homes and other suitable spaces throughout Le Chambon-sur-Lignon—a hotel, a house that was under construction, administrative buildings high in the hills above the town. Dispersion helped to make German raids more difficult.

Among the attendees at the Cévenol School were several of the children from Les Grillons: Peter, with his sparkplug and his winning smile; Rosario, with her silky black braids tied on top of her head; sweet Régine of the fuzzy hair in barrettes; Suzanne, with her math problems; and

Fanny, who dreamed of angels and cathedrals. These were the crickets who gathered by the hearth at night with the others, who needed help with their schoolwork, who were cold or warm, hungry or fed, depending on the efforts—*il faut tout faire*—of their director.

Who can imagine how much the normalcy of school meant to children like these at a time like that? Many of the Jewish children had lost, years earlier, the right to go to school openly. What was it like to have a place, far from the barbed enclosures of wartime, for freedom of the mind? One boy from Paris named Serge—finally safe in the Plateau and living with a Madame Jouve, who, marvelously, possessed two cows and bees and fresh butter and a great deal of kindness—had this to say about his time at the Cévenol School:

> I had the feeling that the fog was lifting in my head. Everything was becoming light. Math. Chemistry. Literature. I devoured . . . the seventeenth century! I discovered, at fourteen, a world: the intellectual life. I was globally, profoundly happy. . . . For me, Le Chambon was the town that made me happy, that gave birth to me . . . intellectually and religiously. Bizarrely, it was there I became Jewish.

After the war, the Cévenol School—in the French system, a *collège* and a lycée combined—would continue to thrive, its reputation as an innovative place of learning, focused on peace and internationalism, spreading in the decades that followed. Some remarkable people were first educated there, during and after the war: the philosopher Paul Ricoeur, the mathematician Alexander Grothendieck. In the 1950s, American alumni raised funds from the Quakers to create permanent structures for the school in the exquisite wooded setting where it now lies. And lo and behold, new foreign students began to trickle in again— among them, those whose families had fled newly troubled countries like Hungary, Chile, Laos, Madagascar, and Tibet.

Over the years—and as it competed for students—the Cévenol

School broadened its mission to include a focus on openness, accepting students who might have difficulty with their schooling elsewhere. The idyllic environment, with its woods and clean air and distance from city troubles, was seen as a kind of continuation of the region's history of taking in children who needed, literally and figuratively, fresh air. As of now, there are, among the students, children from the Middle East, Eastern Europe, the Americas, and several African countries. They come from a wide range of socioeconomic backgrounds, some of them rather privileged, others dependent on scholarships. I've seen them around town with their massive scarves, their short Afros, their long unwound hair, or their pants slung low—sweetly incongruous here in the land of practical fleece and pixie cuts.

If you think the solution for how to fix the world could never be to return blows with blows, you could do worse before a great war than to create an institution that set about to prepare children for other ways of fixing things. And once that institution was born, you could do worse than to give it air to breathe, fresh and clean, and to nourish it with young people from all over the world, class after class, year after year, decade after decade.

It's a little miracle, the Cévenol School. And now, a teacher named Sandrine has invited me to spend the day with her students there. I've been waiting a long time for this chance.

SANDRINE TEACHES POLITICAL ECONOMY at the Cévenol School. Slim, with an athletic grace, she has spiky light brown hair and a mild, pleasant face, and a kind of clarity in her blue eyes. Right away, she feels like what the Russians would call *svoia*—a grammatical pirouette of a term that I've never quite been able to translate into English. The best I can do is this: *svoia*, "one's own." She looks you in the eye when she speaks, Sandrine. There is something steely behind the mild mien.

Sandrine's own mother had been a student at the Cévenol School.

She'd grown up in Le Mazet-Saint-Voy, in a family of farmers who had been in the Plateau for many generations. The family still owns an expanse of land—now divided among siblings—right at the foot of the triangular Lizieux peak. Sandrine spent her summers here on the Plateau, picking raspberries at her uncle Jean's farm, learning about the relationship between hard work and spending money, but also about the kinds of trees and woods and mushrooms and animals that flourish here; learning to long for the ineffable gifts of the natural world.

Within minutes of meeting me, Sandrine had offered to bring me up to see the Cévenol School. Minutes after that, she'd asked if I could put together some kind of lesson with her for her kids. How about this for an idea, she said: What is anthropology?

And so here I am on this bright, cold winter day, climbing uphill through new snow. I've been to the campus a few times already—to meet some of the faculty, to go to an alumni meeting, to talk to first one and then another director of the school—but today, the forest beyond the campus, now hushed with white, feels different. It feels like I'm about to witness the past of the Plateau for the first time, really. The living past. In the course of settling into the Plateau, I've met—with Muriel's help—a small number of people who were alive during the war and who have been uncharacteristically willing to talk about their experiences. They have been charming and kind and have told me vivid stories about that world of their youth: the refugees sleeping one room over or hiding in the rafters of the church; the babies who became new "little sisters"; the shared moments in the forest among the men and women of the Resistance; the songs by the stone fountain in the center of town, as clothes were washed; the father's gift of a carved wooden horse; the sudden death of a friend, whose last words were "I wrote a little poem today." Many of these stories have been published, and they've been told to groups of schoolchildren, and recited on camera. They are good for all of us, these remembrances, even as they have grown patinaed, over time, with use.

But the Cévenol School is not a musing about a tumultuous past; it is not an archive; it is not some fading talisman of what was once good and true. It is still taking in foreigners, still teaching nonviolence, still transmitting powerful ideas to young people. In that way, it is a being still in its prime, an institution of social memory, par excellence. It's alive. And the anthropologist in me knows that a living institution is sometimes—in its day-after-day, year-after-year ways of being—a better bearer of memory than an individual, who might forget things. Who does forget things. Who, one day, will leave this world with all her memories in tow.

So HERE I AM, in a bright, cold classroom, still a little soaked from my long walk. Sandrine has quieted everyone down and asked me to talk a bit about what an anthropologist does.

"Okay, well," I say to the class, looking out at their pretty faces in various shades of pink, cream, and brown. Some of the children are doing an animated wriggle in the front of the room; some are sitting slouched in the back; most are elegantly draped in scarves. Three boys huddle by the warm radiator, their faces fixed in an amiable expression of boy-teen doofus.

"The key question," I say, "the beginning of all questions in anthropology, is this: '*Qui fait quoi avec qui?*'" Who does what with whom?

There is a pause, the room lit up by all the new snow outside.

Bahaahaaaa! Tee hee heee!

Oh right. Teenagers! I laugh, too.

Who does what with whom? I draw a couple of circles on the whiteboard in the front of the room.

Okay! Where do we go from here?

We'd been talking about what culture means and doesn't mean. And how you can be many things at the same time, really, and how none of those things alone defines you. You can come from a particular country, but you aren't defined by that alone. You can speak a language, but you aren't defined by that, either. Same with your religion. Or your profession. Or your class or your ethnic group or your gender or anything else.

I draw another circle on the board and let the kids experiment on me for a while. I tell them some bits of my background—random bits about where I've lived and worked and things about my parents and my siblings. So what am I?

They call out all kinds of things: *Russe! Juive! Américaine! Chrétienne!* I write those things on the board.

I crack a grin to myself, reminded of how you learn in high school that an atom is built like the solar system, with a nucleus like the sun, and electrons like the planets rotating around in circular orbits. How elegant it is, that mustard seed for the mountain—and *ta-da*, here are some equations for that! And then you learn in college that this model is kind of an expedient lie—there are no real rotations in electrons, there are no circles, there are no actual linear movements of energy (though it seems so in the regular laws of the regular Cartesian world). There is just the mad beautiful blinking of probability fields, the bursts of energy that act in patterned ways in the aggregate, ones that you can never stop, ones that change irrevocably by the very fact of your looking at them.

Ha. It's not fair. I'm mentally pulling the tracks out from under these kids even as I'm leading them on this identity train.

I can't say this to those pretty faces out there, but it's true: What is anyone? I don't even use the word "identity" analytically anymore—it is a linear word for a blinking, beautiful aggregate of a probability field.

I look back up at the whiteboard, with its circle and the words that now surround it: *Russe! Juive! Américaine! Chrétienne!* What am I? . . .

I think: I have no idea. Country. United States? Northeast, urban. With long, long stretches of many years in the cold in Canada and then in Russia. Ethnicity. I guess ethnically, I'm the kind of person who, once comfortable, talks animatedly and with my hands, and then, afterward, feels vaguely embarrassed by that fact.

What else? I'm an anthropologist. A professional stranger, who for many years traveled to foreign places, barely understanding anything at first, learning from other people, longing for a sense of place, a place of home. Mule-like, I labored forward for many years toward solitude and homelessness: living in corners of log cabins in the snow, or compounds with scratchy Middle Eastern pop music on in the background; until recently—until Charles—never owning much more than you could stuff into a car.

So, I'm a stranger. A rootless cosmopolitan. One who has made a habit of longing for home.

What else?

Religion. Religion is . . . delicate. Ha. Once, when I was an undergraduate student myself, I went to a talk by an eminent anthropologist of religion, Talal Asad. As I sat in a row of chairs hugging the wall of a packed seminar room, I found my heart pounding with a question: What does one gain or lose in the study of religion, if one is not religious? After the talk, I went up to Dr. Asad, and as I was gathering my many messy thoughts, he stopped me and pointed at my face: "Look!" he said. "Why, there's something on your lip! Why"—and to this day, I can still hear his voice squeaking on the last word—"you're *bleeding*!" It seems my personal question about religion, in the setting of science, could not be expressed without some discomfiting gore. A bloody nose.

I grew up with a Jewish mother, a Bahá'í father, a Christian grandmother, Buddhist aunts, Muslim roommates, and the stories of Quaker ancestors—the Paxsons—who sailed to the New World with William Penn. Plenty of intimate friends with deep and beautiful lives and no religion. Plenty of ways to get along. I'm a Bahá'í myself, a faith that teaches the essential oneness of humanity and the essential oneness of all religions, including, of course, the Jewish religion of my birth. But "Bahá'í" is not a term these kids are likely to know and, though I doubt I'm still susceptible to the bloody nose, it's not something that is easy for me to talk about in a setting like this.

I shake my thoughts away. The children are so sweet. Just look at them. These words—"religion," "ethnicity," "class"—are still too big. How can I get at the smallness of things?

"Well, okay. . . . Let's think about this some more. . . . It seems like I'm a lot of different things at the same time. And what about you? I know you come from lots of places and speak lots of languages. . . . What about you?"

"Wait, hold it!" says a regal-looking boy, suddenly animated. "I'm from Guinea. And my blood—it's not been mixed with any other blood! *Je ne suis pas coupé!*"

"And yet, here you are in France," I say to him, laughing. "So you've already been a little diluted just by being here, right? So now what?"

Ha-ha-ha, the kids join in.

Let's push this, I say. In fact, if you think of yourself as just one thing—or other people as just one thing—some big problems can arise. So what is anthropology? It's a way of opening your eyes to see what kinds of things people actually do—what groups really exist by their actions, not just the things we think exist, like nationality and race and ethnic group and religion. And then, once we know what groups actually exist, we think about how resources flow and power flows and senses of love and hate and belonging flow. And these tools from anthropology, they give us a way of shaking off our preconceptions. Give us a way of starting fresh.

So, who does what with whom?

You could say it's the foundation of all the social science questions. Groups can act, and they can think, and they can feel, and they can resist . . . and with this one question—who does what with whom?—you can start figuring out the bigger puzzles: the overall contours of group action; the conceptual frameworks that overlap within individual people and communities; the emotions that fill their social world.

But for this question to reveal important things, you have to keep your eyes open! And you have to really listen to the things that people say, really watch the things that people do, if you hope to figure out these bigger puzzles.

Sandrine's plan was that, after some background, we would make mini-anthropologists out of the students for the day. We would have them think of stories that they'd heard as children, about the faraway past, and then tell their stories to the group. And then we would, all together, think not just about the countries and religions and languages in their stories, but about the social groups that meant something in what was said. We'd open our eyes and ears together. We'd fill in the social circles that we drew up on the whiteboard in the front of the class. Who does what with whom?

Sandrine starts. Her grandfather lived in Le Mazet. Once, in the 1930s, there had been a very hard winter. Her grandfather would take the doctor to see people when necessary—like if a woman was having a baby. That winter, the snow was so high, her grandfather had to walk in front of the two-horse sleigh to shovel a path so they could all pass. The snows are no longer this fierce, says Sandrine, no longer this high.

So, what does this tell us about, say, who works together? I ask. What does it mean to help a neighbor in this context, someone who is not in your family? In the Plateau, were there—or are there—kinds of work you do together with your neighbors? Ooh, yes! says one girl from the Plateau. When you kill a pig! It's called the *tuaille*. Sandrine smiles. That's a local word. And when you wash lots of clothes! And when you build something! And when you grind the grain . . . and when you plant the potatoes and hay the fields. Everyone helps!

Sandrine sees everything, guides everything. She asks the girl to tell everyone more about the *tuaille*. The kids from other countries—and even other regions of France—won't know. You wait all year for it. You slaughter the pig after the hard frost, in February. You spend the day with the animal, separating the meat and the entrails, rendering the fat. There is music; there is a big feast. A party!

Then Clarice, from Brazil, just can't hold herself back anymore. Open-faced, round-eyed, quick-talking, Clarice is full of ebullience, full of energy. When we were talking about travel earlier, she exclaimed, "The Germans! They are so warm! You have to get a car there! . . . I love

Canada! . . . Oooh, the Spanish!" She's traveled a great deal and seems to love all of it and everyone. Now she chimes in with the observation that *tuaille* is just like the festivals back home in Brazil—Christmas and Easter, when everyone cooks together.

And then Ami speaks. Ami, from Guinea, is reedy and erect. She and Clarice sit together in that way that best friends do at that age, draped closely, finishing each other's thoughts. Ami has elegant features, with a gap between her two front teeth, and long black hair braided into a ponytail. She is reserved, but also ready with a smile. Now she is telling us about what Ramadan is like at home—the huge banquets when the sun sets—and also Tabaski, a joyous festival to honor Abraham's willingness to sacrifice his firstborn, Ishmael. It's a great big feast, she says, in her contained way. And the women do one kind of work, and the men do another; and the old people do one kind of work, and small children another.

Then Sandrine asks me to tell them all a story about living in Russia, so I start saying what it was like to live with a healer there—a sorcerer. "Oh . . . NO!" exclaims a Haitian girl, hearing the word.

Well. Okay, maybe I shouldn't have led with that word. But sorcerer— *koldun*—was what this man was called at times. And let's face it, it was a good way to get the attention of a group of teenagers.

The facts: In Russia, I lived with a couple. The wife had been a child orphan who'd lost her father to one of the many battles on Hitler's Eastern Front, and her mother to a botched abortion. The husband, the sorcerer, was a local man who'd learned magical practices from his father. What that meant, in actual life, was that people, often strangers from far away, would come to see him, day or night, mostly without notice, with a sore arm, or general lethargy, or a colicky baby, or with a mother-in-law who was cursing them, or with nightmares of ghosts, or with cancer, or—having been used up as soldiers in Chechnya—wanting now to kill themselves. People would arrive, and the sorcerer would listen sympathetically, diagnose their illness, and then make a potion of water with words whispered over it, before sending them on their way.

This sorcerer had been a Communist Party member in his day, and was an all-around straight-arrow kind of person. But he was, mostly, a healer. And for that healing, he used every tool he knew—from the secret powerful words his father passed to him, to the water he would whisper those words onto, to numerological diagnostic charts he found in random magazines, to the icons of saints in the corner of his tiny home.

This man, the healer, was dedicated to being right and good in his magical practices—to doing white magic, that is, not black magic. He didn't take money for his work; never made love potions; never messed with someone's will. He always urged people to forgive the harm that others brought them, to answer evil with good. *Dobrom dobro*, this principle was called: Good, through good. I came to understand that all this magic, all these incantations, all these icons, supported, together, a form of religion, really, with ethical principles and broad social impact, not to mention a frightening, bountiful, shape-shifting set of powers with which to interact.

In my own time in the village, I—with my deepening dark circles under my eyes, thanks to my restless sleeping at the far wall of the log cabin—was, on occasion, diagnosed as being under the influence of curses. And so I myself sipped waters laced with incantations and thought about how big the world is and how—who knows?—maybe the generous will to heal is enough to make the waters work. Who knows.

What a beautiful mess this healing was in the Russian village. What a lesson in seeing how a people can take whatever tool they have—we are large, we contain multitudes!—in the interest of fixing other people's hearts and bodies and minds. How these multitudes can't be contained by small words like, say, "religion."

But the Haitian girl needs a simpler answer. So I tell the class how people would come to this healer—he didn't like it, in fact, when people called him a sorcerer—because they were sick in the body or in the mind or in the heart. And how one of the big illnesses he would cure people of was a kind that you get from envy—whether from feeling it or being the recipient of it. This way of being sick is in fact related to what, in many parts of the world, is called the "evil eye." There are nods. They've heard of the evil eye. The healer I lived with in Russia, I say, was the kind of professional who could fix the social body, cure it from the harmful effects of envy. Give it some equilibrium. Make things right again.

It's nice when things make sense.

Sandrine, who sees everything, says, well, there are healers and sorcerers like this around here, too, but the church is against these practices. Clarice adds that, in Brazil, there are traditional healers who give you foods that are supposed to cure you, but they don't actually work and people end up dying. And, she adds with a click of the tongue, there are Creole methods, too, but she doesn't believe them, either.

Local kids bring up healing stones they've heard about in the area: Do they work? One girl went to a healer here when she was little, but a woman was yelling and moving weirdly and that scared her. Ami volunteers that there is some kind of evil tree back home where there are supposed to be djinns, but she doesn't believe any of that at all.

I laugh. "Ladies and gentlemen, we have here in Ami a real scientific spirit!"

Who does what with whom?

I watch and listen. And soon, like fish in water, like little crickets by the hearth, the children watch and listen, too. Here is the messy world of real people, young as they are, their personalities made of still-forming pieces—the girls draped over each other, one a lovely chatterbox, the other elegantly still; the regal boy whose blood has already been diluted, like it or not; the local children who are quieter than everyone else, but who pipe in shyly now and then about the Germans here on the Plateau during the war, and their grandparents, and how lives were saved back then. One girl—modest during the class itself, but now eager to speak— approaches me when the day is winding down. She tells me why she comes to the Cévenol School and not to the regular public school in Le Chambon. It's all farmers in her family, and she wants to be a farmer someday, too. Here, she gets to take care of horses right nearby. Would I ever want to come and see them?

Oh yes, I say, I would. Very much.

Il faut tout faire. But now, as this Brownian jiggle plays out in front of me, I feel like a door has opened and a fresh breeze has arrived, along with the newly minted snow.

The bell finally rings, and the students tear out of the doors of the classrooms—*Merci, au revoir! Au revoir!*—thrilled to be free for a moment and together with each other until the next bell rings. Off they go, finding the door outside, just for a moment, to take in a deep breath themselves, out in the white hush of winter.

Who does what with whom?

The children, being themselves, make the anthropologist happy.

———

If you were living up in the Plateau Vivarais-Lignon in late 1942, you might not yet have sensed how the war was changing. But it was.

By this time, Germany, together with its allies, had occupied most of Europe. Its armies were advancing steadily eastward, and it had established footholds in North Africa, crucial for blocking Allied access to the oil resources of the Middle East. Europe was choked.

But a shift was coming. For months, the Soviet Union—one of the few countries in the region that had not yet submitted to Germany—had been pressuring the United States and Great Britain to open a second front in Europe. But where would that make sense? And how could it be accomplished? The solution was to begin in North Africa. On November 8, 1942, British and brand-new American troops landed in Morocco and Algeria. Within days, they had claimed these territories for the Allies. Then, in swift retaliation, on November 11, Germany pushed down into nominally independent Vichy, seizing it with no real opposition. And so, in two single moves, the chess game advanced, with the enemies now facing each other on either side of the Mediterranean Sea. And as much as this might have seemed at the time like an equal and reciprocal show of strength, the fact was: There was now finally a place—under the clear desert skies of the Sahara—where Allied troops could amass, and train, and wait for the proper time to move into Europe. This made for a real problem for Germany. It was now only a matter of time before those fresh troops would be able to contribute their full force on the European theater. *Tick-tock-tick-tock.* The war had changed. Who would be winning, soon?

And there was another shift, equally destabilizing to Germany—though somewhat less visible to the rest of the world at the time. From June 1941, Hitler's armies had been pushing steadily into the Soviet Union. The SS mobile killing units, Einsatzgruppen, went plowing into western Ukraine—then occupied Poland—and then Belarus, stopping at village after village to identify and then murder, face-to-face, hundreds of thousands of Jews. The regular German army claimed cities, towns, and hamlets, and along the way identified eager local collaborators. By the summer of 1942, Germany had made a serious advance into the Soviet Union itself. Though the rationale for this push eastward was sound enough—the North Caucasus of Russia held rich oil supplies—it was, in fact, a fateful move. Fighting a land war in Asia meant fighting the vastness of the steppe, the unforgiving ice and cold. It meant stretching an army thin, far from home, deep into a country that covered fully a sixth of the earth's surface. And it meant fighting a perplexingly valiant enemy that, no matter how hard it was pummeled, simply would not give up. From August 1942, the Germans were facing the Soviets in the southern city of Stalingrad. But they were now also facing the furious white winds of winter. And their own thinness; and the vastness of it all. Hitler, seemingly at the height of his powers, was, newly, weak. And like many weak leaders, he responded, as day followed day, with more brutality.

And so, if you were living up in the Plateau in late 1942—up among the sheltering pines, far from the beating of the war drums in the world below, amid the children in momentary rest from their flight—you might not know it, but life would soon be more dangerous than ever. Soon, there would be no going back to that time around the hearth.

. . .

EARLY IN 1943—just after the Allies successfully took North Africa—the world was introduced to a child who would become the best-known refugee in modern history. This child wasn't hidden in an attic, like young Anne Frank, writing a diary in gifted prose. He wasn't ill-clad, or unfed, like so many of the hundreds, the thousands, the millions of those displaced in recent years by the advance of armies. This boy had a corona of blond hair and wore a royal uniform with shiny buttons and a sword. He had arrived in the Sahara Desert, all alone.

Now, if you let your mind linger at that image of the solitary boy, it doesn't take much to imagine the sound of Allied planes flying overhead in the African deserts that surrounded him. It doesn't take much to imagine how brilliant the stars would have been at night when the nameless child—known only as the Little Prince—arrived softly on the desert sands. Or by now—with his story published in over one hundred million copies, and translated into more than 250 languages—the soulful strangeness of the first words he uttered to the first person he met on planet Earth: "Please. Draw me a sheep. . . ."

The author of *The Little Prince*, Antoine de Saint-Exupéry, was himself a French refugee. He had grown up in Lyon, only to be attracted—like Daniel—away from a staid and privileged upbringing, toward Africa. And so, in the 1930s he became a pilot, flying mail over the Sahara, back and forth, learning the contours of the desert at night, accustoming himself to solitude. Once, he crashed. For days, he struggled desperately to fix his plane, but after the water was gone, and the food was gone, and the sun kept blazing, it seemed more and more likely that he would perish. Then a Bedouin nomad came and gave him water and food, and saved his life.

When Saint-Exupéry wrote *The Little Prince*, he was living in New York, thinking of that crash, and his work at fixing the plane; thinking of his troublesome darling wife, Consuelo, his rose; thinking of his Bedouin rescuer; and thinking of his "best friend in the world," a Jewish man named Léon Werth, who was then, in early 1943, "in France where he was hungry and cold." It was to Werth that Saint-Exupéry dedicated *The Little Prince*, writing that here was a grown-up who could—and this was the highest praise he could offer—certainly understand books for children, adding, "He needs to be comforted."

Please, draw me a sheep. Please, sing me a song. Please—there might be nightmares tonight—read me a story before I go to sleep. Please find me some gloves, find me a hat, warm my room. Please give me potatoes and butter—food, fit for a king!

Please, help me with my math, the child would say; please point out the stars to me, far from all that darkness below.

The child is a stranger—golden-haired or olive-skinned; a chatterbox or a soulful one; naughty or nice. The child is in need. The child is from Africa or the Middle East or Russia or Poland. The child wants lessons and wants comforts. But who, in the end, is comforted? Who, in the end, learns?

It's as if my vision is starting to blur a little, here in the snowy, starry reaches. Who does what with whom? Did Daniel rescue the children, or did they rescue him?

IN JANUARY 1943, Hitler declared total war. In February, a new round of raids was planned all over France. André Trocmé, Édouard Theis, and a local school director, Roger Darcissac, would be arrested and sent to an internment camp at Saint-Paul-d'Eyjeaux in Haute-Vienne. Soon, the forests of the Plateau would be full of parachutists and other Resistance fighters. Soon, there would be new reams of documents, typed by hand, hunting for a child named Klaus, or Peter, or Alexander, or Étienne.

On February 7, Daniel wrote home: "I am terribly single or, more precisely, a widower. I'm the father, as I like to say, of twenty children, and I am forced to admit they have no mother. How long will this last?"

Many years later, the Little Cricket named Suzanne would remember that long stone house where they all were, momentarily, protected:

"Daniel was so loving toward us and his loyalty was unending. Very often he would watch over us during the night. Was he afraid that there would be Gestapo raids . . . ?"

And that's where I leave Daniel for now, as the children sleep as best they can, up on the sheltering Plateau, behind the great stone walls, as the hearth embers die down and chill for the night.

Watchful in the dark. Waiting.

Chapter 6

HANDS AND FEET

On my hobnailed shoes, I have crossed
The world and its misery . . .

—FÉLIX LECLERC, "MOI, MES SOULIERS"

HAVE BEEN WATCHING an old woman who lives near the apartment I
rent on the edge of Le Chambon. She is in her seventies, and is wiry and
strong like a bird, and she works outside much of the day. In her leggings
and knit cap, I see her dragging fallen tree limbs, or wrestling with a
clothesline, or fishing something out of a small tractor. She has a face
that is as fresh as the outdoor air, and big bobbly plastic glasses and long
gray hair pulled back in a bun. She gives kisses hello, holding your face
up close to hers so that you can feel the soft fuzz of her cheek.

I've heard that this woman might have some stories to tell me about
her family during war. Up to this point, I have spoken with only a small
group of storytellers here, practiced in recounting tales of adoptive
baby sisters, and next-door German soldiers, and running around the
forest as fighters—stories sure to enchant busloads of schoolchildren
or tourists. Here and there I've been attempting to find others who might
be willing to share something new. But true to the Plateau's reputation

for general silence on these matters, my efforts have gone mostly no-where.

A local historian agreed to talk with me after an innkeeper I knew assured him that my research was really quite different from the usual fare. In the dim light of his stone home, deep in a forest not far from Le Chambon, he told me about the region's history of farming and industri-alization, its habits of interdependence and secrecy, the varieties of resistance during the war: nonviolent, violent; religious, a-religious. Eventually, I found the courage to ask him if there were any stories in his own family about sheltering strangers.

"Yes, there were," he said, and then added, after a pause: "In this very house." I looked toward the stone hearth beyond the kitchen, the cozy fire giving its glow into the dark. Then he said, "But these were my grandmother's stories, and she isn't here to tell them." I waited a little in the quiet that followed to see if he'd say more, but he didn't.

There are a few names that are very common here, and I'd seen them in books about the Plateau, in the graveyards, on the walls of the Righ-teous at the Holocaust Museum. But each time I've encountered a per-son who bears such a name, they've deflected, or denied any connection to themselves or their parents or grandparents. Not my stories. Not us. Not ours.

I know I have to earn their trust. I know these things take time. Still, I keep wishing for the vivid pictures—the spontaneous ones, the palpa-ble ones, the ones it seems you might be able to reach out and touch. So when I heard that the old woman who lives near me might have stories, I girded myself, walked over to her house, and knocked.

She opened her door with a big bright smile. But when she heard why I had come, her face fell.

"During the war," she said, after a pause, "when I was a girl, people showed up at our door at night, covered with blood. I was very afraid, and my father was very brave. And that is all I will say. No more."

I left her threshold, mortified. Ashamed. I couldn't bear the way her beautiful face fell, because of me. I went to see her again a few hours later, and apologized. She was so kind. She patted my hand and said not to worry; I did the right thing not to press her.

Over the years, in Russia, faces have fallen so many times, in front of my face. . . . Over the dead father, the dead love, the beaten mother, the raped girl, the botched abortion, the child ravaged by war or drink or prison or anything else. The faces have fallen over the hideous war in Chechnya, the murders, the arrests, the bribes, the lostness, the wishes for speedy, merciful death. So many tears.

And so now I realize, I just cannot bear to make any old woman's face fall because of my questions, ever again. If people want to tell me their stories, they can; but I won't ask. I can't. If the past wants me, it is going to have to come and find me itself.

So, here on the Plateau, silence has won again. But it has given me a parting gift: the image of a dark night, a brave man, a door, several bloody migrant strangers. And a child—her fingers folded around a wall—looking on. A decision to be made.

I will watch my neighbor, as her eyes meet the winds of the Plateau. I will see what she and her kindred spirits say, without words.

It will never again be late 1942 in the Plateau Vivarais-Lignon. Daniel Trocmé won't be climbing up and down and up and down and up the road to Les Grillons, making shoes from old tires at night. The Little Crickets won't be exploring the forest, debating whether a girl should follow her beloved to Tonkin. My neighbor will never again be a little girl, standing behind her brave father at their threshold at night. That door called 1942 is closed forever.

But then I learn that there are asylum seekers living on the Plateau today.

This might not seem like such a striking thing out in the regular world. After all, there are signs of migrating people in need everywhere these days. But when I tell my social science friends back home about it, their jaws all drop. Yes, strangers have been sheltered on the Plateau periodically for hundreds of years. *Data point, data point, data point, data point.* Because of that, I can already understand something about how those practices have persisted over time. But this shiny new data point means that the dimensions of the *knowable* explode open. It's all up close now, all vivid in time and space. I don't have to imagine, or suppose, or draw causal lines like castles in the air. I can watch and see. I can accept or refute things, *thus.* It makes all the difference.

It is Caroline who first tells me about the asylum seekers. Caroline grew up in Montfaucon, on the far edge of the Plateau, and has taught English at the Cévenol School for many years. She has a mane of long brown hair and wears hoop earrings and has a cackle of an infectious laugh; she is the kind of person who breaks into song for the slightest reason; who kisses you on the cheeks, squeakily; who can't take more than two paces in a grocery store before another person wants to talk with her. At a family dinner at her home in nearby Les Tavas, she tells me about the local branch of the national organization called Centre d'Accueil pour Demandeurs d'Asile, or CADA. Welcome center for asylum seekers. The asylum seekers who come to CADA are from all over the world. They live in a residence compound not far from the center of Le Chambon, about fifty to a hundred people in all, at any given time. The parents in the asylum-seeking families spend months filling out their paperwork, waiting to learn if they will be given refugee status or sent back to their home country. And, in the meantime, their children go to local schools, including—for the strongest students—the Cévenol School itself. In fact, Caroline says that Sandrine is facilitating some kind of volunteer program between Cévenol students and CADA children. They do art projects and schoolwork together. For this program, Sandrine is working with a woman named Amélie, one of the CADA staff.

You should probably get to know Amélie, Caroline says to me, as our evening winds down.

And now, this is what I say:

The Second World War is over. I know that most everyone who

remembers the war on the Plateau is gone from this world. And so, they are silent. And the few living who remember it are silent, too.

But knowledge of the asylum seekers living in the Plateau today lets me draw a brand-new circle in my head, and I can—and I do—ask the question: Who does what with whom? And with that question I can now prepare myself—with new faces and new stories and new conditions, and new doors, and new countries and new children—to see how strangers are taken in here.

I am a blind person bumping up against the world in the dark. And the world answers.

Centres d'Accueil pour Demandeurs d'Asile were first created in France in 1973 to house the waves of refugees who arrived from Chile after Pinochet's coup d'état. Soon, the CADAs were also serving the so-called boat people of Vietnam and elsewhere. In the 1990s and 2000s, new streams of asylum seekers began arriving to France from sub-Saharan Africa, from Eastern Europe, some Middle Eastern countries, and from the territory of the former Soviet Union. Today there are more than three hundred CADAs in France—spread among the many *départements*—serving seekers of asylum from all over the world. Their key function is to make the rather arduous application for asylum more rational and more humane. There are tens of thousands of applicants per year in France, after all. If people find their way to a CADA, they are roughly twice as likely to be granted asylum, and to be allowed to stay in France, away from the risk of death back home.

There has been a CADA right here on the Plateau Vivarais-Lignon since the year 2000. Monsieur M—, the director of the local CADA since its founding, had been working at a similar center down in Saint-Étienne, one with a thousand beds and barracks-style living with shared kitchens and no real privacy. Here on the Plateau, he aimed to create something smaller and more dignified, far from the chaos of the city. Monsieur M— now works with a staff of around ten: with social workers, like Amélie, and educators, and legal and administrative assistants. And it has been going pretty well, all in all. In many places, you'd see foreigners treated with fear and suspicion. Here, it's different; there are lots of local volunteers who teach French or offer music programs or art programs. There are even a couple of independent organizations that support the families if they are refused refugee status.

Sixty-three residents from thirteen families now live at the CADA. They come from Congo, Rwanda, Angola, Guinea, Albania, Armenia, Azerbaijan, and Chechnya. Many had long and perilous journeys to get here, having been crammed into cars or trucks, having spent weeks or months sleeping on the streets or in dirty hotels. Most arrived utterly traumatized, some without speaking a single word of French. At this CADA, each family gets its own apartment, with a door and a lock, and a key, since Monsieur M— made a point of creating a place of privacy for the families. Asylum seekers are permitted to live here for the months and sometimes years it takes to put together their legal case for asylum. They also get monthly allowances for food, since they're not allowed to work. But you never know who will be awarded asylum and who won't. It can be a new kind of torture, the waiting.

Now, after talking with Monsieur M— on a couple of different occasions about the mission of the CADA, after meeting his staff, and explaining my own work to the group of them, I have been invited to go with Amélie to the CADA residence to meet a family of asylum seekers. This family comes from Armenia. I have never been to Armenia, but I've lived on the northern side of the Caucasus mountain range that Armenia is wedged to the south of. And I know something about the bloody—and some would say senseless—war that has been waged between Armenia and its neighbor, Azerbaijan, since before the collapse of the Soviet Union. As for the details, however, I know only that Amélie has been helping the family with paperwork for many months now, an especially complex process for people whose first language is not French. She hopes my knowledge of Russian will prove useful.

. . .

I'VE BROUGHT A BOX of cookies along, as an offering to the family.

"Is that weird?" I ask Amélie, before anyone answers the door.

Amélie has dark, smart eyes and short golden hair, parted into a flop on one side. She is wearing a leather jacket and a big scarf.

She gives me a wry smile. "I think you'll find there will be plenty to eat," she says.

On the second ring, a middle-aged man with brownish skin and grayish stubble opens the door. Standing just behind him is a woman in her forties or so, with big, expressive eyes and long, luxurious dyed-black hair.

At the sight of Amélie, their faces open up.

AMÉLIE! Amélie, Amélie!

At the secondary sight of me there is a little one-two, up-and-down glance. Then back to Amélie.

Come in, come in! No, no, no!! Keep your shoes on! Keep them on!

She is Lalik, and he is Arat.

Somewhere between thirty and forty thousand years ago, human beings began stenciling outlines of their hands onto cave walls in Europe, East Asia, and Indonesia. Using pigments of red, or rust-orange, or violet, they created permanent shadows of hands of different sizes: of both men and women; some with fingers splayed; some missing a digit. Some of the hands were clustered together in compositions, perhaps, of an entire family or residential group, or clan.

I am here, says the hand.

We are here, say the hands.

We are here, many of us—all our fingers pointed up, like flowers toward a hidden sun—says the group of hands.

One of the earliest examples of hand stencils is found in the Chauvet

Cave, just two hours of snaky roads south of the Plateau Vivarais-Lignon, deep into the Rhône Valley of the Ardèche. The hands in the Chauvet Cave, discovered some twenty years ago, are special for many reasons— not least because they were found together with a few of the most astonishing and earliest examples of cave art the world has ever seen. By the dappled light of fire or lamp, spectacular images of horses, deer, and bears leap off the walls. But there are also cave lions among the vivid beasts, and panthers, and rhinoceroses. It's Africa on the Rhône, deep in the darkest recesses of the Chauvet Cave.

Thirty thousand years is a long time; it stretches into our evolutionary history. Right when those cavemen in the Ardèche were marking their existence in silhouettes of violet and red and rust, Neanderthals— another branch of our genus, *Homo*—were also living in France. In a different cave of the Ardèche, called Moula-Guercy, there is evidence of how Neanderthals—with their big brains and heavy brows and brawny frames—once ate both deer and each other. And now we know that all those thousands of years ago, the Neanderthals of Europe fraternized with *Homo sapiens*. The two species made children with each other—a commingling that left permanent traces on human DNA.

We are here, say the hands.

Thirty thousand years ago, there were hands, uplifted, right . . . here. Those hands hunted and gathered and scraped meat off bones in front of fires in a cave. They practiced some kind of worship; even their Neanderthal cousins might have thrown flowers over the bodies of their dead. On and off, these human beings—the owners of the hands— would come out, to live in the light. Here in the Ardèche, the wind would blow fierce in winter; the river would run cold in the spring. Tens and hundreds of years went by, and then thousands, and tens of thousands; humans learned how to cultivate plants—chickpea, emmer wheat, barley—and they learned how to fire metals; and they learned to make more tools and travel more broadly over land and down rivers; following the seasons, they moved; following the stars, in set patterns in the sky.

They moved, those humans. They moved to find what they needed, to flee from the cold, or from disease, or from an enemy. They moved, and on the way they met each other and mixed with each other and traded and married and, we presume, loved.

It took a long stretch of history to create the modern nation-state, and the idea that something called a country, with a past and some documents and a set territory, somehow springs from the natural order of things. It took a long time to create something called the République Française, with its borders and armed border guards, and papers and black-and-white photographs that say—*snap*—this one belongs here, and this one does not.

It took a very long time and lots of hard work to imagine that somehow, the gorgeous barbaric yawp of the handprints in the cave were made by French hands. That those hands and that gorgeous yawp didn't, in fact, belong to the world.

MODERN NATION-STATES ARE far more—and far less—than we now imagine. They are far more because of the broad, specter-like reach of their colonial empires. We forget where riches come from. Despite our narratives about hard work and gumption and the spirit of innovation, the United States grew rich on the institution of slavery. In Europe— despite its own narratives about blood and soil and God and kings— countries grew rich on colonialism and colonial extraction. So in France, it's easy to forget that the country is made not just of Parisians lolling at a *dîner en blanc*, with their lovely flopping hats and long gloves. It's easy to forget that France isn't the republican spirit, either, with fists raised— *en grève!*—in some industrial town. France is made of shadows of its broad colonial past—in the Americas, the West Indies, the Middle East, South Asia, the Far East, the Pacific, and, so importantly, in Africa. France is much more than we think.

But it's also much less than we think. Why? Because those very narratives about the national past effectively cause us to suppose that countries have been there forever. Always an England. Always a France.

Always a Germany or Italy or Poland or Bulgaria. But of course, those countries weren't there forever. Sure, there were kings and wars and alliances. Sure, one by one, each of those countries had a shot at dominating its own region of the world. But most of the countries of Europe didn't exist in anything like their modern shape until the late nineteenth or even early twentieth century. And because of the peculiar, stupefying ideology of modern nationalism, we beg to differ, even when faced with the fact that Prussia wasn't Germany; Rome wasn't Naples; Poland was for a time part of Russia; Bulgaria, say, together with a huge swath of southeastern Europe, was a single arm of a massive Ottoman Empire.

It doesn't take a long dive into literatures on the advent of modern nationalism to date the peculiar way of seeing countries—as having defined territories and senses of belonging—to somewhere around the end of the eighteenth century. Before that, yes, there were lords and kings and royal families, and battles over territories. (That's our river! No, ours!) But the equation was different before modernity. The lord was a proxy for the king, and the king was a proxy for God, and the closer you got to the lord, then to the king, the closer you got to God Himself. It was a topography of proximity, getting good, better, best as you approached your liege.

But now, in modernity, the king was diminishing in his grandeur and would soon be almost entirely gone. Now—O science! O dissolution of the master narrative!—the map would flatten out, and each country would get some nice smooth color, becoming, in the aggregate, a nice, even pastel puzzle. Italy, red; France, blue; Germany, pink; and on it went. But what that map had lost of its rich, kingly glow, it had gained in the seeming solidity and permanence of its borders. The national anthem replaced the hymn. A country, not God, was forever. Now you died for your nation, not your lord. And you killed for your nation, not your lord. And maybe, just maybe, if nationalists could get it just right, you wouldn't even notice the difference.

The ideology of nationalism works. It makes us believe some things are large and forever, when they aren't. A pretty flimsy sleight of hand, if you think about it. But France—like Germany, and Russia, and Italy, and on and on—is less of a country than even what remains after that abracadabra. It's less on the inside.

What if it was the eighteenth century and you lived, say, in a village up on a high plateau towering over the Rhône Valley, with a religion unlike that of your neighbors and a patois they couldn't understand? Let's say there were still no rail lines connecting you to big cities, and you were wholly unaccustomed to strangers, and the king—say, the weak, womanizing Louis XV—was so far away, he barely had any glow at all in your mind? Were you living in . . . France?

In *The Discovery of France*, the historian Graham Robb tells the story of an eighteenth-century geometer who traveled into La Haute-Loire, a part of France still virtually unknown by the king. The geometer arrived in the village of Les Estables—just fifteen short kilometers from the edge of the Plateau—loaded with equipment. The locals took one look at him, with his strange instruments, and assumed he was a sorcerer and therefore a great and immediate threat to the health of the human and natural worlds. They butchered him on the spot.

Were those locals, so far from Paris—with their concerns so vivid and urgent and complete in their own terms—were they, in any meaningful way, French? Could France, at that time, honestly claim their bodies, or their minds or their hearts or souls?

The world is huge and ancient. And there was never a time when people weren't, in effect, coming out of the caves, following the rivers, fleeing from the wind, looking toward the rain, hoping for bounty. These countries we live in, they are mere artifacts of a long history of walking and stopping, and walking and stopping again. Our maps are just snapshots of that walking and stopping, and then mixing and trading and fighting sometimes, and then hoping for the best. No country is made of a pure kind of human; no border—however high or however intimidating the barbed wire wrapped around it—surrounds a real thing. It's a fairy tale to think that it does.

AND YET, there is today a country called France. And in that France—and its territories in South America, the Caribbean, Africa, and Polynesia—live around sixty-seven million people. So who are they?

For centuries, people here mixed with their neighbors, creating a lively Celtic-Italic-Germanic mix, with Moors and Vikings to boot. And then there are Jews—both Ashkenazim and Sephardim—who have been living in French territory since the Middle Ages: protected, then persecuted, then protected again. As France built up its colonial empire in the eighteenth, nineteenth, and twentieth centuries, it also built and strengthened ties to what would become powerful migration routes in the future, particularly from North Africa and Asia. The Second World War brought in people from all over Europe and beyond. Today's France is rich with migrants—a lucky counter to the demographic crisis facing most of Europe, where too few babies are born to replace the generation dying off.

It is illegal in France to collect statistics about the racial or ethnic composition of the country. But rough, recent data suggest that all of those colonial traces—and the brutal, attendant decolonization wars that followed—have produced robust pathways into the country. In the year 2010, more than 27 percent of babies born in France had at least one foreign-born parent. Among the ethnic communities, the largest trace their origins to the Arab and Berber lands of the Maghreb—Algeria, Morocco, and Tunisia. In cities mostly, there are also significant numbers of people of sub-Saharan origin. There are those who trace their roots to Vietnam, Turkey, and Madagascar as well. In the past twenty years, these enriching waves of migrants have grown rapidly. The fall of the iron curtain in 1989, the collapse of the Soviet Union in 1991, the Yugoslav Wars of the 1990s, the enlargement of the EU, the after-effects of 9/11 in the form of refugees—all brought wave after wave of people into Europe, with France considered a first-rate final destination.

But all this demographic richness has come with its burdens and dangers. Recent economic crises have added a dimension of new pressure in Europe, making it harder for people to feel at ease sharing their country's wealth; making the whole enterprise of taking in newcomers feel like a zero-sum game—if I win, you lose—and making the fiction of the clean, pure nation, where everyone looks the same and talks the same and worships the same, seem newly attractive. France's right wing is on the rise; likewise its anti-Semitic outbursts. In a brand-new strain of anti-Muslim violence, pig feet, pig heads, swastikas, and the words *Sieg Heil* have desecrated graves and mosques. Muslim practices like women wearing headscarves and covering their faces have been banned by republican French law. Women who cover themselves, in accordance with their own or their family's interpretation of holy writ, have been beaten by strangers.

So on it goes, the movement. On it goes! Out of the cave, into the light, down the stream, and into the chill of the wind. On it goes, toward the rain, away from the war, toward some hope for safety, toward some hope for thriving.

And, one more time, on it goes, now, into a train station, onto a bus—coins jingling in a metal plate as you pay your fare—up a creaking hill, the air growing colder, the trees growing higher; falcons overhead, magpies in the grass, swallows darting from branch to branch. On it goes, up into the land of stone houses and blue eyes and quiet stories.

On it goes, for new travelers—from which of the round earth's imagined corners?

Lalik and Arat are from Russia, but came to Russia from Armenia. They speak French only slightly, haltingly. Amélie, it is clear, speaks brilliantly with her hands. As we stand in the entryway to their apartment, she tells the couple, pointing to me, that this is Maggie. That Maggie is here, for a time, to learn about how foreigners experience life in the Plateau. Eyes up; eyes down. And that I used to live in Russia, so I speak Russian.

Really?

At their threshold, I bend down to unlace my boots. "Don't you DARE take off your shoes! Don't you dare!" Lalik hollers, in response. Interesting. Though I don't know every region of the former Soviet Union equally well, I certainly know the ubiquitous dance-of-the-shoes. Here's how it goes: You are never supposed to leave your shoes on when you enter a home, at least not in any place I've ever lived or traveled in the region of the former Soviet Union—north, south, east, or west; city or countryside; Christian or Muslim; apartment or log cabin. Street shoes are pretty much considered filthy everywhere—not befitting the clean inside space of a home. But still, as you enter a home, people will, at times, tell you not to take your shoes off. Why? Herein lies the dance: People do this as a sign of deference to you, their guest. But you, the guest, are supposed to take your shoes off anyway, as a sign of deference back to them. Once the dance is all done, everything becomes nice and cozy and kosher, as it were, with everyone satisfyingly receiving a proper dollop of respect, right there at the door. But the whole ritual can get rather dramatic—not to say baroque—in certain circumstances, like when relationships and hierarchies are unclear. Like now.

So, after several rounds of don't-you-dares, I swallow hard and, like Amélie—innocent of the shoe dance—obey Lalik.

And so we both enter fully into this new territory, shoes on.

Inside the apartment, we are sent straight to the small bright kitchen, at a little table wedged into a corner, and Lalik opens up my package of cookies (Why did you bring them? she asks. *Za chem*, what for?) and starts cutting up all kinds of fruits.

Amélie and Lalik are speaking in French, and in hands. There is much to discuss. Arat has been trying to reach their lawyer, but the lawyer doesn't answer. Amélie mimes a huge pile of letters that this lawyer—a very good and popular one—is already dealing with. Then, Lalik and Arat strain to explain that they found something on the Internet about how, if you join the French Foreign Legion, you can get automatic status in the country. Should their son try for that? Amélie, her face kind but alarmed, mimes the dangers of joining a mercenary army; mimes the love their son has for them, embracing herself, *"J'aime Papa! J'aime Maman!"*; mimes the fact that their son might do anything to please them. She says something under her breath.

Oy. If we could just get our papers, Lalik says. And she says it again.

As Lalik cuts the fruit, she gives us a lesson straight from a first-year medical anthropology class, telling Amélie about foods that can be used for healing purposes: for coughs, diarrhea, fever. I know many of these formulas from Russia—honey or raspberry jam for colds, mustard plasters for fever, fire cupping, with those dreaded, medieval *banki* that only ever made me scream. But here are new ones: drying pomegranate peel and then breathing it in, for infected teeth. Pear seeds in a tea for a cough. Cocoa butter for fever.

How many of these conversations did I hear in Russia, over the years? How urgently did people wish to tell others—even in the first moments of acquaintance—how to cure what ails them? How to fix things that were broken in the body or the soul? The sorcerer I lived with in the village was no expert in this kind of healing; but his small, soft-spoken wife knew more than he did—as was often the case with women. When people arrived, sick, at the door of the cabin, she always had ideas of her own—besides the magic potions of her husband—about how to make visitors well with plants, steam, honey. Hers was a soothing art.

Amélie sips her coffee. They've offered her every kind of food, but Amélie warned me beforehand that she just can't eat every meal offered to her. The residents—that's what they call the asylum seekers here—all want to be generous with her. But she just can't eat every time. She has daughters at home, who need real meals. No matter; Arat and Lalik clearly adore her, even though she doesn't take what is offered.

But I'm hungry, so I do.

Now, Lalik begins to glance over at me. She and Arat have some questions; they're testing out this business of the foreigner-who-speaks-Russian. I tell them what I learned about the Plateau during the war—how people from many countries were sheltered here, when it was very dangerous. And now, I understand people are living here again from all over the world.

The response is a blink and a change of subject.

Soon, though, Lalik, and then Arat, are speaking a little Russian to me. Though it's a second language for them—and Arat has an especially strong accent—they are quite fluent. Before long, they are speaking only in Russian, and very loudly and very quickly, and I do my best to translate for Amélie. What about the *bumazhki*, the papers? they ask, now in Russian. The *bumazhki bumazhki*? And to me, Where do you live? Where is your husband? Where are your children? And, oh yes, Yerevan is beautiful, a great cosmopolitan city, nothing like this backwoods here! Why in the world would you live in a Russian village? Or any village? Yes, the air is clean—so clean we could hardly breathe when we first arrived. But can you believe how people dress here? They look like *bomzhi*: bums!

The food is piling up on the table. Lalik flips her long black hair. She sets down some sunflower seeds. Eat!!! Eat the fruit! Eat the fruit, it's good for you! And it all is starting to feel rather familiar, being stuffed around a table, being ordered around, being yelled at with the formulas for secret elixirs. . . .

I am seized, in a moment, with how I miss Russia: the small, warm table when it's cold outside; the potatoes and onions crackling on a skillet; the intimate questions coming fast—yes husband; no children—and hearts heading right out onto sleeves. I miss the poems, recited out of nowhere with the nod of a knowing rhyme, full of grace. And the cures themselves—from fruit tree and honeycomb—because there will always be pain, and something must be done to repair it.

Now, as I sip my tea and eat what has been offered at this table, I realize I feel oddly at ease here in this home, among the strangers—or rather I, the stranger, among them. Which is it? I find myself exhaling, sinking into the moment, taking in the known contours of this food and this talk: the bossiness, the benevolence, the warmth.

Finally, I allow myself to look around. The apartment is modest and neat. There are couches and chairs. The television is blaring, in Armenian, I assume. I notice there are lots of teddy bears, all over the apartment. In fact, the longer I look, the more teddy bears I see. They come in all kinds of colors—blue teddy bears, pink teddy bears, orange teddy bears. Most are faded, like they've been through the wash, or caught out in the snow or rain. They are large and small. Some are propped onto chairs, others are perched onto shelves or hung on the walls, in patterns. In the bedroom, off the living room, there is a large circle of bears on the wall. One has a head that has been re-stitched with black thread.

I look, I listen; they talk. Lalik begins to just talk and talk. Amélie lets the Russian float past her for a time, sipping her coffee, nibbling at a cookie.

And now, a story begins to unfold.

A girl, Lalik, is born in Azerbaijan, one republic in the Soviet South Caucasus, right on the Caspian Sea. When she is still small, her family moves to Armenia, another republic in the Soviet South Caucasus. She grows up there. Her father, an Azeri, was once a Soviet officer, beloved of many.

At some point, the girl goes from being a cherub, the apple of someone's eye—a girl with a big bow perched on top of her head—to being, as far as her Armenian neighbors were concerned, simply an *Azeri*. Not a girl, not a cherub. Just an Azeri. An Azeri to be feared, hated, distrusted. Now a young woman, with long, plush black hair—she works in a sewing factory. She meets Arat. "He cut, and I sewed!"

Soon, Lalik and Arat are married and living in Yerevan, a city surrounded by beautiful mountains. Then one day there is some political shift in the wake of the collapse of the Soviet Union—a mountainous piece of Azerbaijan called Nagorno-Karabakh is claimed by Armenia, and everyone gets murderously upset about it. *Poof*, the couple is in grave danger. Because Lalik is Azeri, Arat is getting beaten, again and again, sometimes to a pulp.

The couple eventually flees Armenia, selling everything. Only when he is forced to sell every one of his two thousand books, each of which he had read, does Arat finally break down and weep. They find themselves in Moscow. At first things are okay. But soon, their status changes. They become stateless people, living underground, bereft of citizenship and without documents. They are now vulnerable to every sort of corrupt practice imaginable at the hands of the Russian mafiosi—with their track suits and their empty eyes—and the Russian police, and the Armenian diaspora, too, that never gave up hating this couple because he was Armenian and she was Azeri. By now, in Moscow, they can never go to the doctor, so they have to use things like pomegranate tea and pear seeds when their teeth are infected, aching through the night.

I now see that Lalik is missing several teeth on the side of her mouth.

In Moscow, there are everyday cruelties, large and small. Arat is beaten in the stomach with a hot metal rod. They have two children, a boy and a girl. Their boy, Avedis, is now almost seventeen. That's him, Lalik says, pointing at a figure that comes in and out of the shadows of the apartment, blushing and pale. I can't exactly see him in the French Foreign Legion.

That is their boy. But their girl is gone.

The Armenian music on the television is blaring. The teddy bears look on.

Their girl is dead. *They* killed her. Arat was in the car with her, when they hunted him down, those Armenians, and crashed his car. After the crash, he was in a coma. When he woke up, the girl was already buried.

Gathering together thousands of euros, the couple found a driver, a *passeur*, who could smuggle them into Europe. They had no idea where they would be going. When they arrived in France, they went straight to the prefecture's office and gave themselves up, and officially requested asylum.

Their boy was still in a state of terror when they first arrived in Le Chambon. Would scream like a girl when he saw a spider. He is still afraid to speak, says Lalik. Yes and no, that's all you can get from him now.

But their girl. She's dead. Gone.

Lalik tells me how she plucked all her eyebrows out with her own fingers, one by one. Tells me how she was once slim, but is now fat. Look at me! She covers half of her mouth to hide the missing teeth. *Akh*, you can't even buy proper clothes here. *Akh*, this place . . .

Amélie is taking all this in. I've been trying my best to translate. I can translate words, but how do I translate this: That you can love a place that might someday break your very heart?

The evening is winding down. And I begin to assess—within the storm of words—what I can really know:

Lalik and Arat lived in secret for years, and now they are momentarily safe. Lalik and Arat lost a daughter. She is gone forever. And now they are waiting, waiting, waiting for papers. Would that they had their papers! They say this and repeat it again and again. *Lish' by byli bumazhki. Bumazhki. Bumazhki.* The papers. There is no respite from the wish for papers now. No real peace until they know about what will come of these *bumazhki.*

Arat soothes his wife. She cooks. She cuts more fruit. She starts insisting again that Amélie eat. She blinks. She eats the sunflower seeds that have been placed on the table. She eats and talks and eats some more: fingers, mouth, bowl; fingers, mouth, bowl.

Her mouth, an O. A poor crooked O. Her eyes look down, then up, then out.

The days go by; the weeks go by. Things have changed for me here on the Plateau. The doors have opened.

I go to CADA now, and I meet people. I knock on doors. Bring my cookies and chocolate bars, hope for the best. Word has gotten out that I'm okay, I guess. That I speak Russian—which is useful to all the families who come from the former Soviet Union—and can translate. And though I'm far from perfect at it, I don't cost anyone anything, so Amélie, who is always greeted with the same happy chant—"Amélie! Amélie! Amélie!"—has been putting me in her agenda for meetings about the *bumazhki*. Or next week's visit from the electrician. Or for setting up a doctor's appointment.

I meet a family of hardscrabble Albanians with kids who always look like they've been crying all night long, and a single woman from Rwanda who walks erect and frowning, her little son in tow. I meet a glamorous young couple from Armenia with three children. Their eldest daughter volunteers to help the little CADA children with art projects together with kids from the Cévenol School. One of that family's few keepsakes, rescued from home, is a photograph of their son, with a bird slipping from his hands, in front of Mount Ararat.

Worlds open up.

Rather often, I visit a Congolese family, composed of seven exceptionally beautiful people—a wife, a husband, and five children. The wife, Rosine, has creamy skin and smooth long hair and a low, scratchy voice. Years ago, her husband was arrested for handing out flyers; he was gone so long she was sure he was dead, but then it turned out he wasn't. The wife was later arrested, too; she was tortured in prison, and raped. Finally, a church group got them all out of the country and into France. "Oh, when the children saw snow for the first time! They couldn't believe their eyes!" says Rosine. "The snow came out of the sky and they reached out to grab it, to eat it, to pour it over themselves, as if it were the sands of Africa!"

Her husband's eyes bear yellow scars, I see now. Before his arrest he would travel for his work, walking from Congo to Angola to Namibia and back, through the countryside, through the jungles, along rivers, the back ways, borders blurred, trips measured by where the sun would be when you arrive in a certain hamlet along the way. What is a border, anyway? He tells me that when you travel like that, by foot, the chief of the village comes out to join you, and everyone comes out to welcome you, and you have the right to all the fruits of the village, brought out to you in brimming baskets by the armful.

I look at his hands; they are textured, also scarred. With all they have carried, and all they have begged, and all they have borne, his hands are finally here.

And so now, when I lay me down to sleep in the quiet of the night, there are images I see not only from Nazi Germany or Occupied Poland, or the concentration camps where parents were left behind. Not only of Daniel's solitary waiting by the dimming embers at night in Les Grillons, safe for a moment, in late 1942. Or of Magda Trocmé's doorway—from which, they say, no one was ever sent away.

Now there are snapshots of a city—Yerevan!—surrounded by mountains, as beautiful as my mind can conjure; and of a boy releasing a dove in front of Mount Ararat, where Noah once crashed ashore, with all the beasts of the earth spilling out to start anew; and now, too, a snapshot of a river, winding through West Africa toward the ocean, women washing their clothes there, on the edge of Kinshasa.

CURIOUSLY, as soon as I begin spending time with the asylum seekers and learning their stories, the stories I'd originally sought in the Plateau begin to arrive as well. People start telling me things, without ceremony or hesitation. At CADA, the guy who helps with the legal papers tells me how his wife's family sheltered Jews. A graduate student from the area mentions that a relative of his was blamed for trading with the Germans during the war. A friend's mother was evacuated here from Saint-Étienne; another friend's grandmother lived just past Le Mazet, at Panelier. A beautiful old woman with bright white hair and berry-black eyes tells me of her girlhood in wartime, and sings me a song her mother—a washerwoman—taught her at the fountain in the town square.

The stories are everywhere, just below the surface, and it seems pretty much everyone has them. Oh yes, well, maybe my grandmother said something about some refugees during the war. I don't know. I'll ask my uncle. I think I heard they fed some people in the barn? They'd sneak food out. They'd hide them in the wall cabinets—here, these cabinets here—all those police would come but they didn't give them up. They'd hide them up in the church bell-tower, across the street from the butcher. I don't know if they were Jewish or not. No one ever said.

The stories come now, without hunting, without digging, without any faces falling. They are fractured, spontaneous, sparkling with tiny aspects of life, flowing like water. They aren't the kind of stories you would offer a busload of tourists, but intimate, real, tied to moments of life's own urgency.

This is a favorite so far: Sandrine and I are walking with her tow-headed little boy one day in a field at her uncle's farm. The boy is chasing frogs and looking for mushrooms—at seven he's already got a masterful eye. Sandrine tells me that she'd heard how, during the war, some Jewish children had been taken in by one of her relatives. "And these children wanted to please the family. They knew how much we like eating frogs' legs here. So the children went out into the woods, hunting for frogs. But they were from the city, and after they were out for a few hours, they came back with bunches of toads. Not frogs, toads!"

Sandrine, with her eyes like water, laughs. Toads! Ha-ha. They did their best, the poor ones!

So now I know how to spend my days. I go up to doors, bearing cookies, and listen. There is so much to hear.

But something else is happening. It's as though some new logic—with a strange new shape—is forming in my peripheral vision. It goes like this:

I didn't understand the Law of Silence on the Plateau, but one day, I obeyed it anyway, and was silent. And then people began to speak.

And like this:

I stopped going to violent Russia because I needed to study peace, but then Russia returned to me anyway, here in the land of peace. The map of my world bursts open, down new rivers, up new mountains, into new countries, and new continents, with new wars, new conciliations under jungle leaves, new hands stretched upward in supplication and hope: We are here!

And like this:

The past was closed to me, and the present now comes rushing toward me, in a torrent. And then the past arrives in its wake.

What physics is this? What conservation of matter? What fluid dynamics? That when you close one door, another, greater one opens? That when you reach for the cloak, you are given the coat as well; and hoping for one mile of companionship, you are given two.

I'm so grateful for all of this, and a little dumbfounded. It's hard not to blur Magic and Law when you see this: That when you finally melt into your purpose, your purpose melts, right back, into you.

One day, not long after our first visit, Lalik and Arat invite me back to their home. Lalik has been to the Resto du Coeur, the food bank the CADA residents have access to a couple of times a month, and Arat tells me he wants to make *shashlik* for me—shish kebab. He wants me to taste the real thing. The visit is calmer, easier this time. Lalik wants to tell me about her life back home. She had several fur coats back then, and Arat always liked to dress sharply—"You don't have to be the boss to look like the boss!" Yes, this village life in France is calm, it's true, but so slow for her, so tedious. No, she doesn't like walking around the village, or into the woods. You should have seen me before, she says. I was slender.

Here, nobody cares how they put themselves together, she insists. The Frenchwomen, they don't care; they go out with their hair still wet. They never wear heels. She has another friend from Russia in the area. That woman once got dressed up and went out to an event in makeup and proper heels and a pretty dress, and people were looking at her as though she were some kind of prostitute.

Arat lets me help with the *shashlik*—I put the raw onions on the skewer next to the chicken. Lalik is still in a good mood from her trip. The food wasn't the best this week, she says, but it was okay. She got fish and canned ravioli and chili; boxes of "American" milk; frozen fish fillets; some sardines; some fruits and vegetables. A CADA woman from Africa who was waiting behind her in line had started touching her hair! Lalik didn't like that; she wriggled and told her to stop. The other woman didn't have much hair of her own—probably because the Africans braid their hair so tightly, she says, that'll make your hair fall out. Well. I wondered about the other things that could cause an African woman's hair to fall out. But I didn't say.

The *shashlik* is delicious. Arat and Lalik take pictures of it and of me. The glamorous young Armenian family comes by for a visit.

At the end of the evening, I tell Lalik and Arat not to worry about walking me back to my apartment at the other end of Le Chambon. It's nearly a half hour to get there, uphill for part of the walk, and they'd have to go both ways. But they insist. Lalik puts on a bulky sweater she says she wouldn't have been caught dead in back home.

The moon is out, fat and white behind thin clouds. It follows us as we walk, first down the street where the CADA residence is, flanked by tall pines. We pass large houses, all closed up. You'd think no one at all lived here, Lalik says. You see not a flash of light coming out of any of the houses. But people are there, inside. Here's the big house, dark almost, where a woman lives alone. Not even a dog lives there with her. If we get papers, maybe we can buy this house.

Then, there is another big, dark place behind some trees.

And here's where that man hanged himself, Lalik says. No one lives there now. Back in Armenia, when someone dies, we lay them out in their house. Here, they send the bodies right to the church, but we don't think it's respectful to take the body away from the home.

We're getting closer to the train tracks.

Here is the place where the father of the music person lives, she says. Down the hill, now, in the center.

It looks so different here in the summer, she says. People come out, dancing. People bowl in the square.

Here's where I go to the doctor. That's my doctor. Here's where you can buy clothes.

Here—she is pointing at a small public square where there is a plaque dedicated to the Righteous of the Plateau—is where there was some summer festival. I don't remember what. Something about flowers. She looks at the Protestant church coming up on our right. I haven't been inside any of the churches yet, she says.

We round the bend toward the river. A bright star has appeared. It seems to blast light on the three of us as we leave the center of town, pass over the bridge and along a quiet highway, surrounded by fields and trees. We walk, and walk.

Lalik narrates her tale of the large, dark houses, the quiet here, the suicide, the church, the women with their flat shoes and unkempt hair: This is what she sees, as she walks. This is her Plateau. She knows nothing of any righteous past here. But why should she?

The one moon follows us as we walk, down finally, toward my own door, and my own little light that shines above it at night.

Lalik has her eyes; I have mine.

Chapter 7

THE HUNT

Thus ev'ry kind their pleasure find,
The savage and the tender;
Some social join, and leagues combine,
Some solitary wander:
Avaunt, away! the cruel sway,
Tyrannic man's dominion;
The sportsman's joy, the murdering cry,
The flutt'ring gory pinion!

—ROBERT BURNS, "NOW WESTLIN' WINDS . . ."

JANUARY 18, 1943. MONDAY.

On that day, the Red Army finally broke through the German blockade of Leningrad. Behind the blockade, for three years, Soviet citizens starved to death, sometimes at the rate of one hundred thousand human beings per month. Those who survived ate bread bulked up with sawdust, weeds that grew in the once stately gardens of the city's imperial past, and—in the delirium of starvation—they sometimes killed and ate one another. January days in that northern metropolis are short and dusty dark, the sun barely piercing the thick layers of clouds just overhead. Maybe the winter of 1942–1943 was Russia's darkest ever. But on that January day the blockade was broken, and food and the sun would slowly come back, and life would slowly begin again, over the bones of the more than one million who finally perished.

Also on that day, hundreds of Jewish inhabitants of the Warsaw ghetto rose up for the first time, in order to thwart a mass deportation to the Treblinka extermination camp. The ghetto dwellers used their hands, their fists, whatever they could turn into a weapon—a gasoline bottle, a smuggled pistol, anything. The deportation wasn't prevented in the end. Still, eight thousand people were meant to be rounded up, and when it was all done, the German soldiers had managed to round up only five thousand. So the fists and hands and bottles meant that three thousand lives could keep being lived. For a while at least.

And meanwhile, on that same day of January 18, 1943, dead in the middle of winter, in an office high up on a plateau in the craggy back-woods of France, someone sat down at a desk to work. Maybe he or she—shall we suppose a she?—touched her hair lightly before begin-ning. Maybe she adjusted her chair. Who knows. What we can be abso-lutely sure of, though, is that at a certain moment that person picked up a piece of paper, rolled it into a typewriter, and began to type, right at the top of the page:

13ième LEGION DE GENDARMERIE. COMPAGNIE DE LA HAUTE-LOIRE. SECTION d'YSSINGEAUX. BRIGADE DE TENCE.

These were the basics, in capital letters, probably typed countless times before, identifying the police station where the typist sat, the *départe-ment*, the section, the brigade.

Then, *ka-ching*, the bell ring, and the slap of the carriage return.

Liste des israélites étrangers en residence dans la circonscription de la brigade. List of foreign Jews resident in the brigade precinct.

Was the radio on? Did the typist hum along with whatever was play-ing, maybe the sweet tenor sway of Tino Rossi in his recent hit: *"Quand tu reverras ton village, quand tu reverras ton clocher"*—When you see your village again, when you see your bell tower again. . . .

The document she was creating—a table, really—was for the commandant of the brigade, a man named Dubreuil, who had himself been ordered to furnish this information to the departmental capital in Le Puy-en-Velay. We know this because right around that same day in January, scores of other forms—amounting to hundreds of pages of documents—were created in the *département* of Haute-Loire with the same information, some also typed, some written carefully by hand. This was just one piece of paper in one typewriter. Just one among the newly minted mountains of them.

So much had changed since November, when the Germans first occupied the South of France. The German soldiers had stretched thin into this mountainous country. It isn't easy to take over bureaucracies and businesses, even in puppet regimes, but the occupiers did what they could. The Eastern Front kept bringing bad and worse news—broken blockades and ghetto uprisings—but finally the soldiers had settled in and begun to make new plans.

On this January day, then, all over France, strategies were now in place to corral Jews toward the center of the country, concentrating them into a small number of city centers and camps in order to limit their movement. Since December, every passport, every ration card owned by a Jewish person had been stamped JUIF, and all the Jews had been ranked according to their status as French or foreign, and whether they were part Jew or full. Trains were finally ready again for large-scale deportations that could ship about a thousand Jews at a time to camps out east.

Strange to think how you couldn't have had a Holocaust without an office, without a typist, without a train, without a plan.

So, the typist had her task: to create a list of foreign Jews, with accompanying details. How to make it look right?

She types a long line of *m*'s:

mmmmmmmmmmmmmmmmmmmmmmmmmmmmmmmmmmmmmmmmmmmmmm

This makes a clear break from her title to the start of her columns: Last name, first name, parents; date and place of birth; nationality; profession; place and commune of residence; evidence of Jewish identity. It's a lot of information, but the typist has come up with clever ways to divide up her columns (with exclamation points) and rows (with dashes). Everything fits.

Now, the names. ABRAHAMSON (Herbert), son of Albert and of Rosenthal (Elsa); born 15-1-1903 in Berlin. German. Without profession. Living in Tence, at the Freydier house at the train station. Abrahamson's insurance card and his food ration card indicate that he is Jewish. Next, Herbert's wife, Olga. Next, a German Jewish youth named ALEXANDER, born in Hamburg, who has JUIF also stamped on his *récépissé*, his refugee document. Next, seventeen more like those three, all living in Tence.

Then, the names begin for Le Chambon-sur-Lignon. First, ALLALOUF (Jacob), son of Menaen and Eskenazi (Esther), born in 1903, in Salonika. Then the boy, Rudi APPEL, from Mannheim, who, having been fished out of the Rivesaltes concentration camp in September 1943, is living in a home for children, sponsored by the Swiss Red Cross. Rudi's mother is in a hospital in Perpignan and here he is—as our typist spells his name wrong—on a form that says he has no profession, and that he is known to be Jewish because he is identified that way by his food ration card and his insurance card.

BLOC, BRAUN, BERGAS, GRONNER, GOLDENBERGER, HENE, HERMAN, HIRSCH, KALLMAN, KAUFMANN, KOHN, KRAMRISCH—at Les Grillons, with Daniel—LASSERSON, LEVI . . . All typed neatly, all adorned with the dashes and exclamation points that are being used to delineate person from person, datum from datum.

Then there's LEWIN. Two Lewins, in fact. Brothers: Martin, just nineteen, and Jacob, not quite eighteen.

I know Jacob Lewin. I feel like I do, anyway. I've followed his story now for a long time. Jacob Lewin, also Jacques. Also Jack. He's a boy still, not quite eighteen.

Jacob arrived in Le Chambon after a long journey. First there was Kristallnacht in Kleinlangheim, when his mother's teeth were punched in and her coat stolen, and his dog, Waldi, was killed by German soldiers. Then there was the relative anonymity of Berlin, where he kept his yarmulke tucked in his pocket when walking in the streets. Then, the road to France, where Jacob was with his parents again, a witness now to the German invasion from the land and from the sky, bodies of dead people and horses strewn over the ground. And then, the French concentration camp at Saint-Cyprien, the town named for the holy comforter, but besieged with infernal mud and floods in which corpses washed up on the shore, causing Jacob to throw up. And then, another camp called Gurs, where a worker from the Swiss Red Cross found him and his brother and said there was a place where the two might live in safety.

I feel I know Jacob Lewin because I've been reading about him for years. And because I've seen a photograph of him taken just four days after he arrived on the Plateau from Gurs. In it, he is perched on a rough-hewn fence, just a log and another log, with mud fields behind him, and a strand of pines behind that. And he is smiling broadly, it seems especially broadly because his face is razor-thin. And his hair is combed back. And his limbs are razor-sharp, like a scarecrow: He weighs only eighty pounds, and his belt is cinched to a tiny circle. The sun is so bright, it makes black shadows under his chin and along his narrow temples. Here, he is a boy who once had a mother with all her teeth and a nice warm coat. And a dog named Waldi. And who once was able to feel safe in the world. And so, heartbreakingly, he smiles into the sun.

And now, in this office, on this January day, when a pretty typist—shall we call her pretty?—might or might not be sitting in front of a typewriter, as the sweet lilt of Tino Rossi might or might not be wafting in the air around her—"When you see your village again, when you see your bell tower again, your house, your parents, the friends of your age, you will say, 'Nothing in my home has changed'"—now, this Jacob, this Jacques, this Jack is just a name that comes pounding out of a typewriter. *Tap-a-tap-tap-tap-tap.*

LEWIN (Jacob), son of Anode and Sondhelm (Irma). Born May 5, 1925. German; no profession; staying at the home of the Swiss Red

Cross in Le Chambon; Jewish identity on social insurance card and on food card.

Nothing more.

It wasn't the first time Jacob's name had been typed into documents. Nor would it be the last. In the thousands of pieces of paper created and duplicated, and then placed in the file cabinets of Haute-Loire in those months of 1942 and 1943, his name would slip in and out and in again like a silver fish in the ocean, like a woodland creature scurrying up a tree—now a flutter, tail pulsing; now you see it, now you don't. All different pieces of paper. All fitting, sooner or later, into some folder, some plan.

In late August 1942, when Jacob was already in residence at a home called La Guespy, a raid was planned on the Plateau. But it was staved off by a set of simple evasion techniques that had been established there—a warning phone call, the barking of dogs on the arrival of trucks, an administrative foil by the director of a couple of the homes, August Bohny-Reiter. The refugee children scattered into nearby forests in time to escape. While they were gone, their rooms were raided, and policemen made detailed notes, in pencil, of each. Because of this, I know that Martin Lewin and his roommate in room number 18, a boy named Koranyi, owned, together: two pairs of pants, one in flannel; one pair of overalls; two overcoats; two jackets; three shirts; a leather bag; a large cloth bag (empty); a pair of shoes; a pair of sabots; a pillow; five books; one notebook; one bottle of ink.

Jacob himself ran off into the hills near Le Chambon and stayed in the woods, eating berries and wandering until the sun set again, when, finally hearing a telltale whistle, he knew the coast was clear. From there, he and his brother hid for several weeks in a farming village on the Plateau, and then returned to Le Chambon to live with Dora Rivière, in her home just up from the railroad station. With her nom de guerre "Monsieur Lignon," Rivière—square-jawed, handsome, in and out of Nazi concentration camps—was one of the great heroes of rescue and resistance on the Plateau; she and her family shared all they had with Jacob and his brother, but, for the danger, could not permit the boys ever to look out the window.

Jacob was safe, for now, in the Plateau, and his brother was safe, and so was a long list of children at a home called Coteau Fleuri and another called La Maison des Roches—its name oddly echoing the name of the École des Roches, where Daniel was born. But the police—who'd botched the raid—were clearly in trouble with their higher-ups, and upset about it. Their failure triggered whole new reams of paperwork—stamped SECRET in their upper-left quadrants—where the justifications for not finding the children were listed, saying that they must have fled the country since "the intemperate climate and the cool nights will no longer allow them to sleep over in the woods, and if they were still in the region of Chambon, we would have found most of them." Attached to their paperwork was a new document, "Activity of the Police of Haute-Loire in the Search for Jews in the Period Between August 27 and September 28, 1942," where the bosses could know that, in Le Chambon-sur-Lignon alone, police had questioned 879 people in buses and trains and 496 in hotels and inns, had conducted 625 home visits, and made two arrests outside the town, on the basis of "furnished information."

New lists were made. They were a little different every time. Sometimes they were lists of all foreigners, or just of Jews, sometimes by country of origin (surprising how many Turks made their way to the Plateau, and who even knew that there was a distinct people called the Saars?). Sometimes the profession of the foreigners was highlighted—there were architects among them, painters, sculptors, lawyers, and judges. Or their sex or age. The typist used punctuation in newly creative ways: a dash, then a division sign, then a dash again made an attractive divider, as did creatively employed brackets. The names were foreign, so they were spelled differently here and there. They were also, often, false.

By December 1942, after the Allies invaded North Africa and Germany made its descent south, an important and inclusive new list was made right there in Le Puy-en-Velay, this time in an official form with the stamp of the prefecture, for all of the foreigners living in Haute-Loire. Among the 174 names on that list were those of Jacob and his brother Martin, and also that of the future math laureate Alexander "Grottendiech," his last name spelled wrong. And there was the Little Cricket Hélène, with a blond bob and a lopsided smile. And there was the trim mustachioed Yehuda Basnitsky—in the list he was called "Walter"—who was also, secretly, a member of the maquisard. And there was Kurt Grossman, Peter Feigl's friend—though Peter's own name was not there. And there was August Bohny-Reiter, the Swiss director of two children's homes on the Plateau.

That cold Monday in January—when the Leningrad barricade was broken and the Warsaw ghetto was in flames—a person sat at a desk and stared at a piece of paper. Germany was panicking with its losses in the east and with the new buildup of fresh Allied forces. Our typist sat facing that sheet, rolling it in the machine, just as tens, hundreds, thousands, were sitting elsewhere in France, elsewhere in Europe, elsewhere under siege. Like them, she was trying to make her list look nice and clear. Maybe, like thousands and thousands of others then and there, she was just trying to finish her day.

On the Plateau, it was cozy inside even as the winter winds blew. But here, as all over France, new roundups and deportations were about to unfold. *Tap-a-tap-tap-tap.*

THE FORESTS AND THE HILLS of the Plateau are full of animals: wild boar (who root annoyingly through gardens) and deer, birds and hares. Pheasant. When someone catches sight of a boar, a hunting party is called. Together, the group heads to the forest. They beat on drums, loose their dogs out into woods. I have seen them all after, along the winding roads where the cliffs drop down to the Rhône Valley, trees lit up with orange and fiery red leaves swirling down, the men's leathered skin darkened by the cold, their guns bent over their arms, a pack of dogs around them, sniffing madly, climbing, bellowing. In the trunk of a car lay the body of a wire-haired boar, its face toward the forest, its skin bearing patches of bright pink, all its movement gone.

We can eat all kinds of things in this life, but we don't hunt just anything we can eat; after all, we can eat the bugs that slither up trees, or our pet kittens, or rats, or eagles, but we rarely stalk them as game. And when we choose to hunt, we don't always eat what we've killed—we sometimes put its remains up on a wall to gape at, or place it, still living, in a cage to look at.

And sometimes, we don't hunt animals, but we hunt people. And not because they are a danger to us in any real, immediate way.

So. What are the rules? How do we know who is the hunter, and what or who is the game? What does it take to divide up the world into the bearers of guns here, the bellowers there, and the still bodies beyond?

It seems like a patently obvious point that within the social world, there are people who are labeled as "us" and others labeled as "them." Our family! Our country! Our team! Our church! And that you could put, say, plusses next to the *us*es and minuses next to the *them*s. Or binary ones and zeroes instead. And you could then map out, with some ease, who does what with whom, with a mind to who is in the in-group, and who is in the out-group. And from there, you could make assumptions about who might live with whom, or fight with whom, or die for whom. The question of us and them is central to any study of social life, but ethnography—the up-close, detailed description of groups we do in anthropology—shows that belonging and not belonging can't be characterized by zeroes or ones, or plusses or minuses, alone. Reality is more complicated than that, more plastic, more fluid.

Language gives us hints as to the possible breadths and depths these concepts travel in different parts of the world. The words for the ins and the outs, after all, carry not only binaries, but sets of associations and feelings and even colors and textures. They carry layers upon layers of history, evidenced in their etymological foundations. And they also carry, sometimes, rich dream logics. The English word *foreign*, it turns out, shares a Latin root, *foris* (outside), with the English word *forest* and the French word *forêt*. Foreigners are outsiders, but they are also, say, under thick canopies of trees, under tangles of thickets, where you might be lost among them, and alone. And if in English the word *stranger*—like the French *étranger*—nearly always feels dark and threatening, the Russian *chuzhoi* resonates with the words for both "monster" (*chudovishche*) and "the miraculous" (*chudesnoe*). And in Kabardian, the language I studied in the northwest Caucasus, the word for "stranger," *khame*, is neutral, meaning simply not-family, not-villager, not-clan, bearing no distinct aura of fear around it. In that world of ancient lowland kingdoms, *khame* is just someone or something that is not your business. It is another word entirely, *bi*, or enemy, that carries fear and danger and the threat of violence.

As we orient ourselves through the words and pictures that languages give us, we see how the next order of questions is also oriented: Is a stranger . . . going to kill me? Or wait in a dark room for me with a blade? Or, perhaps, bring me a gift and transform my life? Or enter my home only when accompanied by rituals of protection? Along the way, and in a flash, we also decide how to treat that stranger-person, how to feel about him, how to elect if he can cross the threshold and live among us.

Beyond those associations, there is also a sense in each society of how one can become an insider or not. In Russian, a person who is *chuzhoi* may slowly become *svoi* (one's own), through spending time with a community—sometimes years. The *khame* could become an insider to the family or clan by, say, the elaborate ritual of marriage. These take time and effort, but they are possible in principle.

And the stranger, the *étranger*?

How could I know, in any depth, what these words and concepts mean? What could I ask, in a place—here, or anywhere—to know how a person sees and feels and accumulates a sense of belonging and a sense of the barriers to belonging? Taking nothing for granted?

I could start with questions about belonging and then work my way out from there: What is a brother or a sister to you? Are those large, warm words? What is a friend, and what does that word feel like? Or a neighbor? Or an acquaintance? Or a coworker? What do you see in your mind's eye, when you conjure them? Do they look like something particular? Do they have a kind of skin, or a kind of hair? Lacking that skin or that hair, do they scare you, or me? Do you think that they are dirty, that you can't eat food that they have touched? Do they bow down in prayer in a way that seems reverential, or somehow primitive? Do they raise their hands? Do you not like how loudly they speak on the subway or in a cinema, or the smell of their food? Do they cover their heads when they walk in crowds? Do they all look alike to you, or to me, those strangers? Would you prefer not to be on the street where they live because they are too poor, or too rich?

Are they a he to you, or a she? Or, maybe, an it?

These are empirical questions, not rhetorical ones. Questions that tell us about how a full person—with a whole life and history, and with things they love to do and people they love to spend time with—becomes a one or a zero, and nothing in between. How they might, someday, become a neighbor—to whom acknowledgment and an open kindly face is due—or a *tap-a-tap-tap* on a list.

During the Holocaust, communities all over Europe worked to solve the problem of the stranger. People who were once neighbors and friends, and fellow countrymen, and fellow human beings, no longer belonged to one another. Over time and in degrees, they became strangers—lurking, monstrous, thicket-dwelling, dangerous. You make lists; you arrest them; you corral them; you don't feed them. Soon, they are eating on the ground, soon they are covered with mud, soon they are hungry and thin and hollowed, soon their hands are outstretched. They become strangers to their fellow creatures, barbarous in their eyes; thinking makes it so. And with that whiff of barbarity, they can be hunted.

And on the Plateau? Was there a special language there for who is ours and who isn't? For whom we should help and whom we should fear? Were there special words that people drew from as, one by one, name by name, fellow human beings were hunted down in their midst; as that mountain of typed pages became a mountain of real people, real bodies, real suffering, real imprisonment, real deportation? There on the Plateau, were the wells of language deeper than French alone? Were they sweetened by other sources?

There must have been something. If the law of the binary had held, how could you explain what happened to that skinny German-Jewish stranger called LEWIN (Jacob), when the bus and the police finally followed all those typed pieces of paper, and came for him?

Without those sweeter wells, there is no explaining it.

It is a cold winter's day on the Plateau Vivarais-Lignon. A man walks up a road. He has brown hair and liquid hazel eyes and a beard. There is a grace in his gait, but he is walking slowly. Each of the man's arms is stretched out to hold the hand of a little person, and he keeps glancing at a third little person to be sure she is safely coming along. These little ones, one-two three, are bright creatures, all. Together, the group is stopping and starting. One of the children, with long shiny brown hair, keeps dropping something, picking it up, dropping it; picking it up again.

The road inclines steeply. The small group walks up, along a stone wall, under a canopy of pine trees. It's been a long cold spell. They walk past the house where Dora Rivière once lived, where Jacob and Martin LEWIN were once forbidden to look out the window. They walk past another house whose entry is marked with a plaque dedicated to the life and death of a certain young doctor Roger Le Forestier.

The children all have big eyes and long eyelashes. They wear bright colored hats and mittens. The tallest is fair, like the man, with greenish eyes. The two smaller faces are milky brown. They bounce as they walk. Bounce and chatter. Soon, they reach a gate to a compound—the CADA compound. They walk in. Other children are running around. Small groups of men are clustered together, smoking and talking, hugging their leather jackets closely to themselves. One boy is zooming the length of the courtyard on an old bike, this way and that, this way and that.

The man with the graceful gait and the liquid hazel eyes ascends a set of stairs with his children, one-two-three. They scramble over the threshold of an apartment and disappear behind a door.

Now, what if you could just sweep away all the categories of person, of nation, of border, of religion, of ethnic this or that? Of us and them? What if you could just plain see the man and the children, walking? With no words to interfere?

You are watching the man and the little one-two-three. Maybe you are a citizen of this country. Maybe you have bright blue eyes, and a mild mien, and skin of brown leather. Maybe you wear fleece or are birdlike. Maybe you work in a field; or in an office, at a typewriter. Maybe you are an anthropologist, even. Anyway. You are the hunter now.

And what is this fluttering, luminous game?

EVERY TIME I arrive on the Plateau after an absence—I now come as often as possible from Washington and stay for a month at a time—I see Amélie first thing, if I can. Amélie tells me how things are going at CADA—gives me news about which families have gotten their papers—leurs papiers, ikh bumazhki—and which have not. When I arrived this winter, the news was mixed: There was a yes, miraculously, for Lalik and Arat, who left immediately and gleefully for Montpellier (a place where their son would never have to join the French Foreign Legion, and where Lalik might just get to wear proper heels and lipstick again); a maybe for the Congolese family, now working on court appeals and praying; and a no for the glamorous Armenians, who have begun the undocumented life, farther afield.

Amélie tells me about a young family just arrived at the CADA: a father, a mother, and three little children. They don't speak much French, but they do speak Russian, so maybe I can come along with her to visit with them and translate a bit?

The family, it turns out, is from Chechnya. Chechnya, of the North Caucasus in Russia. Chechnya, with its dark, unpronounceable consonants and vowels that can, all by themselves, repel people from its complicated story.

Chechnya. What business do I have knowing anything about that place, anyway? I, from Salisbury Street—with its elms, all dead; its boys smoking pot up on the roof at Calabrese's bakery; its city dotted with rusty billboards of poor little Michelle Maenza that should have scared me away from the world for good. What business do I have knowing how to pronounce Chechnya properly, let alone having met a man who wanted to kill himself for what he'd done as a soldier there, or having lived in a village where—at the worst moments, years before I ever arrived—you could hear the explosions from its wars?

What business do I have in this? None, I guess. But there it is; I do know something about the place. I lived in the Caucasus region for months before authorities decided—as they have decided for pretty much all the (rare) researchers like me—that my presence ought to be vigorously discouraged. And now here I am.

And though I wouldn't say this to Amélie, I admit I have been watching this Chechen family at a distance—the father with his little ones around town. I can't help it. So I set out with Amélie for CADA again, and arrive at a new threshold.

The man with liquid hazel eyes opens the door. Smiling shyly, he scrambles to get me and Amélie some slippers. There is no question of leaving my shoes on in this home. When I was living in the North Caucasus—the Muslim North Caucasus—I once made the terrible mistake of forgetting to take off sandals I had worn outside before entering a living room. The daughters of the family I lived with had to tell me about my error, which was at least as embarrassing to them as it was to me. There is no shoe dance in this Muslim part of the world. There is just the filthy outside and the clean inside. I know what to do.

As we take off our boots, three children, bouncing creatures, one-two-three, clamber to the threshold. They are looking up and calling, delightedly, Amélieeeeeeee, AMÉLIE, AMÉLIE!! The two littlest wrap their arms around her legs.

A small woman, lissome as the stem of a flower, stands in the doorway, too; the children bob toward her, then away. This woman, mother of these children, has long dark hair tucked under a simple kerchief, and a brilliant dark brow. Her voice, like her bearing, is soothing, sweet. *Zdravstvuite,* she says in Russian. Hello. Welcome. Welcome.

These are the Vakhaevs. The father is Akhmad; the mother, Rovzan.

First things first. After introductions, I need to explain to Akhmad and Rovzan about the guy coming to read their gas meter, and the other guy who will be coming to clean the vents in their kitchen and bathroom. Every resident at CADA has the right to a certain amount of money for heat and gas and water. The Vakhaevs are doing fine, according to Amélie, even if Akhmad has been showing signs that he is concerned that it's too cold inside their home; a few days ago, Amélie herself checked the temperature of their apartment, and it was sixty-six degrees Fahrenheit during the day; sixty-four at night. So all is well; but still, some things have to be explained. Meter readers, for example. What is the family supposed to think when some random person comes to their door and starts roaming around their apartment, opening cupboards and making notes on pieces of paper? I do my best, at their threshold, to say what needs to be said.

But there is no way the children will leave things there; they take Amélie's hand and pull, pull, pull, stretching her arm, until she is solidly in the living room and responding to their observations and questions and notebooks with pictures. They are bursting to use the French words and phrases that they have already absorbed with lightning speed. So, before I can even, really, get my bearings, they are stretching their arms to bring me in, too: *'garde! 'garde!* They can already say: Look! Look! Over here! Look!

The children are each ravishing, like their parents. Fariza, the eldest, and the one most like her father, has long blondish hair and a big toothy smile and a very slightly wary expression. Zezag, the middle girl, wears an impishly crooked grin and has fiercely intelligent eyes. She is carrying around a balloon that she's drawn all over, bonking Amélie with it, bonking me with it. Ha. She reminds me of a Russian cartoon of the Uzhasnaia Printsessa, the horrible princess, who defeats a man-eating ogre by scaring him with all her marvelous chaos, sticking her tongue out at him, and clonking him with a bone. Yay for the horrible princess! The boy, Dzhamal, is the littlest. He has the largest, prettiest eyes, and his older sisters abuse him in ways that are familiar to me, as a middle sister: putting his hair in rubber bands at the top of his head and then laughing at him, leading him around with a string on his wrist, or on all fours. They draw, he draws; they dance, he dances. They say look, he says look! Look!!

And so, that's it: I'm in. We begin to talk. Amélie fades once there is too much Russian and too little for her to do, busy as she is. So she leaves me behind, and the children bounce around, and Rovzan, in her lovely low voice, invites me in to sit, to drink tea, to stay.

One visit becomes another and then another. I stop by with cookies or other treats—Dzhamal gets chocolate all over his face—I bring my notebooks to scribble things down in, hand notebooks over to the children for them to draw in. I translate messages from the kids' school (permission slips are perplexing), or from a doctor, or from CADA, on some official business.

And though, cosmically speaking, I have no business knowing anything about Chechnya, I'm now inside a little home in France where—who does what with whom?—a Chechen family happens to live, where a Chechen family speaks and cooks and acts and plays and makes sense of the world they've left behind, and the world where they've arrived, in shock. I come to their home; they invite me in. I put on my role as an anthropologist like an old hat, an old pair of shoes.

In time, I learn the basics of their story. A story that is, at its most painful moments, about us and them—ever so complicated in the land of the twisted consonants and vowels, *chnya*. A story about being foreign, being strange. About being hunted, being in flight.

I come, we drink tea. I listen:

Akhmad grew up in the interior of Chechnya. He remembers how, when he was a boy, the children would go into the woods and gather blackberries and forest grapes—whatever those are—and forest pears. They would collect apricots from their trees and sell them to visitors, making some real money for themselves. They would learn how to farm, how to watch over cattle, how to build things.

I learn that Akhmad is from a village, and Rovzan is from a town—she worked in a stall at a market—and eventually moved to the village for Akhmad. From my own time in the Caucasus, I can picture Akhmad's village, even though I've never been to Chechnya itself. I can picture the cows that roam in the fields, and the forests and mountains beyond, and the compound, with the individual bedrooms you have to take your sandals off to enter. I know what it is like to spend months tying the buds of cucumber plants onto strings in the garden beyond such a compound; I know what it is like to watch the sheep walk by; and to rush when guests come—anytime, day or night—and help prepare a table for them; and be quiet until I am given leave to speak.

And I know this: Being from a village in the Caucasus makes Akhmad different from those who are from a city like the capital, Grozny, where people bustle around and have nine-to-five jobs; where the sexes can talk with each other with no censure; where there is money and there are chances; where you learn to be bold toward authorities. Being from the country makes Akhmad, perhaps, less at ease in the big world—more at ease in a little world. It also makes him, to me, touchingly familiar.

I listen. I adjust my anthropologist hat. I draw circles in my head and declare to myself: village, city; us, them.

I visit again. Rovzan and I sit at the table; Akhmad, more comfortable now, sits on the floor. Akhmad is dying to speak, I think. I listen more:

Growing up, Akhmad's greatest lessons were about how to be a good person in a harsh environment: loyal to family, loyal to clan, loyal to the principle of *iman*.

I, anthropologist, ask: What is *iman*?

Akhmad, who knows Russian only from television and from his limited interactions in bigger cities, struggles to tell me. *Iman*, he says, is something you have or don't have. *Iman* is when your elders are speaking, and your attention is riveted on them. *Iman* is treating a woman who is the age of your sister as your sister, too. *Iman* is helping a woman with her load, whatever her age. It is obedience—fasting when it is time to fast, praying when it is time to pray. It is honesty in your endeavors, generosity with what you have. It is honor. It is not limited to how you think—but defined by what you do.

Iman. In Islam, *iman* means, simply, "faith." I see that to Akhmad, that *iman*—that faith—lies at the very foundation of a good and moral life. Of course Islam is a very great religion, read through many peoples: For Akhmad, *iman* is channeled through his two very distinctive hazel eyes, from his one village in the mountains of his one country, Russia. His *iman*, the one he struggles to explain, guides him to understand about whether you stand or whether you speak when elders are in the room; about how to show honor to women and men alike; about the filth or cleanliness in things; it is perplexed by the need for things like permission slips for school photographs of his child (what is an individual right, anyway?). There are so many possibilities for what *iman* might mean, depending on the eyes, depending on the village. Akhmad struggles to translate his *iman*, and I struggle to understand the yet untranslatable.

I listen more, and Akhmad tells me the barest outline of how they came to leave their home. After the wars began in 1992, life changed for Akhmad in Chechnya. Rockets would land splat in the middle of his village, and if they didn't explode, they could be used for scrap metal. One of his friends lost his hands that way, rifling among the ruins. In their gardens, they used to be able to grow tomatoes and onions and cucumbers and beets, both red and white. But now, Akhmad says, the land is bad. The tomatoes that come up are full of worms. War ruined the gardens, he says, a declaration of horticultural metaphysics if ever I heard one.

Little as the wide world may understand about these Chechen wars, this much I know: They were terrible. They started out seeming almost gallant to some locals in the early 1990s—about building a Caucasus nation after the collapse of the Soviet Union, finally free of Moscow's yoke—but soon they went mad. The Russian army was utterly brutal in its response to separatist actions. Grozny fell in flames. There were merciless acts of terrorism in response. Over time, the wars went from being mostly secular to something else. Something religious, if you can call anything with such violent claims religious. In villages like Akhmad's, people—brothers, schoolmates, friends—would disappear out into the woods, to live the life of guerrilla fighters. Many of them would die.

Eventually, Russia wanted to wash its hands of Chechnya but couldn't: Violence had begotten violence and now terrorist acts were springing up, here and there, in the interior of Russia itself. Now, there were new flows of people arriving from countries in turmoil in the south and the east. Afghanistan. Egypt. Saudi Arabia. Having set up its own sort of puppet regimes in the Caucasus, Russia let those appointed dictators do their thing. This meant weird gluts of wealth and wild bouts of local violence. It also meant that even as those religious extremists—"people of the woods," as Akhmad called them—were growing more numerous, and more dangerous, so were some of the local clans, and the local police, and the Russian overseers, and the plain old mafia.

I look at Akhmad, as I begin to know him. He is a person of the village, not a person of the woods. A husband and a father and a son. He aims morally high, in the scale measure that *iman* sets for him. But how, in the context of the war, could his world continue intact?

One night, in the small hours, there was a knock on the door of Akhmad's house on the edge of the forest. And then masked men burst in, demanding his food or his life; or his food or all his children's lives. In the aftermath of that terrible moment, a neighbor reported having seen black-masked men coming out of Akhmad's house in the morning. So that brought new trouble, and a new round of black-masked men—these, perhaps, police?—came to his door, blazing their own weapons. And then again. And again.

I presume lists were made up in the dusty offices of some downtown capital, with someone typing the name of a man and a wife and three children. And other lists were made up in the minds of guerrilla fighters who needed something to eat and needed to see a doctor. And other lists still were made up in the minds of gangsters who had decided that pasturelands at the edge of the village were also worth killing for. And they made their lists and put on their seemingly interchangeable black masks and burst into Akhmad's life to challenge his world of well-calibrated *iman*.

What was he to do?

Akhmad, of the liquid hazel eyes and graceful gait, says only this: Back home, there is a law of the day, and a law of the night. You can't follow both; you just can't. You can do your best, but there is no *iman* that can cover both of those. All you know is that you are, to just about everyone, them. And so, try as you may to be good, you have become an enemy to all.

When it was finally time for Akhmad and Rovzan to flee their home, or die at the hands of one group of black-masked men or another, their family gathered up every bit of money they could to pay for the *passeur*, so they might travel, in secret, over hills and mountains, across rivers, over borders, the Black Sea ever to their south. They had no idea of where they would land—which country, which region, which city. Only somewhere else. Some other place, far from home, where trouble could no longer reach them.

When they arrived in Toulouse, in southwestern France, they spoke not a word of French. They needed a place to sleep but couldn't find one. Now a brand-new kind of them to a brand-new us, they gave themselves up to the authorities. Rovzan fell desperately ill and was put in a hospital. Akhmad, with the little ones, one-two-three, went to an office where he heard there would be help. A woman typed French words into Google Translate—*tap-a-tap-tap*—and out popped words in Russian: "You are illegal here. Come back tomorrow." And then she handed him a map. And he kept saying to the woman a French word that he had quickly learned: *bébés, bébés*. But the babies. But the children . . .

Akhmad would spend the days in Toulouse under Rovzan's hospital window, with *les bébés* in tow. And eventually, a kind woman, who saw the little family waiting under the window, gave Akhmad some euros for food, just like that.

Now, having made their way to CADA, he and Rovzan and the children bear documents that are still, all these years after the Second World War, called *récépissés*. And their names are on new lists. *Tap-a-tap-tap.* And they wait.

People have been good to them here. The meter reader finally came— an affable man with a ready smile. He has a Muslim wife, he tells me; asks me to tell them. He and his wife take in needy children in the summer, as part of a kind of fresh-air program here in the Plateau. He is very kind. But Akhmad has his worries, still. He wants to be sure the meter reader understands that there are pockets of cold air still in the apartment, close to the floor, where the children play. *Les bébés* will get sick, he says, and I translate. The man does his best to help.

I see how this family receives the kindness of the people in the Plateau with grace. And they love to have guests. But I've also seen traces of pain in their faces when people come to visit but then don't know to take off their boots at the threshold of this home.

Akhmad knows no one means anything by it. He understands that dirty shoes aren't the same thing to everyone, and he is deeply grateful to be here.

But still. "We pray here," he says.

Who is us and who is them? And who, in every age and era, are the people of the woods, choosing the forest, the savage mask, over *iman*? Walking on clean spaces?

I listen. I remember, vividly, the mountainous place where my own name was surely once written on a list—I, the foreign, the *chuzhoi*, the monstrous, the strange: *tap-a-tap-tap*. Where I was understood to be a dangerous *them*. Where I forgot the uncleanliness of my own shoes. Where I, to some, wore a savage mask.

(And, if I am honest, is there not some bit of savagery in this: that some of anthropology's earliest methods were to steal the bones of Native Americans, and to measure the skulls of perplexed immigrant children, and to make hubristic pronouncements about people who had little power to counter them? Is there not some savagery in the very fact that to an anthropologist, a human being is a "subject"?)

I learn new words for things—*barkalla*, thank you; *dik k'ant*, good boy. The children, one-two-three, laugh as I tangle their consonants and massacre their syntax.

What am I looking for here, I wonder—I, the anthropologist? What is it I want to capture? What do I wish to gain?

Just because they are beautiful, it doesn't mean I have a right to their secrets.

After the failed raid in August 1942, things got pretty quiet in the Plateau for months and months. Daniel, having settled in with his Crickets, began falling in love with every little one of them. They played their games, sang their songs, read their books, rushed to be the first on the rope. By February, he had straightened out the mess in the organization of Les Grillons with the help of his cousin André and assumed more responsibility there. He'd made a reputation for himself in the village as friendly and warm and even chic—he could speak other languages!— and now began to feel truly useful. Finally, this worldly young man full of questions, this backwoods cosmopolitan, was feeling like himself.

Then, on February 13, 1943, André Trocmé was arrested. The Gestapo arrived at his door at the presbytery. Magda let the officers in and fed them all dinner—yes, she did—as André gathered his things. Villagers gathered small gifts of food and toilet paper for his journey. Together with Pastor Theis and the head of the public school in Le Chambon, Roger Darcissac, André was sent to a "supervised residence camp" at Saint-Paul-d'Eyjeaux about four hundred kilometers from the Plateau. From his own account, even with the discomforts of the camp and the fear of what would follow, André enjoyed what he called a "wonderful camaraderie" with his fellow inmates, who were mostly communists and other political undesirables. He was even able to conduct a sermon there eventually, after a passage in Hebrews: "Now faith is the substance of things hoped for, the evidence of things not seen." A photograph of Trocmé and Theis from Saint-Paul-d'Eyjeaux shows the two men in a dimly lit room, with books on a shelf behind them: Theis in a sweater, reading a book, Trocmé in a suit and tie, smiling a little and playing a harmonica.

Together with Roger Le Forestier, Daniel raced down to the departmental capital to plead for Trocmé, Theis, and Darcissac. It was a dangerous gambit, and it didn't work; the three would be interned for an indefinite period. And as it turned out, as the mountain of documents with the mountains of typed names piled up, one by one, and as the German plans for total war finally trickled south into occupied lands and then up, against gravity, onto the highest plateaus, it was an important time for Trocmé and the others to be gone.

Because on February 24, 1943, at seven o'clock in the evening, the company commandant of Haute-Loire received a list with the names of eighty-two foreign Jews in the region. Ten of those were living in Le Chambon. Three raids were immediately set in motion that night—with motorcycle escorts and busses, and men with long lists, creeping into the dark. By seven in the morning, the arrests had begun.

The man in charge of the raid in Le Chambon was a young police inspector, twenty-three years of age, named Léopold Praly. Praly was already a known quantity in Le Chambon. With his affable manners, his ease and even flirtatiousness with locals, his fashionably slicked-back hair, and the fact that he was Protestant, he had insinuated himself into life in the Plateau. He'd been in charge of raids before, like the big flop in August 1942, for which he'd clearly caught heat. You see his name all over the documents from those months: his signature, a cipher.

I've never actually seen the final list of the eighty-two, or of the ten. So many lists. So many silver fish in the ocean. But one name that I know for sure was there was Jacob's. Jacob, who—despite his frail frame—had been known to go around the village saying, out loud, *"Vive de Gaulle!"*

This time, when Praly saw Jacob, he said: "I've finally got you!"

I've finally got you, said the twenty-three-year-old policeman with his slicked-back hair and his way with the ladies to a still–razor-thin boy. A boy whose parents, Arnold and Irma, had already left for Auschwitz on Convoy 17, from Drancy. A boy who, when he heard that news, cried and cried and cried.

I've finally got you, said the special policeman, who with his list had traveled, against gravity, up to the Plateau.

Jacob got on the bus. Martin, his brother, got on the bus, too, along with some sixty other people who had been rounded up in other parts of Haute-Loire. And they waited. Waited while the motorcycles came and went, while the arrestees all climbed up the creaky stairs of the bus in the cold.

And then, word went out, into the village. A crowd gathered.

There are several accounts of that day: The crowd surrounded the bus. The crowd began shouting. At a certain point, some villagers lay down in front of the bus, not permitting it to leave.

One witness says that he heard, from the crowd, Daniel yelling, "I accuse this man of being responsible for this arrest!" pointing at Léopold Praly.

Does that sound like Daniel? I don't know. . . .

But all of the witnesses agree on two things that followed.

First, a boy in the crowd dashed off. That boy, another refugee, a half-Jew from a prominent family, ran like crazy to his room at the home where he had been living in the center of Le Chambon. His mother, far away from him now, had given him a bar of chocolate, a gift that grew to romantic proportions in his mind—that someday, this chocolate might save his life! The boy ran off into his room, and without thinking, took the last two squares of his chocolate, put them in a little matchbox, and ran back to the bus. Then he slid the matchbox into Jacob's hand.

And all witnesses agree on one thing more—that the crowd started to sing. To the tune of "Auld Lang Syne," they began the well-known French scout song "Ce n'est qu'un au revoir":

Must you leave us without hope,
Without hope of your return,
Must you leave us without hope,
That we will see you again one day?
It is but an au revoir, *my brothers . . .*
Yes, we will see one another again, my brothers,
It is but an au revoir.

Finally, the police forced the villagers lying on the ground to get up. And the bus left, full of men and women and children who were now descending back down the hills, down into the madness of exile, back into the camps, back to Gurs and, worse, Auschwitz, where they were destined to die.

Was it then that some bell rang inside Daniel's heart? Did he hear it for the first time, then? Did it ring for him, as it rang for the boy with his chocolate? Or for the villagers, lying on the ground, staring at the great wheels of a bus that could, at any moment, crush them?

As far as I can make out from the historical record, Daniel then got into a car with Dr. Le Forestier and raced down to police headquarters in Le Puy. The two of them pleaded, now, for Jacob, who was not yet eighteen and should not have been arrested with the others. They couldn't plead for everyone, but this life they could fight for. This life they could hope to return from the madness.

And it worked.

Which is how, so many years later, in a room full of survivors, a man named Jack, who had once been a boy named Jacob, could tell the man sitting next to him the story about how he had been in Le Chambon, and been arrested, and how the whole village gathered around the bus, singing "Ce n'est qu'un au revoir." And how one boy put chocolate into his hand.

And as Jack told that story, the man next to him, now white-haired and handsome, too, could himself begin to cry, saying, "I was that boy."

THE ROUNDUP OF FEBRUARY 1943 was the first in a series of increasingly aggressive police tactics on the Plateau. With André interned in Saint-Paul-d'Eyjeaux, Daniel was dealing with matters of greater delicacy and also consequence. Jacob had not been a child in his care, but another boy from Les Grillons whom Daniel referred to in a letter to his parents as "a Polish Israelite" was arrested soon after the February roundup. Daniel wrote that he'd gone to Le Puy to plead for that boy as well—he, too, was underage—and the two of them returned to Les Grillons to great rejoicing. Daniel was spending more and more time in tribunals now, traveling in cars, on his bike—thirty kilometers for one tribunal where another of his children was acquitted. "Crazy," he called the work, "but also crazily interesting."

As dangers increased, it was clear that Daniel would need to take on more responsibility. The couple who had been running La Maison des Roches, which housed young men, simply couldn't manage it anymore. They needed help. It was one thing when La Maison des Roches housed mostly refugees from the Spanish Civil War. But now, more and more, it was Jews living there. And so, the police kept sniffing around, questioning, the raids getting more frequent. André had an idea, from Saint-Paul-d'Eyjeaux. Perhaps Daniel could step in.

To his parents, Daniel wrote, "I am taking the direction of a house called Roches, but which will change its name. I would baptize . . . this house 'Centre Universitaire du Lignon' if the initials weren't so disastrous," he joked lamely (*cul* means "ass" in French). At present it held sixteen foreign students, and had capacity for nearly three times that many. "It's a sort of university sanatorium, where one isn't sick. Right now, it's not working at all. And André, since his retreat, has wanted me to take over the direction of studies. So finally, in spite of myself, I'll be taking over the direction of the whole thing. I'll begin my new functions at the end of the month of March."

This was a trickier spot: The young men La Maison des Roches housed would be vulnerable to arrest in more immediate ways than the children of Les Grillons. Still, it was just a few kilometers from Les Grillons, and Daniel had every intention of doing both jobs.

"I'm not leaving Les Grillons," he wrote to his parents. "I don't know if I'm partial, but I find that my kids are simply marvelous in the collective. I adore them, and in return, I can say that they offer me a great deal of affection. . . . Every day they are more precious to me, and my only heartbreak is that I can't give them more time."

And so Daniel was in love, complete with the early signs of heartbreak. Something inside him was sure, even as something inside him was changing. Here: A new piece of paper. At a new desk. Daniel sits behind a typewriter. Maybe he adjusts his chair?

Tap-a-tap-tap.

LA MAISON DES ROCHES

Le Chambon-sur-Lignon . . .

SITUATION AU 1er AVRIL 1943, underlined with dashes. *Ka-ching,* bell, slap of the carriage return. *Information concerning the students,* underlined with dashes.

Carriage return.

Nationality: German, 0; Austrian, 2; Belgian, 0; French, 1; Dutch, 1; Iranian, 1; Lithuanian, 2; Luxembourgian, 2; Czech, 1; Spanish, 10. Total, 20.

Religion: Catholic, 8, Protestant, 12. Total 20.

And the Jews? Where are the Jews?

Return, return, return, return. . . . The paper is rolled out of the typewriter, just like that.

No Jews.

Daniel lies.

Time forges forward. January, February, March, April. You can forget it's not the same story everywhere, always.

Sandrine and I are in Issarlès with her husband, Rémi, their children, and her in-laws. High up, an hour or so from the Plateau, there are no wild daffodils here yet. But spring is coming and they will arrive soon enough, in mad storms of yellow in the fields. Up in the trees, buds are just now appearing.

Rémi's father asks me, "Do you know the legend of the Bloody Inn?"

Once upon a time, the time of troubles after the French Revolution, there was chaos everywhere. And this region where we now sit was still loyal to the king. Once upon a time, not far from Issarlès, there was an *auberge* where the innkeepers took people in, and then stole from them, and then killed them. Bodies were found in the walls. Heads were chopped off in a guillotine set up right in front of the auberge.

Rémi's father tells this story with an April sun blasting on his face, and an April wind sweeping his hair across his forehead. He's looking at me. We are high up in the volcanic hills—with pines and fir trees and dry long grasses rolling toward a drop—sitting next to a stone house built, it seems, forever ago. We are drinking water with sweet syrup and the children are eating cookies.

Rémi's father has the posture of a man who, for a lifetime, talks with his hands; the voice of a man who, for a lifetime, speaks over the sound of the wind. He flattens the *a* in *manger*; but that old patois has disappeared from the tones of his son and grandchildren.

Rémi's father tells the tale of the bloody inn after he asks me why I am here in France at all. I say something about the Plateau, and how villagers there protected people during the war, and how there are asylum seekers living in the Plateau today.

Aw, well, Rémi's father says. That was those Protestants there in Vivarais-Lignon, pointing at Sandrine. None of that here, he says. "Here people would have turned those Jews in."

He eyes me again. There are other legends, he says, leaning in, and pulling me back into the deep past. Like the one about the beast that killed people. So many of them! Was it a *loup*, a wolf? Who knows. It killed mostly children, and mostly women. No one knew what the beast was. It would come out of the forest. And the killings went on and on and they never figured it out.

Not exactly the land of welcome, here! someone says.

Once upon a time, there was a village called Issarlès, perched on the edge of another plateau that drops down to the Loire. And once upon a time, on an April day, Issarlès's village square no longer had any flowers or any green—just those trees that have twigs coming out of their bulbous, knotty branches, close to the trunk. Once upon a time, that same village square was covered with asphalt. And a great cross came up out of the asphalt, too: in filigreed metal, in stone.

Once upon a time, it was not the land of welcome everywhere. And boys like Jacob were turned in to the authorities, *tap-a-tap-tap*. And no one fished them out of any camp, or any prison. And no one lay in front of their bus. No one gave them a last piece of chocolate, a gift from their mother. No one sang, "It's just an *au revoir*, my brother." And no one cried while they sang.

Once upon a time, it is right now.

And documents are being typed. And busses are filling up.

And three little children are bouncing up a hill. And one of them is examining something in her hands. Dropping it. Picking it up. Dropping it again.

And a young man—or woman—who has been around the world but is now, finally, home, is looking at the little creatures at that short distance and is deciding: Who is us? Who is them? Who is a one, who is a zero?

And:

How must I live, now that the answer has become crystal clear?

Chapter 8

HYMN TO SPRING

Then I, Daniel, looked, and behold, two others stood,
one on the river bank on this side,
and the other on the river bank on that side.

—DANIEL 12:5

Je sortirai, bras nus, dans la lumière
Et lui dirai le salut de la terre . . .

—FÉLIX LECLERC, "HYMNE AU PRINTEMPS"

IT IS THE SPRING OF 1943.

In the photograph, Daniel is seated outside. Behind him, the limbs and leaves of trees are outlined in mottled black and white. His face is turned three-quarters away from the camera, his dark hair swept back. Daniel is dressed in a white button-down shirt here, a jaunty striped tie loosely knotted at the neck. Over his shirt, he wears a dark sweater that's been patched with incongruously bright thread near the shoulder. His glasses are round, dark circles, the lenses thick enough to magnify forward the dappled light of the trees. Someone just out of the frame—a woman—rests a hand on his back.

He smiles softly.

Daniel has one of those puzzling faces, truth be told. In nearly every one of the few photographs I've seen of him, he looks like a slightly different person. Yes, there is always the dark hair and the curly big ears. There is always the full mouth, and a wistfulness behind the eyes. But if you hold the photographs up close, if you really examine them, you see many tiny worlds, all different, in that one face. And then, if you pull the photographs back and squint, the aggregate alternates between soft and hard, bright and blank, lovely and unlovely.

As a toddler, Daniel is standing next to his sister Suzie within the crowd of boys of Les Sablons at École des Roches. Suzie and he are both in lacy white dresses; she wears a bright flower in her long hair and leads with her forehead, perplexed. He is looking up, but also straight into the camera, already, at two years old, with a direct, furrowed brow.

Then, at eight years, Daniel tilts ever so slightly away from the rest of his family in the velveteen fuss of the Sablons drawing room: patently handsome, patently intelligent, and pale.

At twelve or so, Daniel wears wire glasses, and his face is softer, more open. By thirteen and fourteen he is in a suit and tie, and something more dazed, and even a little dark, passes across his face. Then, later again, Daniel is outside working on some construction for the school. This could be from when he was diagnosed with pericarditis: His cheeks are bloated, his back awkwardly bowed. I can't see inside his face at all here.

I know of no pictures from Daniel's later years between Verneuil and Paris, when his inner life was growing richer with every passing day, with every passing ponderous walk to the train station, alone under the heavy gray skies, among the single bird calls.

But then there is, from 1934 or 1935, an image of Daniel on a boat off the coast of Lebanon, the sun blasting and blurring his features, turning his glasses to dazzling white circles. And, from 1937 or so, a snapshot of Daniel in Rome—the days of the on-again-off-again pretty little box—where he is standing in a slim suit, wearing white shoes and the hint of happiness. What lies ahead?

The Plateau. The Little Crickets. Decisions.

Daniel's face is different everywhere. But here, on the Plateau where he now lives, seated at three-quarters, looking down, aged thirty-one or thirty-two, a hand on his back, the softest smile, relaxed and full, that face is finally beautiful. It finally contains all the multitudes.

I know what is coming. But I don't know how Daniel did what he did next. I strain to see evidence in the picture—in his face? in just the eyes?—or hear it somehow. I look everywhere for signs, for a cause. In every tiny mote. His face is smooth, like a boy's. I hold the picture close, then far, then close again.

But how do you see the sum of something that changes so markedly with the changing of the light? When, really, the readiness is all?

Spring in the Plateau brings snows and rains, fog and winds, clear skies and then the rush of buttery daffodils that crowd fields and forest floors. Spring comes to the Plateau after the very long winter, after the long, hard, crushing cold. It comes in fits and starts, in the crashing yellows of sun and wildflower, in the harsh new shadows of full light and open winds. It comes with the sticky buds, and the rushing rivers, and the sultry whiff of the morel. It comes in May and then June, the Scotch broom bending brightly and savagely on the sides of mountains. Spring comes in the return of the skylark. The return of barn swallow. The violent sweeping return of the kite. Spring comes and you feel your insides warmed, finally. You sway a little under the newness of it all.

And if you are a young man named Daniel Trocmé, and it is the spring of 1943, you are now spending hours every day walking through this spring, between Les Grillons and La Maison des Roches, which is three kilometers away, over the Lignon River, tucked in a craggy spot under the train tracks. The quickest route between them takes you along a highway lined with large stones and mosses, and then dips you into quiet paths, under the narrow canopies of heavy pines, past fields of pretty, brown Limousins and their calves, wobbling on their spindly new legs. You walk uphill and then down, then up again.

Daniel had agreed to direct Roches with the stipulation that he would continue to spend evenings and mornings with the children of Les Grillons. The Little Crickets, tempest tossed, were now thriving. Whatever glamour there had been in the wild ride of his rebellious youth had finally receded behind their faces, and behind the greater sense that Daniel was, little by little, creating a family with them. That he was needed. He was home here, with them; and this was his very first real spring. The stories of his new charges were harder, though. La Maison des Roches, known formally as the Foyer Universitaire des Roches, had been supported by the Geneva-based Fonds Européen de Secours aux Étudiants, and the American Society of Friends. An enormous old fortified house with thirty-two rooms and enough space for fifty-odd inhabitants, it was now intended as a residence for male students, many of whom had been released from concentration camps in the South of France. They were closer to Daniel's age, more like peers. And, like him, they were often from everywhere and nowhere, all at once.

For years, it had been so strangely safe up in the backwoods of the Plateau Vivarais-Lignon, the war so relatively distant and muted. Even with the total occupation of France, and the new drive to hunt down foreigners, even with all those terrible lists that had been tapped out, one by one, in every town, the population here on the Plateau kept taking people in, kept hiding them, kept bracing themselves when police would come calling, trying not to peer over to the wall behind which a child was hiding. For years, people on the Plateau had gone from sermon to Bible study group, plotting the protection of the refugees. For years, they had brought parcels of food out to barns or corners of the forest at night, and, even more boldly, had brought strangers over their thresholds, into their homes, seated them at their hearths, and shared with them their bread.

Villagers had taken risks, yes, but the risks so far had made sense. Locals had a solid familiarity with the technologies of rescue, knew how to take in families and children, how to use farmsteads as way stations for people in flight. They had warning systems that weren't perfect but had kept the greatest disasters at bay so far. Even in these most unhinged times, they were able to use the directive to "love neighbor and stranger alike" as a kind of living lodestar: Go this way, not that.

But now something was changing. Some center of gravity shifting. Things were somehow darker and prickling. Worse.

In February 1943, when the Germans finally lost the Battle of Stalingrad, a new law was put into place in France requiring all men over the age of twenty to enlist for work for the German cause. This law, referred to as the STO, or Service du Travail Obligatoire (Compulsory Work Service), was a direct result of the devastating human losses to the German army on the Eastern Front. Hundreds of thousands of workers were needed in Germany itself, so by that winter, there was good cause for all young men—not just Jewish young men, or communist young men from Spain, or German young men who had gone AWOL—to rush into hiding and out of the way of the new lists that were being tapped out in every town.

Consequently, the Plateau—with its reputation for shelter, and with its manifold craggy hiding spots, and in its proximity to the center of resistance in Lyon—was becoming a destination not only for children and families who sought quiet shelter from the maelstrom, but for those very young men who were of no mind to go to Germany, of no mind to be placid or defined by their fear. And among those young men, there were plenty who didn't care about philosophies of nonviolence, or loving your enemy, or one whit about the Good Samaritan, and who didn't need or want to take cues from any provincial pastor.

Hundreds of these young men arrived on the tiny Plateau, of all different national backgrounds. Among them were those who had already been in hiding for many years, and those who, by contrast, were only now finally feeling the outrage of displacement. They were not only saving their own lives, but also committing themselves to the violent destruction of a merciless enemy. Many of them were, in fact, quite dangerous to German plans. Coming and going into forests, into schools and homes, then back into forests again, they were hard to account for and hard to control. And, despite the quiet of this place, and the hush of the nights, several of them, angry and afraid, were badly behaved. This, too, had its consequences.

There was the time that "a certain gentleman"—"thin, with slicked back hair" who was known to go around wearing shiny, well-oiled chaps—was overheard saying that it's all "just Jews and Spaniards here, so we have to content ourselves with whatever food we can find."

That complaint, perhaps uttered more than once, then inspired the splashing of graffiti on the walls of Le Chambon, with that gentleman's name and the letters P and D—French slang for *pédéraste*, homosexual. And that P.D., not to be taken lightly, inspired the corresponding outburst from the man with the slicked-back hair: *Je me vengerai.* I will have my revenge.

And then there was the indelicate moment involving the convalescing German soldiers who had been living mostly peaceably in the center of Le Chambon after their time on the Eastern Front. André Trocmé told the story many years later of how those soldiers had a military band that would play from time to time in the center of Le Chambon—*oompah, oompah, oompah.* The leader of the band had an "enormous stomach"—so enormous that it was reported that a young man in a car couldn't even get down the street with it in the way; he had to back up little by little to a wider place before he could get by. Apparently, this band and this belly could not be borne, soberly, by onlookers. The musicians were mocked with great merriment and no mercy.

These days, André Trocmé and the others were just coming out of prison, their future uncertain. Locals were still palpably unnerved by the raid of February, enough so that their unrest was noted in the police reports ("Operations were uneventful but caused a certain emotion in the population"). Inspector Praly, who had finally nabbed skinny Jacob Lewin only to lose him again after Daniel and Dr. Le Forestier pleaded his case, would come around day after day, questioning villagers, making up his lists, putting them in the mail to the prefecture in Le Puy. The young men would watch him, narrowing their eyes. They would laugh, paint the walls, spend the night in the forests when they felt like it.

This was the context in which Daniel took over the direction of La Maison des Roches, which was attached to the Cévenol School, and, like other homes for children on the Plateau, under the jurisdiction of the French Ministry of Labor. The previous director, a Monsieur Pantet, had, after a year of service there, begged André Trocmé to find him a replacement for "health reasons." Even before Daniel arrived at Roches, the police visits had become more frequent. Monsieur Pantet and his wife would labor through interview after interview: Where is Franz Lipschutz? Where is Herman Lowenstein or Klaus Simon? They were here, but they left, we don't know why. Or, on another visit, what about Alexandre de Haan? Or Camille Wouters? What about Henry Mylarz? Gone, we don't know why.

Old homes sited like this had their natural majesty—you could sit outside at the great entryway and look down at the rushing Lignon River—but they also had their practical benefits. From La Maison des Roches, you could hear the trains chugging deep into the night; you could dash into the great pine forest above, if need be. One of the back windows nearly touched the hills behind; you could jump out and scramble up and away. But you could also benefit from one of the oddities of fortified structures like this: In earlier centuries, these homes were often built with tunnels that led out toward safety, if and when the need arose. La Maison des Roches had one such tunnel that led down from a secret door on its ground floor to a waterway below, and then back into the forest. This tunnel had been used, on and off, for centuries. And it was used, to great effect, now.

It quickly became clear to Daniel that the young men at La Maison des Roches would come and go with a kind of looseness that made it awkward when the authorities came calling—raising the question as to whether or not he really had control over them. It was unnerving, on the whole, this large, mutable group with its many agendas. By April 9, on

Daniel's first finance report for La Maison des Roches, there were, among his charges, several young men from Spain, several others who were Jews fleeing Poland, Lithuania, Czechoslovakia, Luxembourg, and Austria. There was also a man named Azizollah Sadigh Ershadi, a Persian from the Jewish and Bahá'í center of Hamadan, who must have somehow found his way across the plains south of the Caucasus, over Anatolia, up into Europe, to France, then, after a stint in Rivesaltes, up into the craggy hills of the Plateau—a marvel of a journey. It was a veritable Tower of Babel, La Maison des Roches, with at least a couple of the young men there nom de guerre–bearing fighters in the French Resistance.

Soon, Daniel was subject to his own police visits about the disappearing Lowenstein and Simon and de Haan, who had now returned to Roches and were under threat. When asked by police why these young men had left in the first place, Daniel would himself now flatly answer: I don't know the motive of their departure, having been director of Roches only since the twenty-fifth of March.

And a number of the young men of La Maison des Roches began, right away, causing extra trouble. Daniel had to answer for that, too. Some of the Spaniards at Roches had "mocked and taunted" the convalescing soldiers. According to testimony by one of the Rocheux, "Furious, a junior officer came to [Daniel] to make a detailed report on the subject of the hostile behavior of the students. [Daniel] managed to appease him, but then he came back, threatening to write us up if the same thing happened again." It didn't look good that his charges were defiant in this way. Didn't look good that they seemed to come and go as they pleased. In late May, one young German named Ferber, a loner who rarely spoke to anyone except to say, quietly, that he was against Hitler and wasn't a Jew, was arrested for having gone AWOL. This gave the police a nice look at La Maison des Roches from the inside—and might well have gotten them thinking harder about what function the home really served.

These new young men, some hardened by years of war in Spain, or in camps, some bearing names trumpet-blasting their Jewishness, were no Little Crickets. They were on their own wild ride—like Daniel, they were in the process of becoming, fully, men.

SPRING RUSHED FORWARD. Daniel walked and walked, and thought and thought. He filled out forms, and he helped with math lessons, or found the right teacher for some stray child, or watched, silently, as children slept. And as danger mounted.

[Late March 1943]

Dear Parents,

Your decision to come and see us, and in particular to spend two days in Le Chambon, transports me with joy. Unfortunately, I am forced to calm myself in front of the kids. Those who have had visits have spontaneously repressed the familial manifestations in front of their orphan comrades. But it's still splendid.

For months and months, Daniel's parents had been trying to get him to come back to them, up in the north of France, back into their world, like old times. But after a series of polite responses from their son that such a visit would be impossible, they finally proposed to come to the mountain themselves, as it were. Daniel filled three picture postcards with his response to them: one of the great stone Maison des Roches, surrounded by trees, and another two with panoramas of where Roches was situated relative to Les Grillons. His world now. He signed his message to them "tenderly, tenderly, Daniel."

Tenderly, Daniel went back to the *grillons*. Firmly, Daniel went back to the young men. Naively, or so it was starting to be wondered, here and there, in the village, Daniel now faced the police, day after day. Did he fully understand the threats that were mounting? Did he not see that with Praly nosing around, and the new police visits, and the questioning, and with the arrival of the good weather that allowed more comings and goings every day, things were getting steadily worse?

Another edict was passed, on June 5, that shifted the oversight of La Maison des Roches from the French Ministry of Labor to the Ministry of the Interior, with its extensive surveillance networks targeting Jews and its close ties to the German occupying forces. This was no school for children, the authorities intimated. Surely, this was a way station for young men who were getting up to all kinds of things. It was time for a much closer look. Still, despite all the warnings starting to come in by way of the young men of the woods, Daniel tried to keep the running of Roches normal, and keep up with his children at Les Grillons.

There is a series of photographs taken of the children under Daniel's care during this period. In one, a large group stands on a patch of ground beyond a bridge, holding a rope. From the dark shadows in the photograph, you can tell it is a very bright day. Daniel also holds the rope, in the center. He is looking down. Then another shot: a tug-of-war has begun. Daniel is on one side—the photograph is fuzzy, but you can identify him still by the bend of his shoulders and the reflection of his glasses. And then, another image from perhaps the same day: Here, the children and Daniel are no longer holding any rope. They are, instead, standing in the bright field, their arms all raised. Behind them is a great stand of pine trees. A boy on the edge of the group arches his back to the sky as he lifts his arms.

While he waited for his parents to visit, Daniel was clearly busy with his own *tap-a-tap-tapping*, keeping straight the comings and goings of the children and young men. On June 22, he prepared a letter to the prefect of Le Puy-en-Velay on behalf of a Polish nineteen-year-old named Léon Cukier, who had been arrested in Toulouse for "an infraction of the law on the circulation of Jews," and who now was in Gurs. Daniel wrote that this young man had been "a student of the school for special electricity and mechanics" in Paris and was, it seemed to Daniel, someone who could "come and profit from our hospitality." He wrote on official stationery from the Foyer Universitaire du Lignon and signed his letter, simply, "The Director," and his name.

The parental visit so delightedly planned would not materialize. Instead, just six or so days after Daniel wrote to the prefect, his brother François came in their stead. François's position running a factory in Lannemezan, near the Spanish border, had become a dangerous and delicate job in its own right. His visit seems to have been one more attempt by the family to finally get Daniel to come to his senses and return home. There was clearly a family program in place to talk about Daniel's future, and the future of École des Roches; to talk with Daniel about what was needed from him and expected of him—and also about that young woman, that on-again-off-again fiancée, whom the family couldn't even bear to call by a proper name.

The visit took place on the last weekend of June 1943. Long after the fact, it is clear that François failed entirely in his mission. The long letter he wrote on June 29 to explain to his parents what he saw and what he heard provides us with a pen portrait of Daniel—of their Dani: beloved, rebellious, prodigal, perhaps—now frozen in a moment in time, neither cleansed nor cleared by the sorrow or the longing that would follow:

> [We spoke of] the Crickets, of "his children." Having arrived at
> Les Grillons, there was a charming welcome by the children and
> Dani's collaborators. Dani is evidently very happy, very useful;
> much less of a boy, in full bloom of his personality, in full
> possession of his qualities. I truly had a very vivid impression of a
> generous and useful equilibrium, of a personality surrounded with
> respect and affection. This is no longer the Dani of Maslacq—
> demanding, generous, but feeling at an impasse. This is a useful
> man, beloved and fully developed. It is equally a director who
> loves his responsibilities, a little young still, but far more
> levelheaded than before. . . . It was a strong impression.

Dani does not feel indissoluble links to the Foyer, nor even the Crickets; but for these children who have been passed from hand to hand, he wants to be a permanent father, not a father in passing. He said with some accuracy that for those who put their filial trust in him, his departure, even if compensated by a man of greater value, would be one desertion more, making them feel ever more grievously their situation of being abandoned, tossed by contrary and always unpredictable winds.

I hold this portrait closer up and farther away. I read it, again and again. Though there is so much richness in the details, I squint, finally, blurring distinctions, to see it clearly:

You turn your face to three-quarters, smile softly, and look down. You know there are better men than you, Daniel.

But still, you forget yourself. You stay.

———

Six-forty a.m., June 29, 1943. Klaus Simon, asleep at La Maison des Roches, woke up with machine guns in his face.

Klaus, nineteen years old, with handsome, even features and a small build, had already been on the run for years. He was born in Düsseldorf—"the Paris of the Rhineland"—where his secular Jewish parents could afford travel and tutors for their son. But by 1933 the beatings had begun at school, and by 1934 he could no longer go. And so, in 1937 the thirteen-year-old Klaus was shipped to Holland to spend his school years with a kind, cosmopolitan family, away from the Nazi fray.

As with so many of the young men of Roches, Klaus had already borne a great deal by the time he arrived on the Plateau. After fleeing Holland, he eventually found himself in a work camp in Brussels and then, after still more running, in the concentration camp at Rivesaltes, in southern France. Rivesaltes was filled with lice and filth and death, but in the case of Klaus, it also offered something that turned out to be miraculous. Fully knowing that he was Jewish, the Dutch consulate there nevertheless gave him—*tap-a-tap-tap*—Dutch papers. Then, that same Dutch consulate found a place for Klaus at La Maison des Roches, where he arrived on November 25, 1942.

Even in the relative safety of the Plateau, the months since November had had their rocky moments, and Klaus—like the other young men at Roches—was getting used to spending nights in the forest, sometimes days and weeks on end, in order to avoid arrest. The police kept coming around looking for him and others—kept asking questions. On April 15, when Daniel had been the director at Roches for just a couple of weeks, the police showed up and found Klaus there. According to their own records, Klaus was Dutch, born in Leiden. He was not suspected of being Jewish. Nevertheless, he was on the run for some reason, so he was questioned, along with five other young men, and forced to write and sign a statement about how he had been sleeping in the woods—he wasn't sure exactly where—and how he was given food by farmers whose names he didn't know.

On the strength of intelligence and rumors coming from the Resistance, several of the young men at La Maison des Roches had recently taken to sleeping outside regularly. When the sun set on June 28, they were already in the forest, finding loamy spots where they could settle in for the night. But not Klaus. For whatever reason, Klaus chose to stay inside that night. It had been cool weather. Maybe he just needed a break, a little comfort.

So the next morning, he awoke to find machine guns in his face. And all around him, people were waking up, shocked, stumbling forward and backward, standing, half dressed, covering themselves with blankets. And all around him, there was bellowing in a language that Klaus knew perfectly well, though he didn't dare betray it, with blow after blow from the butts of machine guns, after each kick to the back: *Ansteigen!* Get up. *Schweinejude!* Pig Jew.

Several witness accounts survive from that day. There are police reports. Agonized letters written to family members of the victims, many years later. In every one of those accounts, there are names. In each name, there are stories—stories that begin decades earlier, often in faraway lands, and stories that end days later, or weeks later or years later, some in France, some in Germany or Poland or Israel. Memory is a din.

But this is what can be known, with some assurance:

Just half an hour after sunrise on June 29, with morning dew still clinging to the rocks outside, fourteen German police officers arrived at La Maison des Roches in two dark gray Citroëns and one dark gray tarpaulin-covered truck. Some of the officers surrounded the building; others rushed in with guns. They woke the residents. Ordered them to come gather for questioning. Then, while four of the officers conducted interrogations, ten others began ransacking the rooms for any items they could find.

There was a great deal of confusion, and a certain measure of violence. At one point, the residents were asked who was in charge, and they answered that the director was one Daniel Trocmé, who had spent the night at Les Grillons, up the hill and over the road. A party was sent out in a car to get him.

At around 7:30 a.m., officers arrived at Les Grillons. Bursting into the home for the small children, they raised their great weapons again. Seeing what was unfolding, several of the children rushed out of the windows and into the forest. Daniel was urged to do the same. The forest was a window away, so close you could almost touch it.

Many years later, Suzanne Heim, the Little Cricket whom Daniel had helped with math, and who loved him very dearly, wrote of that day:

> The people of the SS burst into the rooms with such cruelty. . . .
> With their heavy boots, they kicked in the doors to open them. Of
> course, we were speechless with fear. [They] stood there with their
> weapons aimed at us, giving us warning not to move. . . .

And she recounted, elsewhere:

We told Daniel, "They've come to arrest you! Leave by the back door and slip into the woods!" And he said, "I can't do that. I am responsible for Grillons and for Roches."

So Daniel stayed. Somehow, with those dark eyes, he saw the sign; with those ears, he heard the silent tolling of the tocsin. It was time to act. He stayed.

At some point, making the excuse of needing to use the bathroom, Daniel gathered every one of the incriminating documents at Les Grillons and flushed them down the toilet. Within the hour, Daniel had been arrested and put in a car. Madame Orsi, Daniel's beloved housekeeper, and the mother of one of his favorite charges, Odette, would call that moment—as she watched Daniel go off in that car—the very worst of her life.

As soon as it was possible, Suzanne tore herself away from the house and raced down and down and down the hills, past farm fields and great pine stands, past the bit of the forest that would, in years to come, become the large campus of the Cévenol School. Down and down to the center of Le Chambon and then to the presbytery she ran. There she found Magda and frantically explained that a raid was under way, and Daniel under arrest. Magda immediately grabbed a bicycle and, forgetting herself, left her apron on and sped up to Le Chambon's center and then the kilometers down Route de Saint-Agrève, toward La Maison des Roches.

I can see her now in my mind's eye, the bike wobbling under her with each frantic pump of the pedals, the braids flying up from the sides of her temples, her handsome face steady, her eyes squinting with the rising sun.

Magda Trocmé, her voice low and slow and incantatory, had this to say about her ride to La Maison des Roches:

What a beautiful day it was! You have no idea! These spring days in Le Chambon, with the Scotch broom in flower . . . The sun shining, soft weather, not too hot, these beautiful, clear mountains! It was extraordinary, this beauty, this peace, so calm . . . [set against] the horrors that were unfolding.

Now, having chosen not to flee, now himself under arrest, Daniel arrived at La Maison des Roches in a car, at about eight-thirty a.m. One of the young men there caught a glimpse of him as he entered the kitchen like a shadow, head bent slightly downward. Soon, Daniel would be placed in a line, up against the wall, with the other inhabitants of La Maison des Roches. Because he spoke German, he was able to translate for the young men, who were grabbed roughly by the lapels, pushed and kicked into a room where they would be questioned. There was a sorting of people into this category and that. The police had in their hands lists of "wanted terrorists."

So many of the German and French documents were destroyed after the war, it's impossible to know with full confidence why this specific raid was conducted. The weight of historical evidence seems to indicate that it was not a raid to hunt down Jews, specifically. Rather, in an environment of chaos and increasing pressure on the losing German side, it was part of investigating the irritating, illegal, and probably dangerous presence of the young foreigners on the Plateau, who happened to be pretending to be students. The German police went looking for, well, trouble among the young men. And what a rich feast of trouble they found there at La Maison des Roches: Jews, communists from Spain and elsewhere, Resistance fighters. And who knew what this character Trocmé was, or why he spoke German. Was he himself a Jew? They sorted and yelled at and kicked and punched the young men. They took notes and yelled and kicked some more.

Magda arrived at Roches in her apron, and was improbably allowed into the fray. The Germans served a meal—everyone, including Magda, got the rare feast of two eggs and a portion of bread—a detail that Magda found patently absurd as she recalled it. Because of the yelling and the chaos while the meal was being served, Magda was able to have a few words with Daniel as she carried containers of water from the kitchen. He had some ideas:

First, he said, she needed to go down to the center and talk with the German soldiers. One of the young men, a Spaniard named Guasch-Ramond, had been swimming a couple of weeks before in the Lignon River, when he saw one of those Germans drowning. He saved the German's life. Magda needed to go and get that soldier to testify for that Spaniard, in the name of his honor. Magda said she would do that, and off she went, back on her bike, to face the soldiers on her own, and bring them back to La Maison des Roches.

When Magda returned, the chaos continued, but the room was changing again. She remembered later how the young men whispered to her as she passed by them: I have a letter for my fiancée in my drawer! I have something from my mother! Please take my money and send it to my parents! Her voice echoed with the sorrow of the day when she later reflected on those requests. "The poor ones; they didn't understand that the Gestapo has already gone through everything in those rooms, and it wasn't worth worrying about such things." And she remembered, too, the arresting image of one beautiful boy, a Dutch Jew with blond hair and blue eyes, being beaten with what she suddenly realized were his own phylacteries—the words, again, ringing and ringing, *Schweinejude, Schweinejude.*

For several hours, the questioning continued. Daniel was working hard to plead the case of several of the young men. In the final tally, a group of eighteen of them, including Daniel, were prepared for arrest. They gathered their belongings together in one or two suitcases. Just five who had been questioned that day were not arrested: the one who had saved the German from drowning; three who were sick with high fevers; and that one Persian, whose presence no one knew how to make sense of. Seven of the men the police had been searching for had not been found—seven young men who now, at the end of another day, were perhaps settling again among the mosses and tree roots.

So the story lands here, with a group of young men lined up, carrying suitcases. It lands here, with windows, and doors, and tunnels, and even toilets that can provide ways out, but don't always. It lands in spring, in the glorious days of fresh and clear account. The days when that one face I've grown to love has finally softened into its aggregate beauty.

And the story lands here, now, with eighteen young men—each with his own story, his own name—ducking into a dark gray tarpaulin-covered truck.

And with Daniel leaning into Magda, as he spoke the last words anyone in his family would hear:

"Don't worry," he told her. "Don't worry. I'll go with my students; try to explain things for them. In any case, write to my parents, tell them what happened. Tell them I'm not afraid. This is my work. I love these students very much."

And then, as if in an afterthought, he added:

"Tell them I love to travel."

Chapter 9

LA BURLE

This north wind—crammed with snow, dust,
and clouds—slaps and blinds, buries in ice, uniformly
paints roads and landscapes alike. La Burle is violent,
devious, invading; it transforms the Ardèche Plateau
into an inhuman world.

—JEAN DURAND, *LES CONTES DE LA BURLE*

THIS IS WHAT LA BURLE LOOKS LIKE:
The man is in a sea of white. He is inside a mighty din. He is in front of two shivering horses, frantically digging a pathway through the snow. Ahead of him somewhere stands a lonely stone house. Inside that house, a woman is about to give birth. The man digs for the shivering horses; he digs for the doctor that the horses carry; he digs for the laboring woman. The wind snakes a tunnel wave around them all.

The man is Sandrine's grandfather, long before she herself was born. And the wind that snakes around him, that lifts the snows to blinding heights, is called La Burle.

Sometimes winds get names. In Sudan the Harmattan slashes across the desert. The German Moazagoatl rises in a rotor toward the skies. In Egypt, the Khamsin can make men mad. La Burle is the name for the wind that sweeps across the Plateau in winter. No regular wind, it arrives in ocean waves, locals say. It creeps up over the plains, gaining such volume and power that it scoops snows up from one place and deposits them in another. The massive drifts it creates can block off the world—closing roads, covering whole cars, piling up over the highest windows of houses, shutting you up, stopping you down. "If you are caught on the road during La Burle," people say, "you see *ni ciel ni terre*." Neither heaven nor earth.

Sandrine told the story of La Burle to her own Little Crickets at the Cévenol School. Who does what with whom? Her grandfather—a gray smudge in the blazing white story—digs for his neighbor. Her grandfather, alone, faces La Burle.

YEARS AGO, my thesis adviser sent me off to rural Russia with several bits of general advice. One was this: If you want to understand a place in any depth, you need to live there for the full cycle of a year. In time, I learned how right he was. It mattered to live the length and isolation of the winter; to know the hunger and thirst that come with the slowly emptying larder; to know the sweetness of the first berries, the first greens, the first potatoes out of the ground. You had to learn to worry for the insects that cover crops in the summer, to be anxious for the rain. To know the smell of the dirt in autumn, the hunkering down again. All of it.

Winter, spring, summer, fall; and then winter again.

I learned what it meant to need water but to have no control over the coming of the rains—and to need warmth but have no control over the sun. And, consequently, to look toward the skies with some mixture of fear and hope and longing. Come, rain. Please come. And when the skies would heat and then rumble, or the wind would bend the tallest trees, to ask again: Please, now, finally, come! I learned this prayer. Even when, finally, mean little drops would ping on the roof, then disappear. Please, now. Come.

Spring, summer, fall, winter; and then spring again.

Since the very first time I heard of La Burle, I knew I needed to see it and feel it for myself. Friends would laugh at me for this. They would laugh, and then, if I waited long enough, would begin to tell stories of their own grandfathers and grandmothers, their own horses, their own great drifts. And then other stories, too—*ni ciel ni terre!*—of being on the road or in the blinding light. Of how they would hunker down, down, into the dark of their own stone homes of meter-thick walls, waiting near the hearth, waiting there with barely any light from the window, there, safe from the primal force of the battering wind.

Then my friends would say, stuttering to find the right words, something I also needed to know: Always, after the wind dies down, after La Burle has finally passed over, a silence arrives, and a beauty. The fields then are the purest white; the forest, like some magic kingdom.

So now I am in the Plateau again, and it is February. So cold outside, the pipes are freezing. During the day, I trudge up and down the road to the center of Le Chambon with every layer of clothing I can find, hearing the swish of my nylon coat, the huff of my breathing. Night after night, I soak my feet in the hottest possible water to warm myself for sleep.

When La Burle finally came, it was in a form I didn't expect.

Now, this bitter winter, the birds are gone. And I am lost.

On Wednesday, November 16, 2011, a student at the Cévenol School, a boy named Matthieu, killed another student, a girl named Agnès. The boy was seventeen; the girl, thirteen. Both were French and lived on the Cévenol campus as boarders.

That Wednesday, the two skipped class to hunt for hallucinogenic mushrooms in the forests adjoining the thirty-acre Cévenol campus. Around three kilometers from their classrooms, within a small ravine, the boy tied the girl up to a tree, stuffed her mouth with a scarf, and then, for an hour, punched her, bit her, violated her, and stabbed her seventeen times. He doused her with gasoline and set her on fire. Then he returned to school. He had scratches on his face. He took an hourlong shower.

The girl, Agnès, was from Paris. She was sweet and sociable, with long brown hair and dark eyes, a little rebellious. She had told people she wanted to be a filmmaker, and at the Cévenol School she was known to work hard at her studies. Matthieu, a "brilliant" boy, was from Gard, in southern France. He'd been in trouble before, but no one here knew yet just how much. He had a girlfriend. He was a computer whiz. He did drugs. Agnès was his friend.

Almost immediately, Agnès's disappearance was noticed in the dorms. A couple of the other kids knew about her plans to cut class that day with Matthieu. But as the hours passed and she didn't return, people grew increasingly alarmed. A group from the school set out into the dark to look for her, spanning as best they could into the surrounding forest. Matthieu joined them. Back in the dorm, though, some had noticed the scratches on his face, and his long shower, and his weird answers to their questions about where he had been, and when. Some smelled smoke in the woods. But they found nothing.

By Thursday, panic set in. Official search parties were launched. Posters were put up all over Le Chambon with pictures of brown-haired Agnès, quietly smiling toward the camera, a little warily, and a phone number handwritten below. Families got involved. Some children joined the parties. Off they all went, up into the woods, along the rivers, down the ravines, into the tunnel under La Maison des Roches, among the loamy perfumes of late fall. Off they all went, man, woman, child, to look for Agnès. But they didn't find her.

Already, by Thursday, police were zeroing in on Matthieu, with the scratches on his face and his weird timeline and his increasingly ashen appearance. He was taken into custody and questioned and questioned again.

By Friday, a hundred fifty policemen were at work, with dog teams, helicopters, and divers at their disposal. The local volunteer fire department joined in. Reporters from all over France descended in swarms, pushing microphones and cameras into the pained and bewildered faces of locals.

That Friday, in custody, Matthieu confessed. Agnès's remains were found attached to a tree, charred—*carbonisé*—beyond recognition. The prosecutor determined that the crime was premeditated. As Matthieu described what he had done, he showed shockingly little emotion. Months later, a psychiatrist would tell a jury that Matthieu was a boy whose very body was constantly cold. He could never get warm, even in the hottest weather. Matthieu had, she said, "a winter within."

Soon, it was revealed that Matthieu had attempted a similar crime before. That time, he tied up a girl and raped her at gunpoint, but in the middle of everything, the girl's cell phone rang—her mother calling—and she was somehow able to escape. Matthieu was arrested, only to be freed as he awaited trial. Apparently, with the specifics of his record sealed, one of the conditions of his release was that he find a school that would take him.

WHO DOES WHAT WITH WHOM? The Cévenol School takes the damaged boy. The damaged boy kills the girl and walks away from her charred remains. That's who does what with whom.

In the center of Le Chambon, a woman with soft gray hair is asked by a reporter if she is upset. Well. After a pause, the woman's voice is sweet and slow: "There is a lot of pain for *la petite*, the little one. And for her family. And even for the boy." She shakes her head. "For the two families." Her eyes fill up. "We had such hope. . . . *Voilà*. We are very sad." Nearly silently, the woman begins to cry.

Days after the murder, *Le Monde* wrote, "At the Cévenol School, the end of innocence."

Ni ciel ni terre.

. . .

I RETURNED to Le Chambon three months after the murder, when the worst of the shock had passed for most villagers. The swarms of report- ers, the helicopters, the police and their dogs were all gone. The hunt was over; the howls of pain now quieted a bit. Days after the murder, there was a *marche blanche*, a silent walk up from the center of Le Cham- bon to the Cévenol campus, with hundreds of mourners carrying white flowers, and a blown-up pencil drawing of Agnès, and a sign that read AGNÈS, A NEW STAR IS IN THE SKY. Within that crowd were children from Sandrine's classes—in newspaper photographs, I recognized the Guinean boy who assured me his blood was not mixed!, the other boy who giggled in the back of the room at the radiator, the girl with her beautiful gap-toothed grin who told me all about the feast of Tabaski— their faces now transformed by grief.

Still, the murder of *la petite* looms, mostly silently, behind every con- versation. And friends have been suffering other, more private wounds this winter, too: sickness in the family, anxiety about work or relation- ships. The deep freeze has been bursting the pipes in their homes. As for me, it's been like I've been living one of those dreams where you try to throw a stone with your full force—aiming for a bright, sky-bound arc— but the stone barely leaves your hand.

"It was terrible," a friend told me one night as she made dinner. Her daughter was playing in the living room as we spoke, with two red bal- loons and one orange one; her son was outside in the snow, wresting the remains of a rabbit from a dog's mouth. "The children began asking questions and wanting to go on the search parties, too." This friend, a nurse, is the daughter of a local pastor and grew up in the buildings that are now used to house the CADA asylum seekers. She has lived and worked in the Middle East and in Africa in horrifying war zones, and now volunteers at the fire department. "People were unprepared here," she said. "They didn't know what they were doing."

And then there was Muriel. Muriel told me how she herself went on one of the search parties. I pictured her big blue eyes in the dark of the woods, holding her husband's hand. "What a trauma it was. What a shock. What shame, *honte*, everyone felt. We didn't look one another in the eyes. The old people—those who lived through the war here—simply couldn't believe it. It is our shame."

"No!" I said. "No. This is not your shame. This could have happened anywhere."

Muriel was silent a moment. "Yes, maybe. But that's the view from the outside. Inside, maybe we just don't know the world enough yet."

Sandrine had been away from the Cévenol School when the murder took place, recovering from minor surgery. Now she's back at work and has invited me to come and visit her classes again. There are new groups of kids we could do storytelling exercises with, she says. It might be good for them.

So I will go, anxious as I am to face them all.

The Cévenol School survived over the decades on a set of earnest propositions: All children, from all walks of life, have dignity and can develop their own moral lives; all can come, all can succeed—even children who are troubled, wounded, needier than others. And this: If you knock on the door of the Cévenol School, someone answers. Sandrine told me a while ago that she never looks up the backgrounds of her students. Having struggled herself with grades and authority as a teenager, she makes it a point to take students as they are; to never ask the particulars of their pasts; to look them in the eye equally and with dignity. Today you can regard the Cévenol children from a distance, all mixed together outside the cafeteria in their pretty clusters, surrounded by trees, or hunched up near the doorways to their classes, half outside, smoking, with their long hair and scarves and languid looks and sudden brilliant flashes of smiles: They make for a pleasing, reassuring sight in the aggregate.

But today we also know that a certain child knocked on the door of the Cévenol School just about year ago. A bright French boy with a handsome face. And that boy was let in. So, within that aggregate mix of children, we now know that there was, once, a special kind of child among them, crossing the threshold, then passing along the edges of the cafeteria, maybe, stacking a lunch tray with the others, his blond hair in a spiked arc, lingering at a locker, hunkering in front of a computer in the library, scanning the forest for hiding places. . . . This child, it turned out, was damaged, murderous.

So as I walk up the steps and down the hall once again, the aggregate of Little Crickets look different to me now.

In class, with Sandrine at my side, we return to the exercise from earlier visits—can you tell us a story about the time of your grandparents?—and then, with every story, the analytical question: *Qui fait quoi avec qui?* Hee-hee, the children lightly laugh again. A kid tells a story about how the Germans captured his Alsatian grandmother during the Second World War, but she ended up in Clermont-Ferrand. That leads to talk of work groups and territorial groups. Another kid tells a story about an ancestor who owned an island in the West Antilles. Ah, very interesting! Colonialism . . .

Another boy then tells a story about his grandfather and his great-grandfather, who were captured by the Germans during the war, and tortured. Ah. Okay. I ask, What groups mattered here? *Qui fait quoi avec qui?* Family, says one girl. Culture, says another girl. Class, says another. Yes. We turn each answer over, peeling back layers as we do.

And then, following the train of thought, trying to deepen the discussion, I ask, "What does it take to torture someone? And if you torture someone, are they still a person to you?"

The noise in the room trails off. The boy who told the story, tall with sandy, wavy hair, looks tired, suddenly. His eyes squint a bit.

Agnès, her brown, wary eyes. Agnès de Dieu, Agnès, the lamb of God. Agnès, the new star in the sky. Agnès, whose death augured a fall from innocence. Tortured for an hour before her murder.

Good Lord. What have I said?

Later, in the cold dark of my apartment at night, I keep seeing the sandy-haired boy in my mind's eye. How could I have let the children go on about torture, with the memory of Agnès's still so close and vivid? How could I have forgotten, even for an instant? It was a decent analytical point, worth thinking about for young people: How do our very thoughts about other groups or individuals allow for and even encourage violence in the world? But with the photographs of Agnès's wary face— and the images of men and women in white forensic suits, closing a blue tarp over her remains all still constantly circulating, now indelible—how could I not see, right in that very moment, that it was wretched to push these children back into such dark places? I could have made things better, but instead I made them quieter, darker—worse.

The nights—so cold outside; so cold, still, inside—have become these pictures.

I'd never seen a dead body until I lived in Russia. Unless my eyes deceived me, that first body was frozen solid. I was speeding down the highway coming from the airport, and it was being carried horizontally out of a pine forest, blue-gray and stiff, as if it were a ladder, or a life-size, frozen paper doll.

The second dead body I saw was in the Russian village itself, during fieldwork. An old woman had died one white winter's day, and, as was the custom, she had been laid out in a rough-hewn casket in the icon corner of her log cabin. Villagers, all puffy and round in their cotton padded work coats, fur hats, and boiled wool boots, crowded in to see her lying there. I remember the side conversations about how a truck was coming by with salami to sell. I remember her round little frame, her waxy little face. And how, after a time, her casket was, according to ritual, driven off to the graveyard a few kilometers away. That, to keep the dead woman's soul from flying back and haunting us all.

I was late, in life, then, to death. From childhood, I didn't like the dark, and I didn't like the night, and I felt spaces keenly, and worried about ghosts. And I didn't grow up, like so many, in a land of war or hunger. And I never had a big, teeming family where lives would come and go. Or a religious tradition that thinks much of our waxy remains.

But in that Russian village, death seemed to be everywhere. So I had to just deal with it. And study it. I couldn't wake up and go to the bathroom at night without, once in a while, passing a frozen sheep head on the floor, in all its horned glory, tongue sticking out. There were dead animals: the gentle dog that had been shot for rummaging in the garbage; the dead lamb we ate, named Frederick; dead fish heads, floating in soup. There were dead people, yes, from accidents, or age, or suicide, or murder. And, with more heft and longevity, really, there were dead souls, too, in the form of ghosts and other creatures of the invisible realms—ones that you'd visit in graveyards on windy days, or talk with in your home or barn or bathhouse. And so I, like any anthropologist, however reluctant or squeamish, started learning the contours of how the dead lived among us, right then, right there: how—though gone from the visible world—they could be loving and capricious, both; how they had responsibilities toward the living, jobs to do.

In the Russian village, there were the ghosts that people saw of the recent dead, right there in the forest where the tree had fallen and killed them. There were those they saw in dreams, as admonishers. Right within the house, there were capricious invisible beings, known as *domovye*, who would play tricks on people, and demanded gestures of respect. There were the good dead—usually the relatives you'd loved who had passed on not so long before—and the scary dead, who would haunt your homes and your forests and your bathhouses and your dreams. But mostly there was the collective dead, whose job was to monitor and regulate the natural and social worlds, to keep things going as they ought to. These dead were there with the rain and the crops, and the lightning and the bones. They smelled fragrant and loamy in the spring. They were there, in a bustling invisible army, keeping the great turning world on its proper axis.

It was all very grand and strange when I—with my armor of science, yet timid of ghosts—learned to live in a place where the dead were everywhere.

But now, here, the boy killed the girl. The school opened its doors, and death came blasting in. Cruel wind.

What is this science I'm trying to do? What is this mockery of mourning?

———

Sandrine has invited me to stay with her and her family for a few days in Le Puy. We leave Le Chambon along a winding, narrow road. With every minute in the car, we leave Le Chambon and its recent trauma farther behind. I feel my shoulders relax into my seat. I feel myself exhaling.

And then, Sandrine speaks: "Look, see, there! See those great big plows?" I look over at her pleasant, even face. "See those trucks, and the fans? Once we're higher up, it's going to be La Burle."

She knows I've been hoping to see this. Rémi, her husband, quite an expert on things meteorological, has spoken with gusto about my chances of seeing a proper display of La Burle on this trip. I've learned that even if it's been too cold for lots of snow, it's not the amount of snow that matters. A mere meter of snow, Sandrine tells me, would be enough. It's the wind carrying the snow that matters—the wind that blocks you, that traps you, tunnels you, everything getting narrower and whiter and smaller and more blinding.

Sandrine and I turn another corner on the winding road, finally out of the last craggy hills, fully exposed to the largeness of the sky.

"Look! Up there!"

Here, in the broad, open panorama before us, finally: wind. Wind, creeping up from the fields below. Wind like waves of the sea. Wind, in aerial bursts. Wind slowly, deliberately crafting drifts that will grow and grow.

Voilà, La Burle!

And now they arrive, one after the next, these great waves of wind, sneaking in, soldiering in. I watch them, mesmerized. I think of Sandrine's grandfather, and his shivering horses and the doctor and the pregnant woman, about how he left the safety of his home and its thick stone walls to head into that wind. How could he have known he would be safe out in La Burle? How could he have known that he would ever make it back to his farm alive, back to his wife, to his children?

Of course, you can't stop the wind from coming, I think. But what risks are right to take, and when? What risks, when there are children and grandchildren and great-grandchildren yet to be born? When you leave the dark sureness of your thick-walled hearth and home?

Sandrine's grandfather couldn't possibly have known the answer back then. He took a risk, and didn't know. Magda Trocmé, with her braids, couldn't have known. The thousands here who opened their doors to bloodied strangers, on and off for centuries, couldn't have known. Daniel couldn't have known. No one could have. No one knows. No one ever does.

And I don't know. Risk means facing fears—and I am afraid of many things. I'm afraid of dead bodies and the dark. In Russia, I'm afraid of drunk guys in cars, on trains, in buses, on the street. After a near miss in the woods one summer when I was working at a camp during an electric storm, I'm so afraid of lightning that the very flash of it in the distant sky turns me into a cartoon version of my lizard self: flinching, contorting, darting off. I'm afraid of some pretty ridiculous things—like filling out forms, or touching a fish—but also of real things, like hurting people; or, as a woman, assault; or, mostly, having my life *tick-tick-tick* away in vain. The wind blows, the world is upturned, there's a knock at the door. And I admit: I'm afraid of what might be behind it.

La Burle sneaks over the hills to the right and left of the car as we drive, like the angel of death that felled Pharaoh's firstborn in *The Ten Commandments*. Here, in the little car just now emerging from the great wind, I finally turn to Sandrine and her still, mild face. I tell her, close to tears, how I have been agonizing about the sandy-haired boy, about the students, about my very presence here in the Plateau, about those first questions of mine, questions that now feel a world away, a lifetime ago.

Her words are few, but they are, each one of them, kind. The kids are doing okay. Better, by now, than she thought they would be. And it's good for them to talk. Don't blame yourself, she says, still looking forward.

HERONS PERCH IN THE SHALLOW RAPIDS of the Loire River, looking for fish. It is a beautiful view from Sandrine and Rémi's kitchen window on this cold, bright day.

With this distance now, it's time for facing facts.

When I first came to the Plateau, looking for peace, I thought myself above the worst of the possible illusions. I knew places weren't perfect. I knew that you don't find uniform legions of angels anywhere, just like you don't find corresponding legions of devils. Such supernatural entities—metaphysical beasts—have no bearing on us, the earthbound. Like everyone, I am, in principle, as capable of good as I am of evil; that fact is freeing and dreadful, but it also has the benefit of changing the focus from calcified metaphysics to living science.

Staggering as the beauty of the Plateau's story was and is, I have been working hard to keep my head on straight. To get things written down. To acknowledge the contradictions, to focus. It's true I've watched myself over many months, as I've slid away from structures like interviews or even pointed questions; as I've learned the law of silence, and its fluid dynamics; as I've begun to spend more time with the refugees than with the villagers. But I have marched on.

It's not that science falters, exactly. The murder of Agnès doesn't demonstrate something newly shocking about the capacity for violence. Violence is, of course, possible here on the Plateau, as it has always been. It's possible anywhere. This murder also doesn't threaten how we understand group habit or group action here, at least not yet.

It's not that. It's not that at all.

I believe in the bright light of science. I believe that real science is, in so many ways, our salvation. I have dared ask, What is peace? I march forward because my questions—even in their slighter forms—matter; because they are empirical, and, in small, advancing ways, knowable. It's not science's fault, this dark place I'm in. I'm just so tired and so sad. And I don't know where I'm going.

Something terrible keeps nagging me, filling my sleep with nightmares. It is not only the image of *la petite*, of Agnès. It is also, more and more with every passing day, other images, too, like that pair of scarred dark brown hands from Congo, hands reaching upward to avoid the blows of a captor; or the faces of the bright little Chechen children, one-two-three, looking up at the black-masked men at their door; or of Lalik, eating the sunflower seeds, incanting the loss of her baby girl, with her army of teddy bears looking on. Face after face, hand after hand. "What will become of us," they are all asking, "if we have no papers? Papers, papers, papers. What will become of us if they put us out in the snow?"

Will science help me with any of those faces? Any of those hands?

Such a boundless sea of suffering the wide world has proffered. Who do I think I am, anyway?

SANDRINE AND I SPEND the days together here, talking and walking, making food, just hanging out. We go to a funeral for the man who owned the nearby corner store—yes, Sandrine says, smiling at me with a hint of teasing, it's okay to wear pants to church—and I try to understand the hymns, and sing along, "My little children, let us not love in word, neither in tongue, but in deed and in truth." Later, we go to visit an Algerian friend of hers, another teacher with a moppet bun on the top of her head, who has recently been snowed in; Sandrine brings her gifts of food and cheer, and the two of them tell stories, and smoke, and we talk about how all the religions are, in some ways, just the same. "This is what binds us together," says Sandrine's friend.

In drives to town or in walks, or while cooking meals, Sandrine and I talk about her childhood and the lovely times she spent at her grandmother's farm, and her uncle's farm, while growing up, and what she learned there. A successful and innovative farmer, Sandrine's grandfather had taken risks to build and diversify. And now her uncle Jean, too, is successful. He raises raspberries and sells them, but he also sells jams and juices, and has constructed a set of lovingly crafted vacation homes for tourists.

Once, Jean took a whole blizzardy day to introduce me to some of the farmers in the area. Sitting down with these farmers in their little kitchens, or standing with them in their massive barns, I listened as they told stories—their speech charmed by those flattened vowels—of the old times, and the hidden refugees, and the closed compartments in the barns, and the days when you would walk your cow down to the fair. They told darker stories, too, like the one about the murderous sprees the German soldiers went on at the end of the war, setting fire to homes, shooting a pair of beloved local brothers in the head.

At the end of our day, winding through the blizzard in his car, Jean told me about a neighbor they had while he was growing up. This neighbor's farm was up higher than theirs, and he would let his cows urinate and defecate in the stream that the two families shared. The manure would float down the stream, right in front of their window. It would stink. Inevitably, the day after the cow did its business in their common stream, the neighbor would come to Jean's father, wanting to borrow tools. And, without fail, his father would lend them to him.

He was always teaching us you have to return evil with good, Jean said.

Now, in a kitchen that overlooks the Loire, Sandrine tells me what she remembers most about her grandfather, who opened the door of his dark stone house that day of La Burle, into the blinding snow: that you must love one another, really, through how you live.

MY LAST NIGHT IN LE PUY, Rémi's cousins come for a visit and we are up late. Rémi makes a fire in the fireplace. Later, the children are put to bed, and then Rémi himself goes upstairs to end his day. Now Sandrine and I are left in the glow of the hearth, talking and talking about all of it—the murder and the school and the refugees—as she taps the ashes of her cigarette into the flames.

And I finally say to Sandrine, out loud, that I want so much to tell the truth in my work, not to ignore the contradictions in difficult times, not to ignore things like the murder. And I finally tell her, too, that I am distraught, that I don't know where I'm going anymore.

"But that is *accueil*," Sandrine says. "You see? That is what it really means to take people in. Somebody shows up at your door, you take them in, and sometimes bad things happen. They just do.

"So," she says, after a pause, "you have to have faith."

She is quiet. I am quiet. She taps her cigarette again into the fire. The flames are reflected in her glasses.

"Only it's not faith in the person who is behind the door that you need." She indicates into the shadowy end of the living room, as if it were the far side of a threshold, filled with any dark being, who knows. "It's faith that, in the end, the right thing will happen. That things will be as they should."

I look to her face, and then back into the hearth.

In the silence that follows, her words are shattering. Electrifying.

———

Alexander Grothendieck was born in Berlin in 1928 to true-blue anarchist parents, one a Russian Jew, the other German. At the Cévenol School, he liked his biology teacher, Mr. Friedel, in particular, but he hated how the other children would talk during Friedel's class, and take his focus away. Alexander lived at a home for children called La

Guespy—the same one as Jacob Lewin and his brother—and had a voracious appetite for chess. Years after the war, he would recall how he and the other children fled into the forest during raids, "to hide for one or two nights, in little groups of two or three, without concerning ourselves much if it was good for our health." A photograph from the period shows him gangly, with a thick head of dark hair, hunched over a bike.

He was remembered by his teachers and caretakers. Mademoiselle Usach, director of La Guespy, later wrote that Alexander—known as Alex the Poet—was "always plunged deep in his thoughts," and was terribly good at playing chess. The child "demanded silence" when listening to music, but was otherwise "loud" and "brusque."

What was unusual about Alexander was not the dramatic story of his anarchist parents, or of his flight to France, or a surname misspelled so often in police documents that he might have been Jewish or Dutch or Russian or just about anything—a repeated error that might well have saved his life. No, that brusque child who needed silence was unusual because, many years later, he would go on to create some of the most sweeping, revolutionary theories that pure mathematics has ever devised. In them, Alexander would orchestrate a mathematical equivalent of a unified field theory, where algebraic structure and geometric form—long awkwardly reconciled—were now gracefully intertwined. This required a sublime imagination.

Alexander Grothendieck went on to win the Crafoord Prize in mathematics—comparable to a Nobel Prize—but he turned it down, because of its "corrupting influence." Like many of those who live in the rarefied heights of mathematics, he eventually wrote a series of philosophical, even pseudo-mystical tracts, amounting to many hundreds of pages. In his unpublished manuscript *La clef des songes* (The Key to Dreams), he mused on the meaning of mathematical beauty and form; about the source of new ideas; on the importance of solitude, to which he eventually succumbed fully; and, in that solitude, on the very voice of God.

What did Alexander see, I wonder, those days and nights in the forests outside La Guespy, just over the hill from La Maison des Roches? What did he see when he looked up, between the highest trees, up toward patches of sky? What did he see that I can't see?

As it is, I'm now afraid to go to the forest by myself.

At night, in my own solitude back in Le Chambon, I fill up bottles of hot water, soak my feet, and think. I think about the forest. I think about the hunt of the wild boar, his low gallop deep into the thickets, and the hunt for mushrooms and berries. I think of the boys of La Maison des Roches waking up on a bed of pine needles and moss. I think of the tunnels and the ravines, of little Fanny hiding among the loamy roots of great fallen trees. I think about the miracle of aloneness in the forest; being both captive there, and free.

If I were braver, I would go into the forest myself. I would walk the three kilometers up from Cévenol, to find the scene of the crime. I would go alone. Walking and walking, step after heavy step in the fresh February snow, sooner or later, I might come upon one blackened tree. And then?

Years ago, when I walked to Babi Yar, I said a prayer in the December snow and wind. A prayer I hoped might echo down that awful, stricken gorge that had swallowed the bones of a hundred thousand souls.

Here, in the forests over Cévenol, there would be just one tree, one girl, just one black color to mix forever the matter of girl and tree.

What prayer would I say now?

"God alone is quiet," Grothendieck wrote, "and when He speaks, it is in a voice so low, nobody can ever hear it."

What prayer? A prayer against the wind?

Please, wind, stop!

A prayer for form, for order? I, too, long for the higher dimensions. I, too, am crushed by the beauty of the stars at night.

Please, answers, come . . .

What prayer?

Maybe, just . . .

A prayer that looks like a tunnel of white, with a gray smudge of a man, digging.

And sounds like a voice, still and small, saying:

Everything will be as it should.

Chapter 10

ELSEWHERE

I lean against a fountain. Old women come up to
draw water: of their drama I shall know nothing but
these gestures of farm servants. A child, his head
against a wall, weeps in silence: there will remain of
him in my memory only a beautiful child forever
inconsolable. I am a stranger. I know nothing.
I do not enter into their empires.

—ANTOINE DE SAINT-EXUPÉRY, *WIND, SAND AND STARS*

TELL THEM," Daniel said before stooping into the gray tarpaulin-covered truck, "that I love to travel."

On a brilliant June day in 1943, together with seventeen of his charges—from Spain, Germany, Luxembourg, Holland, Austria, Belgium, and Romania—Daniel began this newest journey, crowded into the back of a stiflingly hot truck, bumping and twisting through the mountains, and then down from the Plateau, nearly everyone getting sick, down and down, detouring into the woods to avoid gunfire, down toward Vichy, and beyond that, toward the ancient Bourbon capital of Moulins.

Near sunset, Daniel and the young men finally arrived at their destination. They clambered out of the back of the truck. In front of them, over a short drawbridge, stood a high and heavy wooden door. Above their heads, a yellowish tower, shooting a hundred fifty feet up into the sky. Built six hundred years earlier, as a palace for the Duke of Bourbon, the structure had for the past few hundred years—and most particularly now, in the age of German rule—served as a prison, where detainees were brought to be interrogated, tortured, deported.

The great wooden doors opened, and then closed again, and then locked behind them all.

Moulins Prison held secrets. For centuries, prisoners had been locked in its dungeons in solitary confinement, and then tortured with water, or kicks to the head or punches to the back, or bullwhips and pincers or— in this more modern age—the butts of rifles. Or simply with hunger and thirst. Once in a while, those prisoners would etch graffiti into the walls of their dungeons: days counted in sticks, Stars of David, the outline of a naked woman—or of a saint. We are here! the hands would say again and again over the centuries, scraping something sharp against a wet, cold wall.

In Moulins, Daniel would become the subject of a new little mountain of *tap-a-tap-tap* documents ("reason for arrest: unknown"). He would sleep on his back, sharing one straw mattress with two other young men, looking up toward the high windows of his cell.

I am here, said Daniel now, at Moulins Prison. Looking up into the damp dark night, he had plenty of time to think.

AT LA MAISON DES ROCHES, the children and their housekeeper, Hermine Orsi, were devastated. Madame Orsi, who had been working with Resistance networks for years, had to figure out quickly how to keep the children safe under these new circumstances. With no obvious resources remaining after the raid, she gathered up all of the jewelry her mother had passed down to her and quietly sold it to buy food for her charges. For the next four months, she made Herculean efforts to place the children and—now that even the little ones appeared to be targets—to smuggle them into Switzerland. Madame Orsi understood the risks she was taking. In the course of the war, she had been arrested, had been under bombardment on trains, had been paraded by German soldiers in the center of Avignon, had worked day after day for years on end to find clothing, food, and shelter for Jewish children she held in her very own arms, one after the next, by the tens, the hundreds. But the day of Daniel's arrest—Daniel, whom she called beloved, whose soul she called beautiful—was, she said, the worst moment of her life.

Four days after the roundup, La Maison des Roches was disbanded and the young men dispersed. Azizollah Sadigh Ershadi, the Persian doctor, disappeared into the woods. Léon Cukier, the young Polish "electricity student" at Gurs whom Daniel had officially invited to Roches just a few days earlier, now had nowhere to go. Cukier's paperwork from his application to Roches declared that he was "without religion [but] of the Jewish race," and soon, with no safe haven, he was swept into a deportation from Gurs to Drancy, and from there, to either Estonia or Lithuania, where he certainly perished.

A couple of weeks later, by mid-July, a heavyhearted André Trocmé—now out of prison—himself went into hiding. Though historical evidence leads to other conclusions, he seems to have felt that, on some level, Daniel had been arrested in his place. And if this complex, looming sense of guilt were not enough, Trocmé had also heard a rumor—by some accounts, a fabricated one—that he and Pastor Theis were being targeted for assassination. Weighing his wish to exemplify moral courage ("I have preached nonviolent resistance," he wrote, "and my duty is to go all the way") against the likelihood that his death would bring massive waves of reprisals, Trocmé was finally convinced that his leaving the Plateau was not only best for the refugees themselves, but best for the overall cause of peace. And so André Trocmé, *le violent vaincu par Dieu*, left the Plateau. He would not return until the war was over.

The roundup at La Maison des Roches, violent and public as it was, left the people of the Plateau in a terrible way. As one witness put it, "A great sadness reigned in Le Chambon. We spoke of nothing but." At the same time, as young men continued to pour into the region—fleeing the Service du Travail Obligatoire, living in and out of the forest, dropping by parachute from the skies—the Resistance was gaining confidence and force. And so a new picture of the Plateau emerged, the quiet and the shattered juxtaposed with the mercurial and the vengeful.

So, it couldn't have been a shock when, on August 6, just one month after the raid at Roches, a small group of renegade maquisards from the foot of the Lizieux peak took it upon themselves to walk up to one Léopold Praly, who was sitting in a café in the center of Le Chambon, and shoot him dead. Down went handsome, affable Léopold, who had once grabbed Jacob Lewin by the skinny arm; down went this informer, typist, signer of arrest warrants. Down he went, right next to the hotel where the convalescing German soldiers had for so long mercifully ig-nored the young refugees—so many of them Jews. Down went Le Cham-bon and the Plateau with it, as a place of notable, if not otherworldly, nonviolence.

Reprisals would surely come.

SOON AFTER THEY ALL ARRIVED in Moulins Prison—on July 12, 1943—five of the eighteen young men swept up in the raid of La Maison des Roches, those known to be Jews, were permanently separated from the group: cuffed, led out of Moulins Prison, sent to a transit camp at Beaune-la-Rolande, and then immediately transferred to Drancy, just north of Paris. Then, at 9:30 a.m. on July 18, 1943, after several days spent waiting in squalor, the five were loaded onto a long train called Convoy 57, where 995 other men, women, and children were crammed with them into sealed boxcars, sixty to a car.

These were the young men from La Maison des Roches who climbed onto Convoy 57: George Marx, from Luxembourg; Jacques Balter, from Paris; Leonidas Goldenberg, from Bucharest; Herbert Wollstein, from Herne, Germany; and Charles Stern, from Antwerp, not yet sixteen. From Paris—Jacques's home for all of his nineteen years—Convoy 57 lumbered east and then north and then east again. At some point on the journey, prisoners in one of the wagons had the idea of setting a fire, which they hoped would force the SS soldiers guarding the convoy to open their car door. Instead, the soldiers told them that they'd better put out the fire themselves, or they would all die.

When they arrived at their final destination, Convoy 57 pulled up to a sandy spot between two lines of train tracks. The captives, pushed out of the cars, were met by soldiers screaming, "Fast, outside—everyone, outside, fast!" waving rifles as they did. Then, one witness remembered, "strange people in striped clothing jump[ed] onto the train like gnomes that had escaped from hell." To their right and to their left, prisoners could see lines of barracks surrounded by barbed wire. In the far distance ahead, there were dark chimneys, and everywhere, a strange, oily smell. Auschwitz.

I bear witness that in Auschwitz, George, Jacques, Leonidas, Herbert, and Charles—not yet sixteen—all perished.

TOGETHER IN MOULINS PRISON—who does what with whom?—the community from La Maison des Roches had changed. With the loss of its five members known to be Jewish came a sense of great existential uncertainty: Where had the five gone, and whatever would become of them?

Then there was the deprivation that they now shared. The food was, as Daniel wrote from the prison, "good, but not abundant." This was an understatement. A Spanish prisoner named Pedro Moral-Lopez carefully recorded their diet: "At 11am they give us soup: One liter of hot water with a few pieces of carrot and dry vegetables, and then they add three to four spoons of noodles or potatoes with no fat. At 5pm the same soup. In addition, 240 grams of bread per day." After two days of this diet, Pedro noted, "we felt a hunger that would never leave us."

In Daniel's very first letter as a prisoner—addressed "Dear Sir," to the elderly pastor Noël Poivre in Le Chambon—he delicately raised the issue of necessities:

> It is still possible to hold on. Morale-wise, all is going very well.
> For the first eight days, we were pretty much all together. Since
> then, I was provisionally separated and placed in another group.
> We can't receive anything here but clothing and toiletries. Might I
> receive some pajamas, boxer shorts, handkerchiefs, soap and toilet
> paper? For food, would it be possible to send a package—rather
> important—of ready-to-eat provisions, directly to the Red Cross,
> where they are distributed?

The group changed shape. The group grew hungry. The hierarchy shifted. Daniel almost immediately gave up his role as the group's director and became "a friend," as André Guyonnaud—former student and future pastor—wrote several years later. As a friend, Daniel lived together with the group in cell number ten, on the top floor of the prison, where they shared their straw mattresses, lying close enough to feel one another's breath and heat against the damp cold of the prison air.

Even now, as their friend, their equal, Daniel brought a set of special skills to the environment—the technologies, say, of keeping spirits up. In the many hours of worry and monotony ("Life went on," Pedro wrote, "while we waited for food"), Daniel worked out games for them to play—like one where they would guess historical names: "We would start with the letter A, and so forth," Pedro remembered. "Sometimes we got all the way up to the letter T." Or Daniel would lead *jeu d'ambassadeurs*, a French version of charades. Though they were not allowed to receive books, at some point they got their hands on the propaganda newspaper *Pariser Zeitung*, and Daniel would translate it out loud, from German to French, and then get a debate going.

Together they learned about the fall of Mussolini, on July 25, 1943. Together they girded themselves against a "drunk man, a journalist and a German" who was an informant, and because of whom they once had their meager food rations taken away. Together they also saw one more of their group, from Luxembourg—most likely Robert Kimmen, "probably a defector"—be hauled off to solitary confinement, down into the basement dungeons.

Even now, at some level, the group shared secrets. Certainly four, and as many as six of the remaining young men from La Maison des Roches, were Jewish, though this had gone undetected so far. Among those were Klaus Simon, who had already been to Rivesaltes, and had already hidden in the woods, and had been arrested and questioned several times; and bespectacled Mendel Jeret, still going by the name Alexandre de Haan.

In this small society of former Rocheux, some novel kinds of bonds were also forming. Though the Little Crickets had been the object of his special affection, Daniel and the others were now intertwining in new ways, and that intertwining brought intimacy, and—though by no means inevitably—moments of generosity. When packages of food finally arrived for Daniel, he shared them with the others in the group—a gesture that was not merely polite or cursory, given that all of them, including Daniel, were now living in a state of hunger they had never before known. After the war, Félix Martin-Lopez, another of the Spanish prisoners, wrote to Daniel's parents in broken French about what it had meant for him to be able to partake of the cakes they had once sent to their son, *le bien-aimé*, the beloved. He recalled packages with "biscuits and prunes," which Daniel had taken care to share with "the youngest and smallest" of the group. Was this Charles—not yet sixteen and not yet gone?—before his terrible journey ahead? More generally, he wrote about what it meant to know Daniel, "honest and brave and wise."

THE YOUNG MEN FROM ROCHES congealed into a new kind of group. Who does what with whom? The prisoner gets sick on the truck with the other prisoner. The prisoner plays charades with the other prisoner, or girds against the informant, or eats the cake. One prisoner and another share the same breath at night.

Even so, I can't help but think how, at the same time, each young man was also living a very deep and very new kind of solitude. And that in each individual solitude, there were brand-new moments of truth—ones that sounded like the question:

Who are you, and who will you be?

If you receive a package filled with cakes, and you look down at it, and you are hungry as you have never once been hungry before . . . you face that package and its consequences alone. And if you are not yet sixteen, and it says the word *Israélite*, right there, next to your arrest report, you face that word and the police alone. And, alone, you make decisions: Will you build a fire in the boxcar, or not? How will you live your last moments? What will be your very last prayers?

Because, always, there is the group—with its technologies of peace or war—that someone like Daniel spent his whole youth trying to figure out. But then there is also the soul, well appointed or not, in its solitude.

Who would you be? Who would I be?

Daniel could easily have escaped the raid at Roches, when the soldiers banged on the door at Les Grillons. Freedom was just a window and a forest away. In his solitude, though, he stayed. And now, in this next phase of things, he—along with all of the others—would have plenty of new chances, one after the next, to witness how his own soul was built.

At one point at Moulins, Daniel demanded that he be allowed to make a statement. He spoke German, which would facilitate things. Perhaps, with an ill-judged aura of self-confidence acquired in childhood among all those elites, Daniel assumed that he could clear things up with the authorities: The young men of La Maison des Roches had been on the Plateau as students, he would tell the Germans, not Jews or communists. They were all there perfectly legally, with support from international aid organizations and global Christian alliances.

But when Daniel faced the German police in those interrogation rooms, things did not go as planned. The only record of what happened comes from a testimony written by Pedro, who survived the war:

> [Daniel] was accused of being a Jew and anti-German. He replied that he was not a Jew and neither was he particularly anti-German. He was accused of protecting a 16-year-old Jewish boy. He replied that he was protecting the weak. They kept asking—did you protect Germany when it was weak? He replied that he'd visited Germany before it became a super-power (1929 and 1934). The Gestapo inspector told him that he was lying.

Did the police think Daniel, with or without his soul, was Jewish? The evidence is thin, but there are several suggestions—as in the testimony from those interrogations—that authorities were trying to figure out who this German-speaking, non-fleeing, oddly confident, and even impertinent young man was. And it is clear from surviving documents that the German police took it upon themselves—with all the myriad priorities of occupation and warfare—to hunt down the marriage records of Daniel's parents and grandparents. Clearly, Daniel's being Jewish or not mattered at some level to the authorities. To Daniel's parents—stunned by the news of his arrest—this was the idea that stuck: that the German police thought he was an *Israélite*, and from that, their sorrow could be framed.

Whether or not Daniel was taken to be Jewish is relevant, perhaps, to the historical record. And relevant, as well, to parents who would long to understand each detail of the fate of their son. But to me, the most important thing in the interrogations at Moulins is not the proof of how authorities were thinking, but rather the demonstration of who Daniel was being. Every time his interrogators pointed to race or religion or country—their own ultimate framing categories—Daniel turned his answers away from their logic:

No, he wasn't a Jew. No, he didn't hate Germany, or love it.

And then, he turned his answers toward his own logic:

He was protecting a boy (not a Jew per se). He was protecting a weak boy (not, particularly, a weak Jew). A boy who needed protection.

It was an honest—if a bit back-sassy—way for Daniel to speak of things, yes. But it was also, if you look at it right up close, profoundly subversive. There, in that moment of stark, interrogatory truth, was just that one soul—Daniel's—knowing how to say, right then and there, that we are not races or countries or religions; we are humanity. Just as Daniel's same soul, in its fluency, had looked down at cakes meant just for him and, in his hunger, decided to share.

What did Daniel get in return for these moments of truth? He told André Guyonnaud that during the interrogations, he was smacked full in the face, with no time to take off his glasses. Did the glasses tumble to the cold floor of the prison? Did they shatter?

I look at my photograph of Daniel from the spring of 1943, smiling in three-quarter view. I imagine his face, now pink and mottled, glasses gone. A new solitude behind his dark, raw eyes.

After the shot rang out in the peaceable streets of Le Chambon on August 6, according to witnesses, a young man cycled off quickly and chaotically, leaving Léopold Praly's crumpled body behind. One more body among the hundreds of thousands of crumpled bodies that had fallen that July and August of 1943, in the bombardment of Hamburg, the siege of Sicily, and the Battle of Kursk—where upward of 380,000 people perished—and in the extermination camps, which each possessed the capacity to murder two to three thousand people per hour.

The assassin came from the base of the Lizieux peak, and had plotted the killing with a small group of maquisards. The group's leader, a man named Jean Bonnisol, was a well-known Resistance fighter in the area. Together, small bands of those fighters had been living in abandoned farmhouses tucked away in that pretty, forested area. New recruits were arriving all the time. Parachutists were landing in the forests, with information and resources.

I imagine that each of those fighters—brave, angry, wounded, righteous—looked into his or her own solitude during those heady days . . . as, say, one of them smoked his cigarettes; or as another posed for a photograph among stony ruins; or as a third watched his Jewish friend start to stand and say, "Look, I wrote a little poem," only to be shot and killed right then; or as the assassin himself aimed at the affable Praly before pulling the trigger. Each of them looked. Each found an answer. And then another answer again.

It turned out that Jean Bonnisol had a friend with decided views on the matter of souls and solitude. This friend, a French Algerian, was living for a time at an isolated old house just a forty-five-minute walk from the center of Le Chambon. He had a connection to the Plateau through his wife, and he had come there for treatments for a long, debilitating case of tuberculosis. And so after a long trip away from the sands, across the sea, up the Rhône Valley, and into the Plateau, that French Algerian—a refugee named Albert Camus—settled into a suite of rooms in a great house called Panelier. Soon, Camus's wife had to return to their home in Oran. But by the time Camus himself felt ready to join her, in November 1942, the Allies had landed in North Africa, the Germans had captured the rest of France, and every southern port was blocked. And so Camus was stuck, far from the sands and the sea; far, too, from the burgeoning excitement for his latest work, *The Stranger*, in Paris; and, perhaps most important, far from the woman, or women, he loved.

Just a forty-five-minute walk from where Praly had been assassinated, this French Algerian refugee peered long and hard into his own famous solitude (who will I be?). And then he went on to write that great allegory of occupation and exile, that great meditation on rats and men and souls: the novel called *La peste. The Plague.*

If the Plateau has gone down in history, among the reasons is this: It got on Albert Camus's nerves. Though he appreciated, now and then, the beauty of the fall in Vivarais-Lignon, Camus found the place cold. He hated the wind and the winter. He was sick. He missed being in the fray. His wife was far away. This was exile for him, and the mountains inspired more claustrophobia than inspiration. *On y respire mal, c'est un fait,* he wrote. One breathes badly there; it's a fact.

Camus did have some friends and acquaintances on the Plateau—among them, members of the Resistance like Bonnisol; and an old Jewish friend from Algiers, André Chouraqui, who became a key figure in the rescue of children in the Plateau, and who went on to be elected deputy mayor of Jerusalem in 1965. Camus also seems to have had a kind of friendship with Dr. Le Forestier, who some have posited provided a model for one hero of *The Plague*, Dr. Rieux. And though there is no evidence whatsoever that they met, it is likely that Camus knew about a pastor named André Trocmé, and had heard of his fiery sermons where he used the force of his charisma to call his listeners to sacrifice.

The Plague is a modern chronicle of spreading contagion. In it, first the rats come sneaking out of corners; then they come in droves. Other than the oddity of the animals' first fluttering appearance, and death, and then a few signs of sickness among citizens in the town, no one sees danger right away. But soon people start dying. And then there is a shocking diagnosis: the Plague. And then there is a quarantine. People are trapped within the quarantine, away from their lovers. The deaths start adding up. As the suffering eventually builds to grotesque dimensions; people decide who they are, and what they will become. A priest, Paneloux (some believe André Trocmé was at least in part an inspiration for this character), offers fearsome oratory and the wrath of God to an increasingly panicked population. But then, before the Plague finally leaves the town, Paneloux loses his faith. Why? Because he finally sees, with his own eyes, the excruciating death-throes of a child. And his faith, such as he possesses, disappears.

Camus kills his Paneloux in the end. But he keeps alive a character named Tarrou—a once-brutal revolutionary who now ceaselessly aids the sick and dying—letting Tarrou utter the question that feels truest to

Camus himself: "Can one be a saint without God?—that's the problem, in fact the only problem, I'm up against today."

Now. This is what I have to say.

It is August 1943. Daniel is in Moulins Prison, sharing his cakes, having his glasses smacked off his face. George, Jacques, Leonidas, Herbert, and Charles, not yet sixteen years old, have been lost to Auschwitz. Some journeys of suffering have ended; others are only just beginning.

I realize I have no choice. I must return again to the place where Sandrine left me last February, after the murder, with the question that hangs in the air, in the glow of firelight and cigarette ash:

Will everything be as it should? Will it?

Camus was looking for a solution to this question, too, really. Right here, seventy-some years ago. He looked into his solitude and answered, no. Everything will not be as it should. Rats will come. Nazis will come. We will see the rats within ourselves. We will. And to counter the problem of rats and Nazis and what they are capable of is to aim ourselves at taking away the suffering that they cause. To work hard at it!

So, we can love people—we can, if we are Camus himself, love women; we can love companionship; we can love "the little people." We can even love a place, a landscape, the unique perfumes of both. And for that, we can fight the Plague when it comes. Fight the rats—the Nazis or whatever other dark form they take—and then, having fought them, wait for their eternal return. Camus's was not an academic answer, or a trivial one. It was an answer that directly faced the grotesquerie swirling around them all in that time and place.

Investing prayer in things being as they should, Camus said through this novel, is just a kind of trained resignation. And behind that resignation is humility; and behind that humility, he wrote, is humiliation. Don't aim your arms heavenward, then—don't fall for that humiliation—as the rats come forward, and they recede, and they come forward again. And again. And, here, again.

Will everything be as it should?

Your soul is summoned. The prison doors open, and then close again behind you.

Maybe suffering is the worst thing in the world not when you feel it yourself, bad as that is. Maybe the worst thing in the world is to bring suffering to any other soul.

So. How about this?

Put down your book, Maggie. Open your eyes, just a little bit more. Open your countenance, and then your heart, just a little bit more.

Then go, travel . . . elsewhere. Enter—really enter—into the foreign empires.

There are no walls around it, but still it is a real place. A real land of its own, ever changing. Right now, girls are sitting on the ground in this place, cross-legged, hard at work at a sprawling chalk masterpiece: flowers, numbers, lines, a triangle lady with Pippi Longstocking braids and a tiny hat. Suns with noses. A boy zooms by on a bike, back and forth, back and forth, his face flashing somewhere between exaltation and tears.

And then Amélie arrives.

Amélieeeeeeeeeeeeeeeee!! Amélie-Amélie-Amélie!

The little girls drop their chalk and rush toward her, arms up, grabbing at her hands and legs and the side of her leather coat: *Bonjour-bonjour-bonjour-AMÉLIE!!*

Women glide over—some in headscarves and long skirts, others looking exhausted in sweatpants, still others dressed up for an appointment with makeup and heels—Amélie-Amélie! they call out, too, with questions about a doctor, a letter from a lawyer, a radiator that isn't working, some incomprehensible field trip their kid was invited on, or

a summons to immigration court. Amélie! Between drags on their cigarettes, clusters of men toss off wry jokes in her direction. She tosses her
head back. Laughs.

It is a place, this courtyard. A land. The land of exile, a land of
elsewhere.

For months, Amélie has been asking the CADA families if they want
any translation help from me. They often do. I get to hear about carpal
tunnel or knee operations or urinary tract infections or chronic headaches. I get to be part of roundelays: Armenian to Russian to French and
back. I translate calls from a lawyer, because even if I am wholly unqual-
ified to do this technical work, I am still better than nothing. I come to
CADA resident events and meetings and help Russian speakers get answers to their questions about Wi-Fi access or school lunches or how
they should be sure and let someone know immediately—immediately—
if ever they see any mice in their apartments.

I sit in the courtyard, children crawling over me, and watch the
scenes pass by: A Chechen woman washing her flea-market purchases
with a hose, slap-slap-slapping them clean with a brush and the force
of a powerful arm. Then, the woman's mother-in-law, in a kerchief and
kaftan, beaming a metallic smile toward a baby boy, cooing, "You are
Grandmother's favorite"—*Babin liubimets*—"you are the one I prayed
for." I try to hear what the locals hear: sounds and gestures that lack the
spark of meaning.

Every once in a while, I notice how the locals walk by the CADA, in
their mild miens and fleece. Most stop and smile. Some say hello.

I must acknowledge this: The strangers can look strange, here within
the empire of their exile. It can seem, to locals, that they don't dress in a
normal way; don't eat healthy foods; have weird ideas about doctors;
worry too much about being sick; use money oddly. They have their silver teeth and kerchiefs; they drape prayer rugs over the gate. They ask
for too much help, or not enough. A doctor rolls his eyes at a patient
who, he believes, is imagining her symptoms, and I muffle his doubt

about her pain. An asylum lawyer talks in exasperated tones about one young woman's case: "Tell the Madame that the judge will consider everything she says is a lie." How in the world do I translate that sentence to this woman, so proud? When I do, mutedly, she just looks up and sniffs at the air.

Day by day, I sit in the middle of this kaleidoscope and translate—trying, as I do so, to erase the tone of strangeness.

These asylum seekers: they, too, write letters home, full of longing. Quarantined from the plagues of the world, they don't know what their fates will be, and they live an uncertain charade. They, too, seek out some relief in orderliness, camaraderie; even as they spend their own nights looking up into the dark, deciding who they are and who they will be.

They are strange, perhaps, but what are we?

What am I? Privileged to a life where I have gotten to carry note-books around and make schemes for things? Where I have received polite applause—*clap, clap, clap*—for writing a book about a group of farmers who have known every dark malady? My analytical wheels keep turning, but it seems to me, more and more, that I am standing on the threshold of something. I will enter, or I won't. And if I do, things will change, and the wheels I have long counted on to bring me along will be loosed.

I come to CADA on my own now, without appointment, pretty much every day. I go from family to family, for visits. Or I just sit in the swirl of the courtyard and talk with folks as life goes by, and see if there's some-thing useful to do. Most often, I leave my journal behind. Leave my questions and schematic drawings behind, along with my anthropology hat, such as it is. Or was.

I stand outside the courtyard, looking in. I enter. I sit and watch. The analytical wheels still turn in my head—who does what with whom? But I realize I just want this: to think it's possible not to bring more suffering into the world than there already is.

Maybe I'm not an anthropologist anymore. Maybe I don't care.

. . .

TIME GOES BY in the land of CADA. Now it is early October. The wind blows in little swirls as I arrive at the courtyard, and Amélie is already here, picking up bits of trash. Normally, the residents know to put only their paper trash outside; there's another receptacle for food. But earlier today, someone put food garbage in a plastic bag right out in the courtyard, and the bag broke. Amélie sighs. Once in a while they do get mice, and of course this doesn't help.

Across the courtyard, she sees a clot of golden pink detritus somewhere on the ground and goes and picks it up. It's the head of a doll, smashed in. "The doll was porcelain," she tells me, sighing again. She picks up little pink pieces of doll face, now shattered, and throws them in the garbage. And then she picks up something else. "Here," she says. And she hands me first one blue eye from the porcelain doll, and then the other. I arrange the two eyes on the palm of my hand in different ways. I put them in my pocket.

From above, we hear a voice, sweet and singsongy: *Amélie!* We look up to see a pretty face and long, long hair and a waving hand, framed by a window. Amélie and I laugh. Look at you, Rapunzel! Look how the birds are flying around your head, singing!

This is Larissa. She is still new to CADA. With her flowing brown hair and her full-lipped smile, Larissa waves and waves again. And laughs. Then she closes her window and comes down to the courtyard and laughs again and smacks her leg heartily at the joke of her being Rapunzel the princess, and hugs Amélie hard enough for Amélie to lose her balance a little. After a quick exchange she says, "Off I go! There are men who need coffee!" Then she looks at me and Amélie both. "Come up another time. Come up anytime! There will be coffee for you, too! And cake . . ."

Here in the empire of exile, I fold my hand into my pocket for warmth as I watch Larissa go upstairs again. I feel two round bits of plastic. Amélie's doll eyes. I look up at Larissa's window.

I recall this: One day in July 1943, not long after the roundup at La

Maison des Roches, Daniel's parents traveled to Moulins to try to see him. They waited at the heavy wooden door. They looked up, searching for windows, only to be told they would not be allowed to see their son that day. So they left a package for him—one with cakes in it—and waited outside the rotten yellow walls, looking up, straining to hear. Later, they told their son François that they were just barely able to make out the sound of men talking inside. Could those have been the sounds of Daniel and his friends? The sounds of *jeu d'ambassadeurs*, the game of charades? Or of those interrogations where Daniel was slapped in the face? Or the sound of the five Jewish boys and men—George, Jacques, Leonidas, Herbert, and Charles—being hauled away for good?

I look up, straining to hear what I can, outside the walls that divide the strange us from the strange them. I strain in part because I sense there are rewards in that land of exile that have to do with the meaning of suffering, and its consequences, and its higher equations. I came here, a social scientist, looking for relief in those lovely circles I know how to draw—in the group. But the group isn't enough. And neither is Camus's Sisyphean labor against pain. Not for me.

It's time I go, myself, on my own now, over some new threshold. Toward a window, up over the wall. Up the stairs. Toward Larissa and her home and her story. With no agenda, no wheels turning, no journals, no plans. Just ears and eyes.

And, perhaps, my very own soul.

I'm alone. *Ding-dong.*

The door opens. Larissa beams.

She is standing at the threshold of the apartment where Lalik and Arat used to live. Gone are the scores of teddy bears. Gone is the clutter and the outsized noise of the television. All is perfectly clean and airy and bright now. She invites me in.

In this new, transformed space, I learn that Larissa was trained to be a cosmetologist—her eyebrows, I notice, have been tattooed on, rendering an expression of permanent openness and semipermanent delight. I learn that Larissa loves the countryside in Russia—she gives me a great big high five when I tell her how I learned to milk cows there—and hates Moscow. Ugh. Me, too! And I learn that Larissa has an Armenian mother and an Azerbaijani father, and that her father, a Muslim, told her that she doesn't have to be a Muslim, no; but that she should turn to God for protection and to ask for His will. And that her mother, a Christian, taught her the same, but with different words.

She tells me how she and her husband fled Russia after she was beaten by a group of men who knew she was of a rogue mixture of Armenian and Azerbaijani, and how she then lost the baby she was carrying. And she tells me how her father, who taught her the difference between halal and haram—the permissible and the forbidden—is dead and long gone. And how her mother is now missing.

Then Larissa says that there are days when these sorrows compass her about. On those days, she can only cry at home, alone. Sometimes Rovzan, next door, hears and comes to her. But mostly, she can't bear to see anyone then. When things are a little better, she will do anything to get people to visit. "Even if it's just for a tiny bit of coffee," she says, raising a cup. "To put my mind elsewhere. You know? Anywhere else."

I have seen how Larissa—of all the exiles here—is the one who will take care of children when their mother is in the hospital. Or when there's a meeting with a lawyer. Or when a parent needs to meet with a teacher or pick up older children at school. Others who live here in their sorrow, in the zero-sum-game calculations of suffering, can hole up into themselves, guarding their share. On the worst days, they'll even fight with each other over the smallest things. Not Larissa, who invites them all in to share a tiny coffee, and some fruit and maybe cookies, offering a wink, a laugh, a slap on the leg.

I start to visit Larissa frequently. *Moe solnyshko*, she calls me, my sunshine. But surely, she is mine. I learn that she loves to sing. I do, too. One day, I bring my ukulele and we sing, together, "La Vie en Rose." And then she asks me if I know her favorite song of all—the one she memorized, line by line, foreign syllable by foreign syllable, back in Russia. The one by Beyoncé?

Please sing it, Larissa.

And, with no need for further encouragement, no detailed sense of what the words could mean, she begins to sing a song about angels, her voice cutting, with its sweetness, through layer, after layer, of solitude:

Remember those walls I built?
Well, baby, they're tumbling down . . .

Chapter 11

SUFFER THE CHILDREN

suffer (v.) . . . : *sub-*, sub- + *ferre*, to carry; see **bher**[1].
bher[1]. Important derivatives are *bear, burden,*
birth, bring, fertile, differ, offer, prefer, suffer,
transfer, furtive, and *metaphor.*

—*AMERICAN HERITAGE DICTIONARY*

LOVE TO TRAVEL," Daniel said. So now, on August 27, 1943—after nearly two full months in Moulins Prison—where did he travel next?

North.

North, where he hadn't been for a year. North, past the line of demarcation that had once separated Vichy from German-occupied France. North, back to the place tens of thousands had fled after May 1940. North toward a place Daniel had once called home.

He was being transferred. It's still not entirely clear why. The French police kept typing *"inconnu"* next to "Reason for arrest" in his documents: Unknown. A shoulder shrug, a pout? The German military commander in France offered somewhat more detail: a document, signed by the SS chief in Paris, reading simply that Daniel Trocmé was the director of a so-called student home and had been rounded up together with a group of *"deutschfeindlichen Elemente"*—German-hostile elements—including Jews and "Red Spaniards." *Feindlich*, as in the English *fiend*.

For two months, Moulins had been dark and brutal, though Daniel clearly worked to keep up his own and others' spirits. Even while asking his parents, in some detail, for food and "pharmaceutical products," and making a general plea for news, Daniel wrote home that *"le moral est toujours bon."* Morale is still good.

But clearly he was growing anxious about the work he had been forced to abandon. What would happen to the children of Les Grillons now? How could they manage without him? In another letter he wrote from Moulins—this one to his fellow aid-worker in Le Chambon, the elderly Pastor Poivre—Daniel optimistically estimated his time away from the Plateau as, at a minimum, a few weeks. And while it couldn't have been easy to write, he added, sensibly, that "no one"—himself included—"is indispensable."

Soon, though, in that same letter, the pragmatic, the optimistic, and even the *bon moral* faded, and a series of Daniel's real anxieties were betrayed, line by line:

"I ask that you would please watch bravely over the Little Crickets," he wrote to Poivre. *Please.*

"I ought to have taken [them] on a school excursion for a couple of days," he added.

But now, of course, he couldn't.

"You *must* equally," Daniel adds, flashing the imperative *devoir*, "do the impossible, so that [the children] can get whatever particular lessons from their school that they want."

The Little Crickets had to work hard in their studies or they'd fall behind—"especially Hélène and Odette." He must have meant Hélène, of the blond bob and lopsided smile, described in class notes as "very literary" and "an artist," and Odette, the daughter of Madame Orsi, who was now selling all her family jewels just to keep the *grillons* fed.

"Send them my affection," wrote Daniel to the pastor, "and also send my affection—and my confidence—to those who watch over them."

NORTH, Daniel traveled first, mile by mile, landscape by landscape, over hills, past cities. North, toward his own past—toward Paris, the city of his higher education, his Left Bank wanderings and rebellions.

But at Paris, the roads split. Had his way tilted west, soon Daniel would have passed a soggy gray bit of rolling country, a place where he himself had once been a curly-haired little boy with big ears; where he had himself once been called *délicieux*; where he once said to his governess, "Don't cry, Mam'selle. Dani is here!" North, and then west, and that would have been the place where his eyes first deepened and darkened and then brightened again behind spectacles. Where his heart first grew sick with pericarditis. Where he had once told his sister Suzie, *"Je veux rayonner."* I want to shine.

As it was, Daniel's parents, Eve and Henri, could not have known that their son was rolling north, toward them. And although they had been doing what they could to help—the packages, with letters, food, clothing, and medicine—their son was in real trouble now. They knew how to maneuver through the worlds of ideas, of politics and the law, of business. *Who does what with whom?* Powerful people *fix things* for other powerful people—even ones who may have tilted toward prodigality in their youth. Such faith in the order of things stands, oak-like, with ever-deepening roots: It is a faith one doesn't abandon—not even under siege, not even in wartime.

But things had changed, the tectonics of the times had shifted. And though that shift had become patently obvious to the Marxes and the Balters and Goldenbergs and Wollsteins and Sterns of the world, it had not yet become so to the Trocmés.

Just beyond Paris, Daniel's road turned away from the soggy gray world of his past, under its comforts and its sure, old ways. Instead it turned *east*, toward chaos and uncertainty.

Many years of studying social memory taught me this: Changing things in the social world is hard. Not impossible, but hard. When you—as an individual or social group—get used to doing things one way, it's hard to create new pathways, new patterns for the future. It's hard to reconstruct the world. So if you are a society that fears outsiders, all kinds of other things can get wrapped up in that fear: your ideas about other people (other nations, other races); your religious orientations (does it get you to heaven to hate other people, or rather to love them?); your economies (slavery, colonialism, capitalism); your habits of power (caste systems of a million different flavors). It all gets knotted up together. Within that knot, everything seems solid, oak-like, eternal. Even if it isn't.

Very early on in my travels to the Plateau, Monsieur Bollon gave me a great hint about the fear (or not) of outsiders here. The CADA families, he said, don't always integrate very well with the local families. The asylum seekers have all suffered in their lives, and when they arrive here, they tend to stick to themselves. But—and here was the revelatory part—*the children are the bridges between the locals and the asylum seekers.*

When I first heard this thing about children and bridges, I knew what to do with it. I created, in my head, two circles—two social circles—with the local French community being one circle, and a group of strangers-in-need the other. I let the boundaries of those circles be nice and fuzzy. I sketched little circle diagrams in my journals with question marks where the circles overlapped, and arrows that pointed down to little smiley faces that, inelegantly enough, served as my shorthand for children. Then, I kept the picture of the two circles and the arrows and the smiley faces in my head and waited to see how and where and when locals interacted with asylum seekers (*who really does what with whom?*). And I waited to see when and how those individual interactions depended on children.

A list of general interactions between the two circles—without children—included some things that, while modest, were worth noting:

greeting one another on the street (instead of always crossing over before that was necessary); *smiling* at one another (instead of having flat faces); *asking* questions of shop owners or market sellers or bus drivers or postal workers or mayoral workers or case lawyers (instead of completely isolating themselves). The two circles would sit in audiences together, *watching* small performances—a local choir, a dance show, a daffodil parade. *Clapping* together.

Once children got involved in those two circles, the interactions grew richer. And sometimes far deeper. Teenagers *played* soccer together. All the kids *studied* together. They would *get crushes* on each other. One teen from Congo, aptly named Séraphin, was so handsome and so widely admired, I imagined whole sets of swooning girls had begun thinking about how they might, if they were lucky, break into his particular social circle. The asylum-seeking children would get invitations to the modest homes of their local friends: birthday parties, playdates. The parents would serve cake or ice cream or cookies. They would all *eat* together.

And sometimes, conversely, local children would get invitations to the homes of asylum-seeking families. When they did, they would walk into the CADA courtyard where the men stood and smoked and little children made massive chalk drawings on the pavement. And then they would walk farther, into neat apartments in the utter midst of the foreigners, and be invited to eat Chechen dumplings or West African peanut chicken or Armenian *shashlik*. On these occasions, the local parents would often come for the visit, too. So now, instead of just *smiling* at the strangers, or *greeting* them on the street, or *answering* their question about a bus schedule or the price of cheese, the locals would themselves take that journey through the courtyard, would themselves walk up into an apartment with new foods and new smells, would themselves sit around a table, eat. Maybe they would even laugh. Maybe they would hear a new story or two.

Well, Monsieur Bollon, of course, you were absolutely right. So, here we have two circles:

One circle of French people: fleece-wearing, rather reserved, and sometimes very kind-eyed.

Then, one circle of outsiders, in colorful clusterings in a courtyard, a Babel of languages, a kaleidoscope of chalk on the sidewalk, children leaping from box to box, children yawping by on some rickety two- or four-wheeled conveyance.

And then an *overlap*, where it is the *children*, from out of the whoops of the shared schoolyard, who pull their parents by the arm, tugging them further and further away from comfort, closer and closer to the home of a new friend. It is the children who cause the parents to *stre-e-etch* themselves beyond natural shyness or wariness or even judgment toward some new zone of overlap and intertwining.

Because of children—and their happy tug toward a benign unknown—strangers are breaking bread together. And with the breaking of bread: a beginning.

A beautiful beginning. Not yet a middle. Not yet an end.

I SIT BY MYSELF in the CADA courtyard on a windy day.

I see Khachik. Khachik is six years old. He is zooming by on a bike, all by himself, around and around, back and forth. He does this a lot. Khachik has dimples on his face—messy little dents that show up in the thick of his cheeks and under his eyes. His hair is a short brush of near black. Now and then, his brown skin flushes pink and the dimples appear: Sometimes, then, a smile breaks; sometimes it's tears.

Khachik's family arrived in France from Ukraine. Before that, they lived in Armenia. I went with Khachik on his first day of school in Le Chambon to help translate for his parents and new teachers. He wept the whole way there, his little hand braced in his father's big one as they walked, tears plopping down onto those dented little cheeks. At his last school in France, his teacher gave him a pencil and asked him to write his name. He couldn't: not in Armenian, not in Russian, not in French.

And so, in anticipation of new pencils, Khachik cried piteously, walking down from CADA; crossing the street from the church, toward the nursery; and then at the school, faced with children at play in the yard. But, as that first day unfolded, it turned out his new teacher wasn't so bad: She had bright blue eyes and a dark brow and a steady gaze. She held out her hand to shake his and, as they sat down at a table, poured out some colored pencils and outlined drawings. Khachik began to color in a house, a yard, a door. Blue, pink, orange. And then, later, at the playground, Khachik was greeted by a full-on din of small people as balls were flung about and chased; with the *psst-psst-psst* whispering, then squealing, of girls in braids and pigtails, hips cocked; with the noise of swinging and careening, sneaker-slapping running, kicking, laughing: the crescendo and diminuendo of mass play.

Maybe things won't be so bad for Khachik after all. Maybe.

I never had children. Not because, like Daniel, I was prevented by war or circumstance or choice; not because I was, more generally, like Anna Akhmatova, "rechanneled by this stern age." But simply because I never ached for one until it probably was too late. I was the kind of girl who played with Erector Sets, not baby dolls, who climbed trees instead of picking out lip-gloss flavors. And I went out into the world, eventually, and worked hard at being a professional stranger, and traveled to faraway places loaded with snow, being only ever partly inside of things, ungrounded, air-bound.

Russian women in the village where I lived would eye the width of my hips, and ask where my own babies were; would look at me first with judgment and then, as the years passed, with pity. But what could I do? I always loved the bumbling sight of little people, with their bright eyes and fresh logics. And—after years of being a little afraid of them—I learned to hold babies in my arms and whistle softly in their ears, until they would pucker their tiny mouths into a tiny letter O. Quietly, I allowed myself to smell the soft air around them.

But until Charles, I never longed for a little being like that, of my own. And this is my secret: On my very first trip to the Plateau—after waving good-bye to Charles at the Gare de Lyon in Paris, and the long train rides south, and the tiny cold hotel room, and with all my worries about whom to call in the Plateau, and what to write down in my journal, and how to solve the big fat science problem—I was, for the first time in my life, pregnant. And I didn't even know. Not long after I got back home to Charles, that child was lost. Miscarried. Leaving an outline, with an ache inside.

I sit in the courtyard and Khachik zooms by. The world of children might save us. It might save me. Khachik's face peels open: those brilliant messy dimples, splashed on the surface. Again, and again, and again.

Compiègne, in the northern region of Picardy, holds a place of significance in the annals of war history. An ancient imperial city—flanked to its south by an exceedingly lush oak and beech forest—Compiègne was the site of the capture (and sale to the English) of Joan of Arc in the fifteenth century; the place of exile of Marie de Médicis in the seventeenth century; and the spot where a group of rebellious nuns were guillotined during the Terror, after the French Revolution.

More recently, it hosted two momentous and ultimately intertwined political events. First, in November 1918, the armistice that ended the First World War was signed there in a kitted-out, Napoleonic-era railcar parked on its tracks in a clearing within the Compiègne forest. Then, in June 1940, sensing a good bit of theater, Hitler himself came to Compiègne to ratify the armistice that signaled the fall of France, right in that same railcar. After signing, Hitler smiled a little smile and stomped a little stomp. And then he rode that railcar back to Germany, where it was put on public display.

That same June, Hitler ordered the seizure of a complex of buildings on the edge of Compiègne that had served as a military hospital in the last world war. By the following summer, the site had been transformed into a fully functioning concentration camp, now called

Royallieu-Compiègne Frontstalag 122. More than fifty-five thousand people—men and women, Jews and non-Jews—would be interned at Frontstalag 122 between 1941 and 1944, with upward of three thousand living there at any one time.

Under the direct administration of the German Wehrmacht—though run mainly by French administrators—Frontstalag 122 served as a transit camp for prisoners of all kinds who, usually after a month or so, would be shipped farther east. Roughly forty thousand people were deported in convoys from Compiègne to camps in Germany and Poland, including the 1,112 Jews of France's first deportation to Auschwitz on March 27, 1942. Compiègne was used for political prisoners: communists, Resistance fighters, and other "hostile elements." Many of those were French, many of them from the elite of French society.

And so it was that on August 27, 1943, after two months and two long journeys in confinement, Daniel Trocmé found himself back north, under an open sky, carrying a suitcase with those few things he had been allowed to keep. If he arrived at Compiègne by train, as most prisoners did, he would have had to walk three or so kilometers from the train station, across the Oise River, past churches, houses, farms, and gardens, as he approached the place that would become the next stop on his journey.

There was so much he had already missed, and now the new world was a big question mark. He struggled to make sense of his new distance from home. In a letter to his parents from Moulins Prison, Daniel recalled a yearly party that they had always thrown back home, to commemorate the birthdays of his mother and his sister Suzie. How he wished he could have been there, he said. He couldn't imagine celebrating those birthdays anywhere but home.

Frontstalag 122 was different from Moulins Prison. The grounds were surrounded by walls and barbed wire, for one thing, with watchtowers perched overhead, but the buildings inside the nine-acre complex were mostly long stone barracks with large windows that let in plenty of light. Daniel could now feel air on his face. There were even some spiky trees and some grass between the buildings where, generally speaking, prisoners were allowed to circulate. One memoirist, Pierre Kahn-Farelle, went so far as to describe Compiègne as "an oasis in the desert," compared with other camps. Daniel was assigned a spot in a group of barracks labeled A—these reserved mostly for political prisoners—and a bed in A3, room number nine.

Daniel's first letter home from Compiègne, dated September 5, 1943, was written on toilet paper. In it, you can feel that his spirits have begun to rise. This place has a "great superiority" to Moulins, he wrote, "in liberty, in food, and in interest." He went over, in some detail, the kinds of packages his parents were allowed to send, asking for any kind of nourishing food in a small volume, raw or cooked. He also hoped they could retrieve his sabots—the strictly rural form of footwear he had grown fond of in the Plateau—from the cobbler in Le Chambon, together with a brand-new pair of boots that should have been ready. Daniel suggested his parents speak with Dr. Le Forestier, figuring that Le Forestier, whom they had known as a former student at École des Roches, might have connections to someone who could help get him released. His case, he wrote, should be simpler because he was, in fact, "unfit" for camps, given his debilitating pericarditis. He signed that letter, "See you soon, I hope." And, "Tenderly, Daniel."

Compiègne, with its big windows, and its air and light, and its possibility for packages, its possibility for hope, had something else to offer: Here Daniel's two worlds—his elite past and his makeshift present—had temporarily come together. Right in that oasis of a camp for communists and political prisoners was a small crew of young men with whom Daniel was already acquainted, mostly from École des Roches in Verneuil. Like Daniel, many of these young men possessed up-high connections and down-deep safety nets, part of the vast rootwork of the old and confident French elite. Among them were young men with double-barrel names like Corbin de Mangoux and Raoul-Duval and Augustin-Norman.

They were the sons of France's leaders of politics and industry and the professions. Here, a pilot; here, someone he'd met in travels in Germany in 1939; here, a pastor Daniel's parents had known, who had already begun the unpleasant business of pestering Daniel right here in the camp about his distance from Protestantism.

But along with these shades of his old life in his new confinement, Daniel was still in the company of a small group of young men he'd been arrested with. Though he had been forced to leave four students from the Plateau behind at Moulins Prison, Daniel wrote to his parents that, to his delight, he had now been reunited with four others: two French students, André Guyonnaud and Jean-Marie Schoen, as well the ostensibly Dutch students Mendel Jeret (still known as Alexandre de Haan) and Klaus Simon.

There was excellent news in this, between the lines, for Mendel and Klaus above all. To have been sent to this relatively lenient camp for political prisoners meant that no one had discovered that they were Jews. Nevertheless, they had vulnerabilities. At not even five-foot-two, neither was physically imposing, and Mendel had worn glasses from childhood. And here in the camp, they had to make their way without the connections that people like Daniel possessed. No packages from home: no food, no clothing, no books, no medicine. This was not a great surprise, given that their own families were in camps and on the brink of survival, but such extras could mean the difference between living or dying, even at Compiègne. Daniel, taking this on, wrote home: "It would be good if one might"—here he used a fancy subjunctive, *qu'on pût*—"send packages to two students from [La Maison des Roches] who haven't received anything for two months." And with that request—*poof!*—Daniel wove Mendel and Klaus into his own network, his own web of connections; into a neat and hitherto reliable landscape of his own deep past.

Their universes—of the refugees and the French political prisoners—were as different as night and day. But together, these men ate their meals, sat for roll call and mail. They spent time out of doors, where summer would soon turn to autumn and a chill would creep into the barracks at night. At Compiègne, Daniel would have been able to look at the one group, and the other, then the one, and then the other again. How far had he traveled? Where had his new compass led him?

From Daniel's letters, we know that despite this relative ease, and the relative pleasure of having the company of the four students and his old acquaintances, Daniel was cold in his room: Even the presence of many men crowded together in long rows of double bunks couldn't offset the deepening autumn chill. We know Daniel read a book a day, and asked for more. We know he was still hungry, and his health was not great. His heart was starting to bother him again in ways he had never complained of when walking his thirteen kilometers a day in the Plateau, up and down and up and down the hills.

We also know he was worrying quietly, persistently, about his erstwhile charges. "Every Little Cricket, how are they doing," he asked his parents. "I've only gotten little bits of news from you on June 23 and August 2, and the letter from Pastor Poivre from August 22, which indicated the closure of Les Grillons." And if Les Grillons was closed, where would the children go? Daniel was starting to remember details—things he'd promised the children, like making a badge for them with the Grillons coat of arms and that motto, *Agir pour tous.* How could he get the badges made? How could he pay for them? How could he make sure each child had one?

Who was watching over them?

It was a year, almost to the day, since Daniel had written to his parents and told them that in going to the Plateau, he wanted to be part of the "reconstruction of the world." Now, with his time to breathe and read and think, and his ability to sort his worries and—behind barbed wire—to sort the limits of his capacity to act, Daniel would compose another letter, this one to the Little Crickets themselves. He would write that letter on a piece of toilet paper, and fold it and hide it within the folds of another, to his parents.

That letter on toilet paper, all by itself, might have been enough of a good act for anyone to live for.

Who, after all, can reconstruct the world, if not children?

Under normal circumstances, babies can learn to produce any sound that any language conceives as meaningful—any click, glide, or gurgle. They can roll their *r*'s. They can pronounce *t*'s heavily in the back of their palate, or lightly in the front; they can curl and flap a retroflex *d* at their teeth, as in Hindi; they can click as in the Zulu languages, or master a series of glottal fricatives and ejectives as in Caucasus languages, making their speech sound a little like water flowing over rocks. They can learn the melodies of two tones in Bantu languages, or four, in Mandarin.

In time, the window of universality begins to close, though. And while toddlers and children can still learn languages with new sets of sounds, it takes them time. By adulthood, only preternaturally gifted adults can sound natively like the speakers of other languages.

It is not a sentimental notion that children can reconstruct the world. It is, if anything, a pragmatic one. They come to life with a universe of possibility—from click to glide to gurgle. In time, sound systems—like ideas about the world, and beyond that, ways of being and acting in the world—fix and harden. Rebuilding a life, a family, a community—a country—might just require forgoing that hardening, that congealing of the universe of possibilities. What if we just put it off? What if we let the clicks and the rolls and the gurgles remain—let some ideas be unset and untrained, a little strange for a while. A bit chaotic, even.

How can we make a new world, pragmatically speaking, without a little chaos? Without a little of that child, wild?

ONE DAY, here on the Plateau, the CADA children put on a shadow puppet show. A couple of local artists volunteered to help them create the stories and make the puppets and the sets. A few days ago, when I showed up at the CADA residence, the large meeting room just off the courtyard was filled with children sitting around tables busy with crayons and large pieces of cardboard. Béatrice—a social worker with pixie hair, enormous clear eyes, and a sweet, rough voice—went from table to table, to see who needed what help. Three little girls were making puppets of princesses and fairies (which Béatrice matter-of-factly defined for them as "princesses with wands"). I asked if I could help. It had been a while since I'd drawn a princess—with or without a wand—and longer still since I'd used children's scissors to cut a princess out of cardboard. But I got to work and soon there was princess after princess, each one with a different-colored dress and face and crown. At another table, older boys from Congo and Armenia were making skeleton puppets. They didn't need any help.

Now, three days later, the shadow puppet show is on, and it is a real event. Families have come down from their apartments dressed up in nice clothes—I see Rovzan in a leather coat, with her little ones, one-two-three, and her long, dark hair tucked prettily under a scarf. The place is packed with the CADA families, but also with the CADA staff, including Monsieur M—, the director. The men show Monsieur M— respect with a nod of the head.

The shadow puppet show begins.

First, it's the princesses and the fairies! Behind a thin white sheet, a light shines brightly. The little girls—themselves hidden from view—lift up all the princesses we worked on the other day, into the bright light. The girls speak so softly you can barely hear them. Their princesses are somehow interacting—can any of the girls know French yet?—with incomprehensible whispers. Like the babble of little birds. That goes on for a while, and then, at some signal, the parents all clap and the CADA workers all clap.

Then, after a beautiful entr'acte performed by the local artists, it is the boys' turn.

How the tone has changed! Now we see a building with a French flag in the background—blue, white, red. Then, in silhouette, the puppet of a man with a big belly enters. It's the mayor, we learn, in the voice of one of the boys. Then, as it happens, a witch shows up.

"*I'm* going to be mayor!" says the witch.

Well, well!

The mayor says that he's not afraid of her.

"If you're not afraid of *me*," she says, her tone rising, "will you be afraid of . . . a *ghost*?" And now a disc-shaped puppet with tissue beneath comes floating by. A drum begins to beat.

"No! I would not be afraid of a *ghost*!"

The drumming continues.

"If you are not afraid of a ghost, are you afraid of a *skeleton*?"

No!

"Then *two*? Or *three* skeletons?"

The drums continue. And the skeletons begin to dance. They dance and dance and dance—in shadow—to the beat of that drumming.

"No! I'm not afraid!"

"If you are not afraid of three skeletons, will you be afraid of . . . a *dragon*?"

From on high, a puppet with green cellophane wings and red cellophane fire coming out of its mouth swoops down! The dragon blows fire onto the mayor. The mayor sinks, dramatically, into the ground, defeated.

The witch gets on the dragon and screams: "NOW! Now *I'm* the mayor of the municipal council!"

Voilà, the denouement, brought to you—in impressively bureaucratic terms—by the child exiles.

We can't see them, but we know the African boys and the Armenian boys are crouched down, with their hands up, guiding the puppets up in the light. With their hands, they are playing out the drama of the terrors they imagine best: one witch, one ghost, one dragon. A mayor, to whom one supplicates. Three skeletons that dance and dance and dance.

Monsieur M—, with his soft, smart eyes, is sitting right next to me. He looks over at me with a smile and raised eyebrows. See? The children are watching us, too.

And I think, it's not just that there *are* social circles with all their abstract overlaps: the locals, the strangers, the fuzzy boundaries in between, the smiley faces in the overlap: The circles are filled! Filled to the brim! A fairy princess here, speaking softly; a witch there, riding a dragon. A supplication, a refusal, a threat, the very order of things turning upside down in the world of their imaginations, but maybe also in the world of what they have already lived.

You don't need a PhD in anthropology to see that these children are working out society, and power, and justice, and the means by which mayors can become witches and back again. Not just in this show, but in the whole of their exile. Theirs is not a world where your birth or your privilege or your family name will solve problems for you. It is not oak-solid, planted by the water. It is mercurial, reactive to light and heat and change. It is a world—sometimes soothing, sometimes terrifying, sometimes electric—where you will have to improvise.

Now I, too—with no real knowledge of children—am improvising. Finding myself sinking into their world, with no plan. I bring little presents. Sometimes I do it wrong, like when I give *three* little toys—two balls and a paper plane—to one Chechen mother for her *four* children to share. That caused holy mayhem. But sometimes, as with the Vakhaev children, one-two-three, I do better. They love to draw, so I bring each of them notebooks and crayons and pens, and they gobble them up. By now, when I arrive at their house, little Dzhamal, age three—with his perfect triangle face of one small chin and two large brown eyes—always comes up to me and looks at my bag and then looks at my eyes and asks what I might have for him this time.

Sooner or later all the CADA mothers ask where my children are. I don't have any, I say, over and over again. Where are they, anyway? One mother asks me, most directly—"If you don't have children, what do you have to live for?"

I give the parents chocolate and the chocolate ends up all over the children's faces. I bring my ukulele and the little ones paw at it irresistibly. There is a world of possibility here. A whole nascent galaxy, among the children. I'm drinking in their presence. It's like honey.

And maybe, just maybe, something else is going on with the children. Something—dare I say—holier?

I am struck, every time I hear it, that Judaism makes provisions, ritually speaking, for naughty children. It's pretty marvelous, really. In Exodus, Jews are enjoined: "Tell thy son" the story of the flight from Egypt. At the Passover Seder, it is the job of the youngest child at the table to ask the question: Why is this night different from all other nights? With that question, the story that lies at the heart of the Seder is set in motion, one that reminds Jews of the bitterness of exile, the meaning of their covenant with God, the awe at God's singular, devastating power, the promise of the holy return, someday, or even "next year in Jerusalem!"

And right there, in the text of the Seder known as the Haggadah, we're told that there are actually several different kinds of children. Four, to be exact: the wise child, the wicked child, the simple child, and the child who doesn't know how to ask. The striking thing is that it's not some special child who gets to ask the question: not one who won the smartness contest, or the popularity contest or the beauty contest or the well-adjusted contest. It's just the youngest who must ask, period. Whatever she is like, naughty or nice. And everyone at the table must adjust their telling to that child.

Together we must witness, together we must share the story, together we must keep things moving forward toward something better, next year. I watch Khachik—his face lately wet with tears—circle around the CADA courtyard on his borrowed bike. The Haggadah makes no special provisions, but I assume that somewhere, in the aggregate of the holiest words, there are words as well for him, the disconsolate child. Or for the child who holds up the skeleton, or for the child who holds up the princess.

And there must be, somewhere among the holiest words, provisions, too, for that one child from Dagestan. This boy's mother, Arubika, had her own rough start. As a girl, she learned to put together and take apart automatic weapons, and once had to sneak out the back door of her grandmother's home, into the forest, to retrieve an address book from her cousin's dead body. Now, her boy, here in the Plateau, can't speak in any language yet, and has a serious thing about Spider-Man; he has figured out a way to tie a T-shirt in a band over his head and then cut eyeholes in it; now, while I'm talking to his mother, he slinks up to the wall beside us and, black-masked, fingers splayed, looks right me, pauses, and hisses. *Hhhhhhssssss!*

To every child, a teacher. I see many here at CADA: Khachik's father offers his large hand to his son's small one. Mariama, little Isa's mother from Guinea, offers her fierce protection, "Nowhere, *nowhere* does it say in the Quran we are to hate each other! And *nowhere*," she adds, referring to the forced circumcision that she fled her country for, "does it say that we are to *cut* women!" Arubika offers kisses and more kisses until they run out and her brow clouds over, darkly. "Pity the children! Pity them!" she says, looking down at her littlest ones, like a mantra. "I pity no one, but I pity *them*."

I, too, had my protectors; I had my teachers—holy to me. Through the gentleness of his face, and the intelligence of his eyes, Allan Levine, our family's first beloved rabbi, made me feel—lifted over the Torah, honey candy in my hand—both seen and safe. Back when we knew him, Rabbi Levine was fresh from jail in Jackson, Mississippi—mug shot number 21217—having been arrested trying to integrate an airport, alongside Martin Luther King, Jr. That, too, was instructive. And, from a little later in my childhood, I can still hear Margaret Lindsay reciting Bahá'í prayers. Her voice was inflected with mysterious dignities, carried northward to black neighborhoods with the Great Migration. Children would sit in a circle on the floor of her home, while Margaret would pray and, through that voice, teach us about what it means to be moved to some great, noble elsewhere.

Then there was Miss Palmeri. I haven't thought of her in many years. For some reason, though, her story comes rushing to me now.

I was eight years old. It was nighttime and I was in the hospital. I was getting a small operation on my ears the next morning. I needed tubes put in them so I could hear better. I remember the shiny brown-orange linoleum floors. Remember wondering if I would get to keep the little plastic things they give you to use in the hospital—a cup, a pitcher, some wipes.

The lights were out in my room, except for the bright yellow one over my bed. There were other children in other beds. The hall beyond was still lit up. I remember being afraid of what it would feel like when it was completely dark.

Only I had a visitor. It was Miss Palmeri, my third-grade teacher, who came in and sat down on the edge of my bed. I was a kind of quiet misfit in her class—the sort of kid the other kids picked on. Miss Palmeri was very young, with thick, wavy hair and bell-bottoms and a purse with leather fringes. She was beautiful. Some days, she would let me eat lunch sitting next to her in the classroom, while the other kids filled the raucous lunchroom.

Here, in the circle of yellow light, surrounded by dark, Miss Palmeri sat and talked with me. I don't remember anything she said—just her calm and her smile. And she had gifts. First, there was a pile of get-well cards, all in pink construction paper, made by every single kid in the class. Even the kids who really didn't like me. Some had even cut out hearts and glued them on the cards and colored them with crayons.

And then, Miss Palmeri handed me something else. A book, tall and thin. Opening it, I saw that there were bright drawings inside—of a yellow-haired boy on a tilted little planet, another with the boy and a baobab tree, another with him planting a rose, or talking with a fox, or a snake. In clear, round letters on a blank sheet where the book began, I saw that Miss Palmeri had written a special message for me. In it, she said that she knew I would read this book many times over the years. And that someday, she believed, I would come to understand the secret of this boy, the Little Prince.

Soon, it would be all blackness in the hospital room. Soon, it would be time to be afraid again. But, by way of response, the Little Prince would offer me an antidote to fear, if I could learn it: *On ne voit pas bien, qu'avec le coeur.*

One doesn't see well—in the light, he might have added, or in the dark—except with the heart.

THE SUBJECT OF MEMORY, which I labored over for so many years, seems to be rooted in the past, but it isn't; not really. The subject of memory is the *present*. It's all about the present. We don't remember together—at a Seder, or anywhere else—because it will somehow change what has happened; we remember together, around all kinds of tables, because we want what happened in the past to guide or shape our world today. When we remember together, when we conjure that past together, we don't call on Pharaoh to return with his chariots, we don't ask for slavery or plagues to come back; but we call on our *children* to learn the covenant—such as it might be—to know it, to re-create it with every new year. To ask the questions, and then, right away, to start answering them, learning as they go.

This, I also know: Maybe, just maybe, the children, all the children—the wise, the wicked, the hissing, the crying, the kissing ones, the ones afraid of the dark—can learn anything at all, if they begin early enough. Maybe they really *must* be the ones to make the world right again, to rebuild it—as in Hebrew, *tikkun olam*—to make it right. Maybe, loosed, they can teach us all, rechannel our age.

Suffer the children! Even the fragile children, the ones who still see nightmares from what they've lived before. They are all our hope.

***

One-two-three. And now, with baby Sulim, *four.* Four Vakhaev children.

"What is this?" I ask Zezag.

"It's a crocodile. A crocodile that has eaten two serpents." The serpents are inside a figure that I now see has two big eyeballs, some big round teeth, and lines of legs radiating outward from it. The serpents are smiling.

Zezag, four years old, the Uzhasnaia Printsessa, the beautifully horrid princess, with her long, brown hair still wet from her first school trip to the pool, goes back to her place at the table and takes the pen again and takes the little notebook again and draws some more, and then comes back to me, looking up:

"These are two *more* serpents. They are hiding in the grass." This second couple of serpents, too, are smiling.

Zezag draws, and draws, making her world. And after every new picture, she squeaks, giggles, and runs over to her mother and then to me to show us, and to describe it in strange, marvelous contours. Here a worm is swimming in the ocean, smiling. Here a house under a smiling half-sun, perched on four skinny flowers. Each time she shows me something, I clap for her drawing, and she smiles a crooked smile—like the serpent, the sun, and the worm—and runs off to start something new.

Here at the Vakhaevs' house, with the kids drawing and Rovzan cooking and tending to the baby, and Akhmad playing with the kids and talking with me, it is happy chaos all around.

Sometimes Fariza, Zezag's older sister, with her long, blondish hair and wary eyes, takes a pen. Fariza draws her father, and everyone laughs because the nose is so pronounced. She draws a little swirl for his chin. It makes him smile. She draws flowers, a tremendous tulip with a huge yellow bulb and a fortress of petals on the top, then a small stem and leaves in green. Then animals! *Hu iu?* I ask, in what I believe to be the Chechen words for *What is that?* A dog, a cat. Fariza makes long-bodied beasts with mouths attached to their heads in a circle with teeth coming out all around it; she makes a dog in brown, with lines for fur, and limbs coming out of its side. And a person with a triangle body and a huge circle over the head, filled with short stick lines, like a dark, rain-filled thought cloud.

Dzhamal joins in. He gets his own pen and now he's drawing his mother: a head and a nose and some grass underneath. Sometimes his father, Akhmad, takes a pen and helps the boy. Akhmad's lines are liquid, graceful. When his sisters draw, Dzhamal draws; when his sisters dance, he dances; when they wrestle, he wrestles. Still only three, he throws himself into their lessons. He's behind, but he throws himself in.

Once in a while, the baby cries from the other room, and someone lifts the light blue swaddled bundle and brings him to me to rock, to hum at, to whistle at like a bird. The baby puckers its lips, calmed. The family coos, in praise of my own soft whistle and the baby's renewed peace.

I visit as often as I can, now. The children wrap their small hands around my neck to say hello. They pretend to do a magic show, with an "Abracadabra and *voilà!*" I find myself patting their heads when they poke me in the side and say, "*'garde, 'garde, 'garde, 'garde!*" "Look, look, look, look!"

Akhmad has his hard days of worry and sorrow, and there are visits when his face is so downcast and he is so jumpy that nothing seems to be able to cheer him, though he always remains kind and attentive with his children. Rovzan has days of sorrow, too. There are the memories of her first days in France—memories I have seen cause the hairs on her arms to stand up. You'd never know Rovzan's sorrow from her face, though. She keeps the memories hidden from her eyes and her bearing. In quiet moments, she holds the baby and talks with me in her soft, low voice.

There are three things from the Quran that must be understood, she says, teaching me. First, that after three days, we must forgive a trespass or we must forget it. Second, that we are allowed to judge someone else only if there are seventy reasons to do so. Since that is never possible, we are never allowed to judge. Third—and this she says looking me straight in the eye—"We are told we must love one another. That is it. That is it. That is what we must do."

Somehow, with all their worry and their sorrow—hidden or not—Rovzan and Akhmad have made a home where there is easy affection, voracious creating, and laughing, and abracadabra and *voilà!* They've created children who are, as far as my eyes can see, perfect. Their compass seems to know the way, with or without suffering, to a kind of true north.

And because of this, I finally tell her, one day, alone, about my childlessness, about my miscarriage, about the outline with the ache inside. I have told almost no one else in the world. She looks at me, all searing kindness under her dark brow.

When it's time to leave their home after each visit, Dzhamal has now made it a habit to carefully bring my blue bag to me—the same bag that used to hold my journal and now, once in a while, holds the small presents for them all. He slings the bag across his little chest, and it's so long it almost touches the floor as he carries it to the door. He then looks up at me at the threshold and says, *"Tu ne sors pas."* You don't leave.

I come so close to happiness with this family. Sometimes I think can't bear it.

It is now early September 1943 at Frontstalag 122, and Daniel wishes to write a letter. He has been at the camp two full weeks now, with more light and air and space, and with better, more nourishing food. Two weeks in which to think.

There is much to say, and only a small sheet of toilet paper on which to say it.

Daniel, teacher, takes a pen and, weighing every word, begins.

Compiègne, September 12, 1943

Dear Little and Big Crickets,

It is on a hot Sunday afternoon that I write you on this deluxe paper. When I was leaving you on that morning of June 29, I told you I would have real adventures to relate when I got back. And that has been true, even if the adventures haven't exactly been wonderful. Still, I believe that this separation brings us closer, in reality, because now I will know a little better the adventures that so many of your parents have lived through. We will have plenty of memories in common. You know well that you are never far from my thoughts, and one of the greatest joys I promise myself is seeing you again. That will be magnificent.

In this letter, I want to tell you two things.

First, those of you who think that I will no longer be interested in them after the war, and that their adventure and their isolation will resume, are wrong. I will never leave you by my own will. You can have confidence; and I hope that I will not have to wait too long before I see you again.

And then, a second thing. This is a recommendation. A recommendation for each one of you, from the littlest to the biggest, and different, in its way, for all of you. Evidently, you all have your worries, your qualities, your flaws, your misfortunes, your melancholies, your characters, your anger, your laziness, your pride . . .

Always endeavor, always try, to master yourselves. Be united among yourselves, and be sure that there are no surprises when I come back, with such-and-such a bit of news.

You know as well as I have, for a long time, that our family is fragile. There are always difficulties to conquer. Our big family is so young, it is necessary for each one of us to take care of it, like a little tree, like one of those little fir saplings you find on the road to Les Grillons. And each one of us must take care, each day, many times, not to break it.

Have courage. Have will. Have generosity. Be wise and good, my dear Crickets, and think of the adults who have endured so much for you, and who love you, too. Nothing creates more evil than an ill-placed word directed at someone we love. So be kind to them, to those who love you. And be grateful.

Very affectionately,
Daniel Trocmé

Chapter 12

SONG OF THE
CHEREMSHA

―――――

It is related that one day they came upon Majnún
sifting the dust, and his tears flowing down. They said,
"What doest thou?" He said, "I seek for Laylí." They
cried, "Alas for thee! Laylí is of pure spirit, and thou
seekest her in the dust!" He said, "I seek her
everywhere; haply somewhere I shall find her."

—BAHÁ'U'LLÁH, *THE SEVEN VALLEYS*

BACK WHEN HE WAS in Beirut in the mid-1930s, Daniel wrote to his
parents that they shouldn't believe that he was "so much of the extreme left." Daniel was seeking then, and he would keep seeking. To a
young European of the time, the left was attractive at least in part because it took very seriously the problem of how to fix the very broken
world. Over the previous century, Karl Marx and then his successors had
offered a clarifying answer, with an entire economic theory that rested
on what Marx assumed we need, most fundamentally: eating and drinking and the like. From those economic fundamentals, it seemed obvious
to Marx that we would end up making a world of perpetual war.

Decades passed; empires crumbled; kings were deposed; revolutions exploded.

In the autumn of 1943, the German army was in retreat. But if you lived in Europe then, you wouldn't have known that to hear it. Pressures of all kinds kept mounting rather than easing—with the questions always swirling of what to eat; how to work; how, in the upside-down world of war, to construct some measure of normalcy. Everywhere, there were food shortages: Bread, meat, cheese, sugar, butter, and rice were all strictly rationed. Nor were the sounds of conflict—from the barking of policemen to the falling of shells—ever far, and canopies of barbed wire still wrapped around the edges of once stately homes and pastoral fields. Young men continued to be called up by a nervous, angry, and increasingly insecure state; not even the velvety golden youth from the world before the war were immune from the general call to the Service du Travail Obligatoire. Those who went to work for the Germans became slaves to that state; those who didn't became outlaws. Everywhere and—unless a person was able to numb himself completely—every day there were small and large moral decisions that weighed on the mind and heart: Do I share? Do I not share? Do I resist? Do I get along?

As the days and weeks pressed on, thousands were deported to concentration camps and extermination camps. Thousands were gassed to death. Thousands fell to artillery, and thousands more to the plagues of war: typhoid fever, tuberculosis, dysentery. And thousands, when given the choice between buoyancy and bitterness, were choosing bitterness.

On the weakening Eastern Front, Germany had new concerns. With the Red Army poised to take back the city of Kiev in the summer of 1943, one especially pressing challenge was how to quickly erase the traces of the Nazis' colossal crimes there. The ravine at Babi Yar—still host to a hundred thousand corpses under a thin layer of dirt and rocks—was a particular conundrum. The normal method for getting rid of this kind of evidence, which had been used by Nazis as a matter of practice throughout the war, was to disinter the bodies and burn them. At Babi

Yar, however, the site was an almost incalculable enormity; erasure would take some planning. So for a month, beginning in late August 1943, Russian prisoners of war were forced to dig up the corpses and place them—fifteen hundred at a time—on great funeral pyres where they would burn for two nights and a day. The prisoners would then collect the ashes and spread them over the fields beyond. Despite this fantastical effort, Bill Downs, a journalist from *Newsweek* who passed through the site in December 1943, spoke of coming upon "bits of hair and bones and a crushed skull with bits of flesh and hair still attached"— a pair of glasses here, a dental bridge there. Babi Yar was not for effacing. And as the months and years clicked by, the site periodically asserted its own terrible remembrance. In March 1961, when Kiev was victim of a mudslide after a great rain, chunks of bone could be seen coursing along the streets of the city, following the flow of mud out of the ravine. Residents said, "It's the Babi Yar curse."

But now, in this autumn of 1943, even as the Russian prisoners of war dug up those corpses and wondered rightly if the very last funeral pyre they built would be their own, a small group of young men in barracks division A at Frontstalag 122 Compiègne, were feeling the first chills of a new cold season and trying to figure out how they themselves might survive this war. What did they need to do? What did they need to have? Who would be next? And in the meantime, while still here in this relative oasis, what could be done to amass all that they needed, or might end up needing—the things that somewhere, in colder or more distant climes, they couldn't live without?

Daniel, who had been at Compiègne since August 31, was working on this puzzle, too. If, early on, he'd pinned his hopes on the fact that his heart condition would make him unfit for camps and therefore set him free, it must have been sinking in that this was not such a sure thing. Though the official paper trail surrounding Daniel's arrest thins out for a while, it is clear that the authorities still didn't know quite what to do with him. Daniel's maternal uncle Charles Rist, an economist and public intellectual with connections, got in touch with a certain well-placed lawyer named Mettetal, who had successfully freed even some Jews from camps, including Rist's own wife. But it was not so easy. Daniel, who had been able to take his own essential freedom for granted for almost his whole life, clearly could no longer do so.

What, then, did Daniel, in these surprising new circumstances, need?

Well, there was food—so perilously limited in prison—for which Daniel continued to write requests to his parents, praising them with lavish gratitude for the packages they had already sent. "Thank you infinitely for the magnificent honey," he wrote with uncharacteristically florid adjectives, "for the splendid butter, the Nestlé flour, the sugar, the cookies or, rather, the cakes." Getting down to business, he also included instructions: "The apples and the cookies are equally welcome, but less indispensable at the present time. If you can, try for more pastas or flour or dry vegetables without neglecting fats and sweet things. Some salt, too, please."

So. Daniel needed food. Of course he did. But what else did he need?

Warmth. His parents had sent him some long underwear; he thanked them for those and said he would save them for later because they had already gotten him a warm blanket and it was really helping. Then there was the pyrethrum powder (or, as he specified, anti-vermin lotion). Toilet paper. Touchingly, he told his parents that he had, at times "nostalgia for a good, small comfort, which I have never known." These comforts now made a simple trifecta: a warm-enough blanket, protection from the mauling of insects, a way to properly clean himself.

What else? Books. Please, please, books. Always more books. These had to go through censors, of course, but he'd been reading Balzac, Shakespeare, and the French Romantic poet Alfred Vigny (who once wrote, as he was dying, *"Seul le silence est grand; tout le reste est faiblesse."* Only silence is great; everything else is weakness); there were bits of Goethe, and *Don Quixote*, and *Madame Bovary*, and Voltaire's *Age of Louis XIV*. Books of poetry, of art, of history. Lesson books. Dante's *Inferno*.

What else?

Daniel thanked his parents, "infinitely," for the cigarettes.

But what else? What more?

If you read Daniel's letters and you didn't know any better, you would think that what Daniel needed most of all was news. He asks for "much" news, "precise" news, "precious" news, "rare" news, news about "every Little Cricket," news about life at home. More news, more, more, more: Words that might conjure a picture of that place where he felt loved and, perhaps most importantly, was himself able to love. Words that could bring back to life, if only for an instant—and then, solidly on paper, over and over again—that place he had come to rescue, that place that may instead have been rescuing him. News! The conjurings of children's faces, of moments around a fireplace, flames flickering them all in warmth. A moment he had managed to teach something. Or solve a problem. Or make peace.

Only news like that, news with those faces, wasn't coming much anymore. After the terrifying raid at Roches, the children of Les Grillons had started to disperse, away from the Plateau. Young Peter had left Le Chambon, together with his friends Kurt and Jean, heading west to a town called Figeac. There, Peter went back to school, but also learned how to pour sugar packets into the engines of motorcycles and delight at how the engines would then pop and fail afterward. Fanny, the oldest girl at Les Grillons, who had greeted the raid so mournfully, also left the Plateau, going back into hiding, back into new unknown villages—once, as she told it later, among a herd of goats—back to a place where she would eventually find her parents. Many years later, that mournful Fanny would say, when asked if she had any message for the future, just, "Love each other. Love everyone. Everyone. No difference of color or race or religion. Just to love everybody. That's my message."

Now, all of these years later, we know something about Peter and Kurt and Jean and Fanny; and we know that Suzy Heim survived to tell the story of how Daniel would help her with her math homework and watch the children at night. But what about pretty Rosario, whom Peter was in love with? Or the brothers who had given Daniel so many headaches, even while garnering his affection? Or, maybe especially Régine—Régine, of whom I have never found a single further trace, beyond that one photograph, with her fuzzy brown bob and her sweet, plain face, and her three-quarter turn to the right.

Daniel needed news about his beloved children. And that news wasn't coming.

It's true that at Compiègne, Daniel appreciated some measure of the companionship of his small group of "outcasts," as he called the friends and acquaintances from the Plateau and elsewhere. They would talk at meals, go on about old times, debate politics and books. Daniel even wrote home about giving a lecture to his campmates on his travels in Syria. And Daniel was still working to secure some packages for his students who were without their own:

"Beloved parents," he wrote on October 10. "Life continues calmly, with less reading, but a marked improvement since you sent the package to [Klaus] Simon. Could you please write to W. H. Follander, P. Kruger-str. 45, Hengelo, Holland, that Klaus Simon is in good health and has received his letter. He waits for packages and will write as soon as possible. . . . Thank you for all these things that are so difficult to find but which truly change our existence."

But all of this was precarious. On Thursday, October 28, at Frontstalag 122 Compiègne, 938 names were called. Among those names were the four young men with whom Daniel had been arrested at Roches, with whom he had shared a floor to sleep on at Moulins, with whom he had shared his food when he was hungry and the news of his own beating, with no time to take off his glasses. And with whom he had become, at some point, friends.

One of these young men lived to describe what happened next. All 938 were loaded onto the cattle cars that made up Convoy 28. They were ordered to take off their clothes, mauled by bloodhounds, and beaten. One man who fell down during the melee was shot and killed because he couldn't get up. There was nothing to drink on the car, so two days later, when the convoy arrived at its final destination of Buchenwald, twenty of the 938 were already dead. But our young man—still alive—was fingerprinted, given striped clothing to wear and the prisoner number 31017. And he was photographed. *Click*. His intake papers from October 30, 1943, say that he was 157 centimeters tall—barely five-foot-two; build, slim; face, oval; eyes, brown; nose, straight; ears, slightly protruding; teeth, full; hair, dark brown. And, with the stamp of an upside-down triangle, colored red, the intake papers also say that he is a political prisoner (and not a Jew). And so he lived.

Nevertheless, at Buchenwald, this young man was required to carry gravestones from here to there. Those who didn't do it properly were beaten. And beaten again. Others were hanged. He learned about medical experiments on fellow prisoners. Heard about how the wife of the camp commandant, Ilse Koch—known to history as the Bitch of Buchenwald—would make lampshades out of the skin of tattooed men.

This young man was Klaus. Klaus, whose intake photo at Buchenwald, *click*, betrayed a face of soft beauty just on the edge of manhood.

Klaus and the others were gone from Daniel now. Gone, these precious friends Daniel needed. And so, as the autumn days darkened, and the cold whipped its northern wind around the barbed wire at Compiègne, what did Daniel need that he might yet be able to find?

On November 9, 1943, Daniel wrote a short letter: "Dear Parents, Thank you for the package. . . . My students, Schoen, Guyonnaud, Simon, and de Haan, have departed on the last convoy, as well as Corbin and Laventure. So, attention: don't send any more packages for de Haan or Simon. Let Le Chambon know."

For Daniel, it was a new sort of catastrophe. A new aloneness in the dark of this new autumn, so different from last year's, when he'd first arrived on the Plateau, full of hope, looking to reconstruct the world. In the weeks ahead, Daniel began to get sick, on and off. Sent to the infirmary, for shorter and longer stints, he began writing home about "indispositions" that took him out of circulation for a few days—though he never mentions that it was his heart that was causing many of the troubles. He asked for news, and again, more news. And nothing came. And he was ever more alone.

⸻

This is my work now: I come to the Plateau. I am invited for meals around tables; I listen to stories; play with children; translate. I take long walks alone through the forests. Then, when I must, I go back home to think.

I'm home now, thinking. Today, I've taken another trip back to the Holocaust Museum. I've got some archival work I need to do that should help me understand the fate of some of the people who passed through the Plateau during the war. There is much, still, to learn.

I am in an elevator with two women from the museum—Regina and Betsy—going up. This elevator, like all the elevators here at the museum, is industrial dark and gray, with streaks of rust red. Regina is fiddling with the chunky green stones of her necklace. Her face is feathery soft and white; she is very small and rather old.

Regina, who volunteers at the museum, was born in Radom, Poland, in 1926; was smuggled out of the Jewish ghetto there in 1939; worked in a munitions factory at the start of the war—where she met her future husband, Sam—and was eventually deported to Auschwitz and tattooed with a five-digit number. On Regina's days here at the museum, she sits at a table at the entrance to the permanent exhibit and fields questions about her life in Poland during the Second World War. Betsy, for her part, works at the museum doing research with the International Tracing Service—a massive database that originally helped people find their lost loved ones after the Second World War—but also tends to the volunteers who sometimes, like today, might need help getting onto and off of elevators.

The elevator begins to climb. Looking down toward the smallest person in this closed space, Betsy speaks with warm, clear diction:

"Regina, this is Maggie. She is one of our research fellows."

Regina smiles up at me with a bit of blur in her eyes.

"And," Betsy adds, bending closer to Regina's ear, speaking just a little louder, "Maggie also sings in a band."

It's strange, but true. Just as I began going to the Plateau, I joined Doc Scantlin's Imperial Palms Orchestra—a '20s-, '30s-, and '40s-style big band here in Washington, D.C. Betsy knows this about me, but not everyone in my life does.

Folks here at the museum—researchers, archivists, and librarians—have felt close, quickly. I guess that makes sense. In a university or research institute you might just pass your colleagues in the hall—greeting each other with polite nods, for years on end—all while guarding your real life, your real self, for elsewhere. But here at the museum, you work together—with your big, urgent questions—inside a wall of images of the worst of what we are. The research projects here are very broad; the work hums with inexorable purpose. And inside that purpose, there's really nowhere to hide—no safe, closed office; no easygoing watercooler. There are nightmares, shared. And tears. And arguments—not the baloney kinds—but real ones, ones that matter.

And so, inside these dark walls, museum folks have very quickly come to feel like a tribe to me, one that welcomed me despite how unformed and ignorant I was at first. They have been with me on some of my most indelible days, like the one when I was watching the video of a long, hard interview with a survivor. That survivor was now an old man with a soft voice, and as he told his story, it began to dawn on me that he had been present at the raid at La Maison des Roches—but due to a simple variation in the spelling of his name, he had been erroneously categorized by historians as "missing without a trace." But now, as I heard the man recount the details of the raid, the beatings, the cattle cars to camps, I realized that he was, in fact, Klaus Simon. Klaus wasn't missing. He had a trace. And for my part, upon realizing all this—with my tribe to my right and to my left, in front of me and behind—I cried, finally and fully, into my hands.

The museum people know things about me that other people don't. And not just the dark things. They know the things that save me from the dark. Like the improbable fact that I periodically put on sparkle costumes and feathers for the Imperial Palms Orchestra, and sing "Skylark" and dance the Mooche. And now today, on this Holocaust Museum elevator going up, Regina—still fiddling with her chunky green necklace—knows this fact, too.

She looks up toward Betsy quizzically, and then up toward me with what appears to be alert, vaudevillian timing.

"A band? Really?" she says, smiling broadly now—her *r*'s rolling thick in the back of her throat. Rrrreeally?

"Yes, in fact, we do a Yiddish song," I say. "Bei Mir Bistu Sheyn."

Rrrreeeally?

"Bei Mir Bistu Sheyn," which means "To me you are beautiful," was originally composed for the Yiddish stage in 1932 by Russian-born Sholom Secunda, with lyrics by Jacob Jacobs. The song grew popular in Nazi Germany—that is, until its Jewish origins were discovered—and soon it also made a splash with African American performers in Harlem, still in Yiddish. In 1937, the song was translated into an English version, with phrases from other languages tossed in—"I could say bella, bella, even say, wunderbar!"— and in that form it became the Andrews Sisters' first big hit. The Imperial Palms Orchestra does an approximation of that Andrews Sisters version, with three of us wearing floaty pink dresses and orange flowers in our hair, and with plenty of reed and brass behind us.

Of course, Regina knows the song. And there in the industrial elevator, with her hand still on her green necklace, she begins to sing:

"Bei mir bistu sheyn . . ."

(In my head, I hear the trumpets that follow, *ba-da!*)

I ask myself: Is this really happening?

I start with the next line: "Please let me explain . . ."

Then: "No!" Regina stops me. "No, no, no . . . You have to sing the whole thing . . . in *Yiddish!*"

Regina starts over. *"Bei mir bistu sheyn . . ."* Her voice wobbles a little with age, but the faintest smile has lit up her eyes.

She sings the song now, syllable by syllable, line by line, turn by turn, in the language of my ancestors. She is looking up at me, coaxing its meaning in my direction. *You are this to me, you are that to me. You are beauty, charm, gold.*

I can see 1937 in Regina's face now. I can see the girl who knows this song, singing every word. And—just like Regina, I bet—I hear the swell in the orchestra coming 'round the bend, at the end:

Bei mir bistu eyner oyf der velt!
To me, you are the only one in the world!

With that last word, *"velt,"* that word, "world," Regina looks up over our heads there in the dark elevator. And, smiling after a pause, she adds a final curlicue to the song—a final high, sly sigh:

Oooooii!

And then the elevator doors of the Holocaust Museum open. And that's that.

I have now seen a photograph of Regina as a young woman—with a head full of dark, thick hair and round cheeks and a girlish face, pre-giggle. I think about how, at that infamous ramp at Auschwitz, this young woman was sent to the right, to work, rather than to the left, to the ovens. I think about how, in the chaos and infinite loss after the war, Regina's future husband, Sam, heard she'd been spotted in Katowice, Poland, boarding a train for Radom, and then—in a grand gesture—sent a horse and buggy for her. And how the two were married in a displaced persons camp, under a makeshift chuppah raised up by hand on four wooden poles, and would go on to have three children, who in turn would give them nine grandchildren.

Regina became the kind of person who lets crowds of children look at her arm with the dusty blue tattoo, and ask her questions—no matter how hard or painful. And she became the kind of person who, in a dark elevator going up, can just start to sing, without inhibition, to a stranger.

Leaving the museum that day, I open the doors to a sunlight that stabs my eyes. And I am left to myself to wonder how any of this is possible.

I HAVE BEEN STRUGGLING so hard to find some bit of light, looking everywhere, in these darkest places, for answers. The light hurts. I think of how the Persian epic hero Majnun (whose very name means "crazy") loses his beloved Layli (whose very name means "night"), and then searches for her everywhere, even in the mortal dust.

Well. This is what my mortal dust looks like right now:

Humanity—in both its individual and aggregate forms—is capable of scales of depravity and baseness that would seem unimaginable if, time and again, they hadn't actually been realized. If anyone were to doubt it, they'd need to just take in one single eyeful at the museum, and there it is: evidence of what even the greatest civilizations, with the most pompous assurance of their own moral ascendency, are capable of. There's no hiding from that.

We need that eyeful. We need that remembrance.

I know depravity isn't the essence of who we are. I'm just so sad and tired and angry these days—that so much of social science is oriented around our ugliness and our selfishness. How we gobble wealth. How we seize power. How we are inclined toward violence and war. Why?

Why, when there are so many corners of human action that can teach us about other realms?

Don't tell me that we all act to maximize our self-interest when there is a Regina who shows her tattoos to children.

Don't tell me villagers in the Plateau risked their lives sheltering strangers—or wayfaring Daniel let himself be hauled off into the desolation of the camps—because it made them feel good about themselves.

Or that the business of eating and drinking, as important as it is, defines the whole of who we are.

I went to school; I can speak logical positivism and Karl Marx; I know about existentialisms categorical, and about the destruction of the master narrative; I can fight in a duel on the side of constructivisms of all kinds, and I can win. I still believe in science. I believe that variables—even in the social sciences—are best served clear and precise, and I know the infernal muck that is created when they are not. I know that when magical thinking pairs with cheap tribalisms—whether of religious or nationalist kinds—we become the worst of who we are.

I know all that.

But the choice isn't between magic, on the one hand, and science on the other. It can't be.

I believe in science. But I don't want to live in a world of science that has no room for *bei mir bistu sheyn*—a science that can't reach deep down into its first principles and find the hallowed place of the things that are, to us, beautiful.

———

Today, it's one of the very first bright days after an achingly long winter on the Plateau. I'm in the courtyard, with Marzet and her family again. Fuzzy-haired and apple-cheeked, Marzet is from a family who fled the conflagrations of Chechnya, conflagrations that caused her husband, Mairbek, to lose a leg, and caused them to live, for years, in near-constant mortal fear. Mairbek sits under the shade of a tree; their three little girls play nearby. Only the eldest girl, Deshi—eight or so, with slate-gray dots for eyes—seems to talk, and she talks in my direction. Deshi has been following me around from house to house for two days now—even to the houses of families that don't particularly get along with her own. But of course, she's too young to know about that. *Ding-dong,* she's at the door, with daffodils in her hand and her silent little sisters in tow, one of whom looks remarkably like a tiny Sinéad O'Connor.

Deshi's voice when she greets me today is whispery and incongruously low. "You said you'd come by. Why didn't you?"

Well, I've come now, and Mairbek is sitting, and the girls are playing, and Marzet waves from a patch of garden where she's been planting something. I'm not sure I've ever seen a woman who is more constantly busy doing immediately useful things. On the days when she isn't indisposed, she invites me in for food and tea and, tossing her mop of curly hair back, laughs generously at my jokes and sneaks a song with me on the ukulele.

But things aren't so easy with Mairbek. I have, in fact, been a little afraid of him. Well, "afraid" is too strong a word. Yes, he's very tall—towering, even when he stands up on the tripod of his two crutches and one strong leg. Scruffily bearded and gruff, with a special flair for the sarcastic. At my first big CADA meeting with all the residents, when Monsieur M— asked me to translate, saying, "I'll let Maggie explain to you why she is here," Mairbek added under his breath, *"za informatsiiu,"* for information, as though I were some kind of spy. And there have been aching moments, like when Amélie needed help explaining to Mairbek what the doctor had said about his kidneys—including details about his poor anatomy that no stranger should know. That day, Amélie looked at Mairbek and talked with her hands, and I looked down at the sidewalk, translating only when necessary, so Mairbek wouldn't have to catch my eye.

I have gathered, without asking, that Mairbek's life had terrible episodes back in Chechnya, and not just the loss of his once-strong leg. There was the time he had to jump out of a hospital window to save himself from who-knows-which killers. There were the constant bombs overhead, which have caused his children, even here and now, to scream at night whenever they hear a plane. In Mairbek's family, there was a murdered younger brother, the apple of his mother's eye; and a cousin who was kidnapped one day when she went into the forest to look for berries, then forced into servitude by the "people of the woods."

It's not that I'm afraid of Mairbek, exactly, but I have certainly given him a wide berth. I can see the pain in his eyes. And the anger. But I've also seen his tenderness with children, how he kisses his own, holds them, balancing them on his half-empty lap, correcting them gently when they need. In his gruffness and his chain-smoking, there is something that feels grounded to me, and real.

And so today, with little Deshi clutching her daffodils, chattering softly—and now getting scolded in Chechen by her mother—I decide I will try to talk to Mairbek.

"How are you?" I ask, directing my question into his patch of shade. I don't know if I should call him the informal *ty* (which I call all the Russian speakers here, except the elderly ones) or the formal *vy*. I try for a *ty* and see what happens.

Plokho, he says, now leaning on one of his crutches, looking up at me. "Bad."

Bad? Why?

Khochu miaso. "I want meat."

I know they've just been to the Resto du Coeur, and that means that the families—including his—each got a pretty big pile of food to take home. So what about meat?

"Can't eat that meat."

"Oh! Right," I say. "It isn't halel."

"Ha*lal*!" yells a smiling Marzet, listening in from the little garden patch, correcting the pronunciation I'd learned in Kabardino-Balkaria.

I went to the Resto myself last fall. There was plenty of donated food for the families in need—including the CADA families—according to the family's size and composition: pasta and cheese and yogurt and desserts, and cans of vegetables and sticky sweet things. And some frozen fish. And milk for babies. And yes, there was a lot of meat for these families, too, but come to think of it, it was, in fact, mostly pork: lardons, pâtés, ham in its many forms.

And of course, pork is not halal. For Mairbek, that means it's not food. Not something you can eat. Not unless you are dying.

Ne mogu kushat' eto miaso. I can't eat that meat.

Right. It's not just that pork is forbidden in the laws of the Quran. Pork isn't this thing that you can't have but you really, really want and sometimes just indulge in—like the bacon that my grandpa Sheldon undoubtedly relished when it wasn't patently disrespectful to do so. In

Kabardino-Balkaria, I finally figured out, pig meat, for many Muslims, is simply disgusting. It doesn't help that pigs, as animals, are seen to be mud-dwelling, dirty, and disgusting, too, even before slaughter. So telling someone from this background to go ahead and eat the pork—eat it if you're hungry!—is a little like telling someone else that they should go ahead and dine on vulture, say, or long-tailed rat.

No. Real meat—that's something else. And without real meat—the clean and wholesome kind—you can be hungry from the depths of your stomach, from the bottom of your once long limbs, from your very heart. You can be hungry for a day, a week, months, a year, watching the snows and winds come and go. Watching the sun finally come back.

When you're hungry like that, all the pigs in the world can't feed you. Just as all the time here on the Plateau, safe from bombs and bullets, won't set things right.

There are many fine things, here in Mairbek's sunny, safe apartment, far from the warring lands of Chechnya—here, where the daffodils have already begun again to explode in the forest and in the fields. Where his daughter can clutch them in her hand without fear. But there is no meat for a tall dark man with one leg who sits in the shade. All hunger; no meat.

Now I learn from Amélie that Mairbek's mother, Kheda, needs to go to the doctor. I like being with Kheda; she reminds me of the Russian grandmothers I knew in the village in the north—the ones who would greet you with kisses after you'd been away for a while and pet you like a cat. Kheda has some serious health issues—ones that I know have caused her to cry when faced with the full tally of them on the forms one must fill out. But today, the trip to the doctor is just to check on her knee, which was recently replaced. And I'm here to translate.

Normally, Kheda wears soft, flowing caftans with old-fashioned prints. Today, for her doctor's appointment, she has dressed up a little, with a soft black sweater and an extra-nice scarf around her hair. She and Amélie and I arrive at the clinic and find three seats in the waiting room. Small talk, such as it is, doesn't last long.

Kheda says, leaning over, "I am sixty-three. Life is over for me. I've seen too much already.

"And some things," she adds, "you can't forget." Like how her younger son—that apple of her eye—was killed years ago. "When Mairbek was wounded, later," she said, "I thought I'd lose my mind."

I see her looking out into the past, and her eyes are slowly filling up. Her handkerchief comes out now. It is white with flowers and you can tell it has been washed many times. She dabs at her eyes.

Kheda's name is called, and in we go to the doctor's office. I do my best to translate. The doctor puts the X-rays up for all of us to see. How much does it hurt? Are you getting massages? Are you walking with a cane? Kheda is asked to get up onto the examination table. The doctor bends the knee that was operated on, and the one that is still not mended. How is that? The unfixed one hurts more, Kheda says. Both hurt, really, but it's bearable.

When it's all done, Kheda thanks the doctor, has me translate that he has wonderful hands. And I tell her that he is impressed with how quickly she has healed so far, that already she no longer walks with a cane. The doctor says she's strong, I tell her, *krepkaia*. She remembers that. Repeats it in the car on the way back to the residence. *Ia krepkaia.* I am strong.

In the car, Kheda tells Amélie that she doesn't know what she would do if Amélie left CADA for any reason. But Amélie, echoing Daniel Trocmé, says we can all be replaced. All of us.

Hearing this, Kheda looks up at Amélie. Her tears are gone, her eyes clear. No, it's not true, she says. We're not all the same. We can't all be replaced. Look at the fingers on a hand, she says, holding up her own. They're all different.

I think about hands, and what—given the choice—they have made, or wrecked, or wrought. Here in the Plateau, there are the hands that fix a knee—wonderful hands, says Kheda. There are hands that wash, and hands that cook delicious food and pass it over to a stranger. Hands that catch a window frame as they are about to jump to safety. Or swing a baby over a half-empty lap. There are hands that reach up, to a face, for a kiss on the cheek. Hands that reach up, in pain, in supplication.

There are hands that make shoes for children out of old tires. There are hands that, farther along, write letters begging for news.

And somewhere, a world away, there are hands that clutch a green necklace, about to sing a song—"Bei Mir Bistu Sheyn."

I have two sets of favorite hands right here in the Plateau. Both belong to women who happen to have long, light brown hair, which they pull away from their faces and fold into buns. Both of the women are in their fifties or so. Both have faces slowly growing soft with age.

The first pair of hands is Esther's. Esther, as it happens, is the niece of a woman who saved many lives during the war. Mild, wide-eyed, Esther volunteers to teach French at CADA, and her hands point to flash cards with pictures—a man, a woman, a city, a dog, a cat, a car—as her students mouth brand-new words. But once, Esther's hands—none of us replaceable!—knitted a blue cap for Akhmad and Rovzan's new baby boy.

Akhmad has repeated the story to me, many times: "She knit a hat for the baby . . . with her own hands!" With her own hands, as if nothing greater could be expected of kindness. "With her own hands," Akhmad repeats, like a song, and the hardness and pain in his own face melt into a raw openness.

The other pair of hands belongs to Marie-Hélène, who manages the apartment where I stay in the Plateau. Marie-Hélène's voice is soft, her gaze sure. Over time, little by little, she has invited me into her home for simple, delicious meals; has told me about how she grew up in the village right at the top of the Plateau, where the cold and wind are ferocious, and the farmwork relentless. People who were raised there understood, intimately, what it means to carry on in the brutal times of La Burle.

She has said, looking straight at me, "We are a hard people. But," she has added, "we know how to work."

And, she has added further, "we have a heart, too."

Now, with those same hands, far from the coldest winds of her girl-hood, Marie-Hélène types accounts. With those hands, she makes clean and beautiful homes for strangers. With those hands, once in a while, she has also left little packages at my door—soup that I can heat up when the wind howls fierce. With those hands on the steering wheel, she picks up strangers along the road—often, as it happens, the CADA families—and gives them a lift to the grocery store or wherever else.

But of all the things her hands have done, this is what I love most of all: One night, when she invited me to dinner with her and her husband, we sat at a cozy round table in the kitchen. Before the meal began, she took my hand gently in one of hers, and her husband's hand in the other—the three of us now forming a circle. And thanks were given for what we were about to receive. And requests were made, for our protection. Grace.

We are a hard people, Marie-Hélène tells me. Words that ring now like something gorgeous, and strong.

AMÉLIE DROPS KHEDA off at the CADA residence. Later in the day, I go to check in on her and the others in the family. I am visiting in the front part of house when I hear a gruff male voice calling.

"You!" says the voice from the back room, where the curtains are closed. "How long have you been in France?" It's Mairbek.

Who, me?

Mairbek has never spoken directly to me before; not without my ad-dressing him first. This man, I've thought, has no time for my nervous cheer. Mostly, he still growls and grouses when I see him. Or mutters under his breath.

But now he's speaking to me?

I tell him I've been here for a week or so this time.

"No, I don't mean this trip. I mean in general. How long have you been coming here? Do you know where to find the *cheremsha*?"

Cheremsha? What is that?

You don't know *cheremsha*? How can you not know the *cheremsha*?

Ah, there it is. I can feel the air in the room shift. Nearly at once, Mairbek, Kheda, Marzet radar toward me and begin talking. How do you explain the thing that everyone should know already? Something so important, so essential?

The *cheremsha*! You have to know the *cheremsha*!

Mairbek hobbles into the bright room toward me—like a great walking tree, limbs splayed, crutches stretched out for balance, taller with every step—and sits on the blue draped couch in front of the window.

The *cheremsha*. It's garlic. Wild garlic you find in the forest! You find it at the end of winter! You gather it. You eat it in huge piles!

Cheremsha, cheremsha!

I know this moment. It happens everywhere I've ever lived as a stranger when people sputter with words for things that are too large for words. How do you translate the Russian *khoziain*—roughly "leader" but layered with qualities of the trickster, and the saint, and long-dead relatives, and even iron-fisted Stalin? Or the Kabardian *guakach'*— meaning that crucial ability, in an intensely hierarchical society, to read people's needs—from *gu*, meaning "heart," and *kach'*, meaning "grow"? Maybe "heart talent"?

It's a very good sign when you see the sputtering over words. It means you're onto something that really matters.

Cheremsha! It's in the forest! It has these buds, these secret buds! It's out there. It could be out there! We tried to explain *cheremsha* to Amélie, but she wasn't sure of what it is, either!

A kind of song begins.

Ohhhh, Kheda incants: We gather it as the snow melts. Right when there are little green shoots. . . . Every spring, but only for a short time.

Ohhhh, Marzet adds, stomping in from the kitchen now: I know for a fact that you can find it in these forests. I saw them sell it in Paris! And I hear it's in Austria, too. I know for a fact it's around here. And the time to gather is now—maybe it's even passed. You gather it and then you can cook it in butter. . . .

Ohhhh, Kheda says again, her face far away, her tongue clicking, "I would trade meat for it. I would trade meat for it. I would . . ."

Trade meat? Trade the meat they are so hungry for? For something wild and green?

Yes, the room has changed. And it is the *cheremsha* that's caused the change, as if the very word cast a spell.

Abracadabra and *voilà*, a moment of remembering:

Remembered, fragrant forests of bright flopping green leaves, low to the ground. Remembered, the wildness of hills. Remembered, a time in those places when things could be both untamed and essential. Remembered, a sharp, dazzling taste that comes only in spring.

Remembered, also, the land you left—poor, battered Chechnya— that is still, so achingly, the land you love. . . .

But then, abracadabra and *voilà*: a moment of forgetting, too:

Forgotten, the doctor's appointment this morning, which—in its way—humbled Kheda again when she saw her own naked, hobbled outlines on the X-ray. Forgotten, Marzet's trip all the way to Paris a few days ago, when five hundred euros were stolen from her in the market in one swipe.

Forgotten, for a moment, the things that Kheda says can't be forgotten. Just for a moment in this room, forgotten. That her beloved younger son was killed, and their lives at home shattered.

Forgotten, for a moment, the things that Marzet, in near hysteria, worries about: the fact that she's bleeding all the time; the fact that there are threats always behind them, or so it seems; the fact that she has to take care of everyone.

Cheremsha, cheremsha. Oh, what to give if only it could be found. And so, forgotten, for a moment: limblessness, bloodlessness, chaos, the death of our best selves.

"Maybe we can get Amélie to go look for it with us," they say.

"Amélie loves the forest," I say. "Maybe we can find some together."

So now I know their forest song. It's not for the mushroom or the berry, so loved in France and in Russia, too, for that matter. It is not made of the musk of dirt, nor of that bright burst of sweetness. This is that other wild thing, under the trees of acid soils, that takes their breath away. This pungent wild flavor—with no words big enough for how beautiful it is.

Soon, Marzet—who has been somehow cooking all this time—serves me fried fish, the only thing she managed to buy in the market after the depressing loss of her five hundred euros. I hold their littlest boy, their only son. I touch his face. I see Mairbek's face in all the children now. Slate-gray eyes. I let the boy down.

Still just wobbling upright, the boy walks toward Mairbek, who is sitting on the bright blue couch. And then he tumbles toward his father's hands. And lands.

Early in his time at Compiègne, Daniel met another prisoner who was also from the big bright old world of his family. This man, Marcel Heuzé, was a Protestant pastor, and the camp chaplain. Like Daniel, Heuzé wrote home. In one missive to his church colleagues on August 18, 1943, he wrote, brightly, directly: "I am in contact with nearly fifty men, most of them young. I have received the communion service. I would need, as quickly as possible, a liter of communion wine, five or six Bibles, thirty new Testaments, and prayer books for the prisoners."

Camp life was as dangerous for Heuzé as for anyone else. Curiously, though, his letter from August 18 carries a sense of forthright pleasure at certain aspects of life at Frontstalag 122: "All is remarkable at the camp from a religious point of view," he wrote. "Many men come to mass. There is an important Orthodox community. There is communion every Sunday evening. Prayer meeting every morning at 10 am. Three Bible studies a week." Then he added, with even more brightness, that he was surrounded by "an ardent group of youth, who are desirous of working for GOD"—he wrote that word in all capital letters, DIEU—"and for their Fatherland"—*Patrie* with a capital P.

"I've been asked to wear the pastoral robe," he added before closing. "If you could send me a used one, I would be grateful."

A book, a robe, some wine, some songs, some meetings, some capital letters that spelled GOD. And another capital letter that began Fatherland. Heuzé knew what he needed, the things that made him firm and fine.

And, it turns out, we know from other sources, that at some point Pastor Heuzé sized up young Daniel Trocmé and decided that Daniel—who was, by now, already growing sick—needed the very same things, too. Daniel's student André Guyonnaud wrote about their encounters, after the war:

> Mr. Heuzé, the camp pastor, tried—not without difficulty—to look after [Daniel] because [Daniel] had firm ideas against our religion. Nevertheless, [Daniel] visited our meetings sometimes later. Sick, he stayed in the camp infirmary for long months. I think his heart was not going very well. Nor was his vision. Mr. Heuzé visited him often.

How strange to see that phrase, "firm ideas against our religion," written down like that, typed neatly in a letter. Our religion? Reflecting on this sentence, Daniel's older brother Charles was later moved to offer a footnote to that tossed-off phrase: "The expression is, without a doubt, improper. Daniel had, from the very beginning, an extreme scruple of sincerity. Not believing in Christian dogmas, he didn't want to pretend that he did. Secondly, he felt a friendship with so many others: Jews, unbelievers, Muslims. Adherence to one and only one community would have seemed to him—thinking of those friends—as a kind of betrayal or abandonment."

Did Daniel need religion? In Beirut, Daniel lived under the brilliant suns of many faiths. It was as though the skies cracked open for him there, with all that light, the world becoming larger than it had ever been for him before. Larger and stranger.

Could you take those suns and put them into a box that comes in a package from home with robes and wine and hymnbooks? Could they ever, ever fit into a box so small?

Or: "Do you suppose," as Rainer Maria Rilke once asked the young poet, "that someone who really has [God] could lose him like a little stone?"

What, then, did Daniel need? I don't think he needed little boxes—or faith like little stones. I think he needed suns.

Soon after Daniel arrived in Compiègne, a convoy took away Pastor Heuzé, who would later perish at Ravensbrück. And then another took Klaus and Alexandre, and Jean and André. And Daniel's eyes were fuzzing up, his heart hurting.

What did Daniel need?

October, November, soon December. As Daniel's health continued to fade, as his friends left—he fixed his thoughts on the *blason*, the coat of arms, that he had wished to design for the Little Crickets along with the motto they had come up with, *Agir pour tous*, Act for all. They could wear it proudly, those little refugees, as if they were at a great boarding school. As if they, too, would live, from then on, among the oak trees.

On November 23, 1943, Daniel wrote to his parents: "If you receive the model of the *blason* that I hope to send in a package, please have fifty sent to a specialized [manufacturer], and send them all to the Little Crickets."

It was so hard to get things done from afar. In and out of the infirmary now, Daniel was weaker and weaker. In time, it became clear that the *blason* would not be made. On December 8, he wrote to his parents again. "Can I ask you to send Pastor Poivre 1,500 francs for the Little Crickets—for them and their Christmas—because I fear that I will not be able to send them the *blason* that I was intending to. Can you ask Poivre that, if he can't get them appropriate individual gifts, to please just give them the cash? . . . If I could have some news that was just a little more precise, I would be infinitely happy."

THIS IS WHAT I THINK:

Beautiful things don't save us because they give us repose, or peace. Or because they fill us with some lyrical longing. They are not essential because they add lovely flourish—nice as that may be—to the truly meaningful things of life.

They are essential because they change everything.

When I was girl, I memorized some words that had just been loosed into the world in 1943, as it happens. These were the words of the Little Prince, who was telling the pilot he met on the African deserts about his beloved flower, the rose he had left behind on his planet. Oh, she was beautiful. And now she was alone, without him. And he was so afraid for her safety. And, light-years away, he could do nothing to protect her.

"If someone loves a flower," he said, "of which just one single blossom grows in all the millions and millions of stars, it is enough to make him happy just to look at the stars. He can say to himself, 'Somewhere, my flower is there. . . .' But if the sheep eats the flower, in one moment all his stars will be darkened. . . ."

Beauty saves us not because it gives us some kind of aesthetic pause, or pleasure, or because it rescues us from pain. It saves us because when you tilt your head back at night, the beauty that lives, alone on one star, illumines all the stars. Because the beauty of one face illumines all the faces.

Beauty saves us because, after a long day of digging into the depths of sad papers that tell stories of our lowest selves, when the lights are shining in your face on a dark stage, and you hear the violins swell, and you open your mouth to sing the question "Skylark, have you anything to say to me?" . . . you see Regina herself—*sheyn, sheyn, sheyn*—dancing with Sam. You see both of their hearts looking up into the lights, too. Because they can now. Because they will.

"Somewhere, my flower is there," makes every sky alive with love. Makes every star—somewhere—a dazzling, crushing sun. It makes of small things an immensity.

Chapter 13

ALONG CAME
A SPIDER

"What are *they*, and where are *you*?" screamed Wilbur.
"Please, *please*, tell me where you are.
And what are salutations?"

—E. B. WHITE, *CHARLOTTE'S WEB*

W HAT I KNOW about all this, I know mostly because of the man who would be called 38222.

On December 14, 1943, a column of nine hundred thirty-three men carrying suitcases walked nearly silently through the streets of Compiègne. Townspeople watched them pass by. After crossing a bridge over the Oise River, the men arrived at a train station. There, they were separated from their belongings and packed into a train, a hundred men to a car.

The doors of each of the train cars closed. There were no windows to look out of, and just the smallest air vents overhead. Despite vivid rumors that had been circulating at Frontstalag 122 of late, the men had no idea where precisely they were heading now, or to what end. At a certain point, they could feel metal wheels squeak and turn below them; could feel themselves begin to move, blindly, over the frigid terrain.

For two days, there was nothing to eat or drink for the men. Every time the train stopped, they would yell, *Wasser, bitte! Luft, bitte!* Water, please! Air, please! For two days, they made every effort to avoid stepping on one another or on the excrement that was collecting on the floor. Outside, it was winter; inside they were choking for air, slowly starving, mad with thirst, their legs ballooning into painful logs. Sometimes, condensation would form on the walls of the car, which the men could then lick. There was panic in the thin air, but also bits of hard-core strategy. In a moment of opportunity when the train crossed the Marne River, several men tried to jump out of the train and flee. A few succeeded. Others failed and were killed.

Now, at five a.m. on December 16, 1943, the prisoners arrive at their destination. When the doors finally unlock and open, their bodies roll out of the cars as if the train itself had been bursting at the seams to release them. Met by soldiers who beat them with clubs and rifle butts, the prisoners beg for water again. Their shirts and shoes are taken from them; they feel the wind with their chests and the mottled, snow-lined earth with their feet.

They begin to walk, with great effort, their next destination a kilometer away. Dogs have been trained to attack the slowest of them; the soldiers walking along burst into mad local eddies of violence now and then. The men's feet bleed.

At some distance, the prisoners see a long brick building with an iron gate in the middle. On that gate, wrought in attractive Bauhaus script, are the words—old and simple—more visible and clearer with every painful step: JEDEM DAS SEINE—to each his own.

And this is how, on December 16, 1943, at around six a.m., the group of nearly a thousand prisoners from Compiègne—minus the few who jumped and ran off toward the Marne, and the few who died right there in the cars among the ballooned legs and the traces of excrement—pass through that iron gate, one by one, to enter a new and foreign land called Buchenwald. To each his own.

Inside the gates they pass an enormous crowd—upward of twenty thousand strong—struggling to stay at attention, wearing gray-and-blue-striped uniforms or just plain rags. They walk by a light-colored brick building with a high chimney that, in the days and weeks ahead, they will learn to fear. The prisoners are then corralled between two barracks and stand there for four hours while they wait their turn to enter a low-lying building. Inside that building—the delousing station—they are undressed, their heads shaved, and then they are dipped in a disinfectant bath and sent under showers. From there, they are driven naked through an underground tunnel toward another destination.

Now the men will be registered into the camp. And to this end, somehow, out of the bewildered chaos of shaven heads and naked bodies, a line forms.

Let us focus for a moment on three of those thousand. To each his own.

The first is young and handsome—twenty-five years old—with a dark brow and flashing eyes. In Grenoble, before the war, this young man studied philosophy, but was also drawn to theater, poetry, and music. After the German invasion in 1940, he found himself urgently swept into worldly matters; soon, he was in and out of prisons for illegal demonstrations, communist activities, and the distribution of anti-German literature. He wrote poems about what had been taken from them all—"the flower and the fruit." In September 1943, he was finally sent to Compiègne, and now he is here in line, filling out paperwork.

Twenty-five years earlier, this dark-browed young man was called Jacques René Laurent. Now, he is given a new name, one that will appear on all documents that refer to him—work lists, infirmary lists, transport lists. It will be sewn into his clothing. Barked at him in the morning and in the evening and when he is in the wrong place, or going too slowly, or when he has disobeyed the rules and been sent into a solitary cell. It will be his, in this strange sea of bald and ragged men, until the day he dies of scarlet fever, not two months later.

He is 38220.

Next.

The second man is bespectacled and quite thin. His eyes have trouble focusing. Against his newly shaven head, his ears stick out in perpendicular shells. This young man is thirty-two years old, and—before the war—lived and taught in Paris, Rome, Beirut, Maslacq, and Le Chambon-sur-Lignon. In Le Chambon, he allowed himself to be arrested in a raid, rather than jump out the window into the forest to safety. As a boy, he had delicious curls and deep eyes. As a young man, he learned to believe that there was not just one civilization, but many. He wanted to be part of the reconstruction of the world. Now, in his own nakedness, he stands in a line and waits his turn to fill out forms, which comes soon enough.

A camp worker in front of him holds an orange card marked up with puzzling, old timey German typeface—like the Bibles you can't read in museums. The young naked man's belongings are noted on the card and stored: Coat, one; Shirts, two; Alpine vest, one; Pair of pants, one; Sweaters, two; Undershirts, two; Pair of underpants, one; Pair of cloth shoes, one; Tie, one; Scarf, one; Suitcase, one. Then, in a scribble, is added: one white watch and white chain.

The man signs the orange card: Daniel Geoffrey Trocmé. The D tilts as it always has, to the right; the T is crossed in a high flourish.

Forevermore, he will be 38221.

Next.

The third man is just twenty years old, and, after his forms are filled out, he will be called 38222. He will live to tell this story—which I will, miraculously, come upon in a French radio recording. From a family of farmers, this third man, too, jumped right into the Resistance when the war began, collecting arms in the forests of Doubs, near the Swiss border, and distributing them out to the underground. Knowing that he was being sought by the German police, this man tried to flee to the Algerian coast, but was apprehended on the Spanish border.

On that fateful trip from Compiègne, he was to have been the twelfth man to throw himself out of the crowded train at Marne, but as soon as the eighth jumped, the train screeched to a halt, and he missed his chance to be free or die trying. In the months ahead—having been starved and beaten and worked down to the nub of his being—this man would cry out to his Christ in the familiar *tu*, "like he was a friend," using "distasteful" language, begging to be taken.

But for now, this man—once named Étienne Bouquet—also stands in line, and waits, and witnesses, recording for his memory and, as it happens, for history, the details of what it was like to walk on gravel and snow after choking with fear for two days on a train; what it was like to feel the burn of a disinfectant bath; or to be naked in the cold. And, further along, what it was like, in the very prime of his youth, to beg to die.

Each of these three young men, like each of the nearly thousand who traveled with them, is now handed one ragged shirt; one pair of underwear; one pair of pants; one jacket; a hat with no visor; and a pair of wooden clogs with no straps. These clothes are not made of the telltale blue and gray stripes—now, at this camp, the striped uniforms are reserved for those assigned a work detail—but each shirt and pair of pants is marked on the back with a great big X, painted in red. The men are also then given cloth triangles, to be sewn onto their clothes. For each man, a color; for each color, a meaning—red, a political prisoner; green, a criminal; black, an "asocial"; pink, a homosexual; purple, a Jehovah's Witness; yellow, a Jew.

Maybe these three young men in a row—each now holding a red triangle and preparing for the walk to their new barracks in their hard new shoes—find a moment to look at one another. Maybe they speak. Maybe, with hours and hours to wait, they notice in one another a flashing brow, or a pair of prominent ears, or some measure of generosity or bravery or poetry. Maybe, in seeing the nakedness, the sunkenness, the pain in one another, they feel a tug of something full and human, to each his own.

Otherwise, how can it be borne? Any of it?

BUCHENWALD WAS CREATED in 1937 on a patch of forest five miles northwest of the city of Weimar, Germany, with the aim of isolating and incarcerating those who might rise up against the new Nazi regime. To put it in modern terms, it was, in effect, a bastion of preventive custody for a paranoid regime, where being identified as any kind of nonconformist—in ideas, in political orientation, in ethnic association, or religious affiliation—could be used as proof positive of the necessity to protect society from you and your kind. Ideally, the camp would be part of the reeducation and reformation of the outcasts—for those at least who could abandon the parts of themselves that offended.

Though Buchenwald held Jewish prisoners—particularly after Kristallnacht—as the war began, and then advanced, and then shifted into a frenzy, the camp functioned more and more specifically as a place for political prisoners who could be used as much-needed slave laborers. The Jews—whose offense, being found in their very lineage, was impossible to abandon—were periodically executed en masse at Buchenwald, or deported to camps in Poland that had been specifically designed for their extermination.

By the time Daniel arrived at Buchenwald on that cold December morning in 1943—with Jacques just in front of him and Étienne immediately behind—the number of prisoners at Buchenwald was a staggering thirty-seven thousand. Most came from Russia, Poland, France, Germany, and Czechoslovakia, among them a mix-and-match of Roma and Sinti, German anti-Nazis, Jehovah's Witnesses, hardened criminals, prisoners of war (including some from the United States), and a relatively small number of Jews, there by clerical error or because they possessed some needed profession or skill. There were Catholics, Orthodox Christians, Muslims, and individuals who, for whatever reason, didn't work at jobs. Buchenwald was primarily a camp for male prisoners. Until 1944, the only women present were workers in the camp brothel, created at Heinrich Himmler's initiative in the spring of 1943, which required each woman to service five men a night at the cost of one or two reichsmarks per man. Open to the racially superior, that brothel was also, at times, forced upon homosexuals as part of their "reeducation."

Gas chambers, as instruments for mass extermination, were not part of the camp design of Buchenwald. That function had been exported mostly to the camps in Poland. But extreme physical suffering—and subsequent death—were nonetheless ever present. As day followed day—with the war advancing and the deportation machinery continuing to expand—the numbers of prisoners at the camp grew exponentially. In these conditions, the bodies of prisoners—and their immediate overseers, also prisoners—were ravaged by filth, by the lack of food and water, by extreme crowding, cold, disease, infestations, and physical violence. Between the spring of 1942 and the autumn of 1944, the camp population ballooned tenfold, from 8,400 to 84,000, with the death toll expanding accordingly. In all, nearly 240,000 people passed through Buchenwald between 1937 and 1945. Of those, it is estimated that more than 56,000 perished.

It was at Buchenwald that prisoners like Klaus Simon, from La Maison des Roches, had to confront the monstrous existence of Ilse Koch, the sadistic wife of the camp commander. It was there where special tortures were inflicted on prisoners—like one called "tree hanging," where a prisoner was mounted by his arms, backward, on a great pole. And it was there where the prisoners would be publicly flogged, their legs bound by a special wooden contraption. There were long and private tortures inside cells in Buchenwald, and murders by the injections of air into the veins. There was an entire barracks dedicated to medical experiments, where prisoners became living petri dishes in the study of typhus, diphtheria, smallpox, and yellow fever; where they were burned and given something called "gas gangrene," and where the organs of homosexuals were operated on, with "rehabilitation" in mind. The heads of a number of murdered men were shrunken and displayed, their expressions frozen forever into small, leathery howls.

These were the fiendish extremes. But every hour of every day in Buchenwald was met with savage hunger, with brutality, and with mental and emotional humiliation. These constants forced every single soul there—whether prisoner or jailer—to witness the descent of other souls into their very darkest places. And it forced them to monitor the shrinking and changing of their own bodies and minds, and, in time, to confront the possibility of their very own souls' journeys down, down, and down toward the mortal limits of what they had once seen as their unshakable convictions.

It was such a very long distance that Jacques and Daniel and Étienne had traveled in those past forty-eight hours—from Compiègne, with its trees and mealtime discussions about philosophy, its roll call of letters from home. Just weeks earlier, Daniel had written delightedly about being moved to a new barracks with more light. Now, in those first moments at Buchenwald, after they had all been stripped and shorn and given their numbers and triangles, could the three young men have heard someone shrieking in pain? Could they have seen their first shriveled corpses on the ground, or caught a whiff of the strange new smell coming from the high chimney of the crematorium?

Of this, we can be rather sure: Wearing their new rags and wobbling on their new wooden clogs, the three were ordered to walk downhill to a place away from the main barracks of the camp. Soon, from out of the dark night, they would have seen a series of long wooden barracks, one of which would have been appointed for them. Someone would have opened the door. And a dysenteric smell would have slammed right into their faces.

Walking inside, the men would have found themselves face-to-face with between one and two thousand other men, all of whom had been packed into a structure originally built for fifty horses. These thousand or so men lay crushed like sardines in filthy wooden bunks in three and four layers, from floor to ceiling.

This was the Little Camp, designed as a quarantine station for new prisoners at Buchenwald who would be shipped out for labor elsewhere in the weeks ahead. The Little Camp was destined, after its liberation by the Americans in April 1945, to supply the West with some of its first indelible images of the full horror of the Holocaust—*click*, the photo of Elie Wiesel peering out from the inside of one of those bunks, a skeletal man standing nearby with protruding hips and ribs, faintly smiling;

click, the photo of a man sitting on the ground with spindly legs in front of him, holding a tin bowl, looking right at the camera, an entire world behind his eyes.

I will leave Daniel—now 38221—here for a moment, at that open door of his barracks at the Little Camp, facing the new darkness that still awaits him inside. I will leave him in that stench, as he begins to puzzle about where he might find a place to sleep among the many strangers.

This is the moment where, I imagine, he finally closes his eyes. Where he thinks of those he loves. And aches for them. Later on, before drifting off, this is where he conjures the sweet small faces of the children he was once able to protect from the night, knowing that he was able to keep at least some of them from harm.

This is where the reconstruction of the world has led you.

───

One-two-three, the children bounce toward the car.

Lunch is over, this chilly April day in Le Chambon, and it's time to take the kids back to school. Dzhamal puts his tiny hand in mine as we get ready to cross the street. Zezag drops her gum on the ground, wipes it, and pops it back into her mouth. She takes my other hand. For months, Akhmad has been walking the children to school and back—from up the hill, down almost to the river, then up again, three times a day. School in the morning, home for lunch, school in the afternoon. Not a very manly stint, in his eyes, that business of walking down and up the hill in the cold.

So now, here it is, the solution he's been saving for: a used car, 340 euros, burgundy, fixed and shined by Akhmad himself, who is stooping with a cigarette and smiling as we cross the street toward it.

The children grab open the car doors and start to settle into their places, and I fumble with Dzhamal's seat belt. Akhmad helps me because I can't figure it out.

I look at the children in the mirror. They are, one-two-three, all wearing cheery winter hats, all bubbling and beaming. It's not this car's maiden voyage with the Vakhaev family, but one of its first here, in Le Chambon, as the first buds swell in the trees. The car insurance question is just about solved—that's why I'm with Akhmad today, to help figure that all out with the bank. Once it's settled, Akhmad will be able navigate all the way to Saint-Agrève, he thinks—or Tence and maybe even Yssingeaux. After that, he will go to Saint-Étienne, and there, finally, he will be able to buy some halal meat on his own, "God be praised."

Akhmad is tall enough to need to duck in his seat just a little as he settles, checking that everything is in place. Have I ever seen him this happy? In Chechnya, he tells me, children are put behind the steering wheels of cars at the earliest age. Even an infant boy will be led, on his father's lap, to an invisible wheel . . . *brrrrrrr, brrrrrrrr, brrrrrrrrr*, right and left and right again goes the imaginary car, speeding down some future road toward some future horizon: mountains, fields, forests on the side, toward some future city, some future market, with cucumbers stuffed into crates in the backseat, the littlest twisted ones the cheapest for sale to old ladies who live alone. There might be a piano strapped to the car, through the mountain passes, a present for a favorite daughter. Or five or six or seven in a family, all crammed into a tiny old Lada, the snowcapped peaks looking close enough to touch, all off for their only ever view of the sea. *Brrrr, brrrrrr, brrrrrrr,* and somehow, someday, there will be no vertigo for you, little man.

The children, one-two-three, are now fully buckled in the back, and the car rumbles to life. Music comes on the radio, too, and it sounds to me like just about any Eastern European pop. No, this won't do, Akhmad says, turning to me and flipping to a CD: "This is what they want. . . ."

The song begins with two counts of eight quick heartbeats, and then the smooth growl of Adele comes in. The children, one-two-three, begin to sing along. They don't understand the words to this song, in their fourth language of four, but they shape every vowel and sing, on pitch, in joy, legs kicking to the driving rhythm. In unison.

Down the hill, we begin to drive—down, to the heartbeat—all the way down into the center, past the Café de Velay, the Banque de Crédit Agricole, zooming past the pizzeria, zooming past the church (AIMEZ-VOUS LES UNS LES AUTRES), then the back of the school. The children sing and sing in their cheery little winter hats, now, at the beginning of spring. Every time the song crescendos, so do they, mouthing those still-mysterious words, every syllable most nearly in place:

We could have had it all
Rolling in the deep . . .

We careen up and down and loop around the village. Akhmad is going fast, his hands sure at the wheel. It's so nice to see him like this. I have watched over many months how this man's face shifts from day to day. How he turns gray with worry or illness, stripped of the community he loves and needs. How he feels like a tree with no roots. I see how the relationships he builds with locals—no matter how good the intentions—feel pallid and shallow compared to what he knew back in his homeland. With no kin or clan, or kith or kind, how can he really live? How can he protect his wife and four children? How can he be a man?

Once, while I'm back in the United States, Akhmad writes me a text message:

Salaam to your husband and all your kin. How are you? . . . You are probably close to your people now? How cozy, how peaceful that must be. How we miss our family, especially at night now when the children are asleep, when we sit and are lonely for them, cry, worry so much, that—could it be possible?—we will never see our parents again. We pray, so strongly—would that we could see our parents one more time. O God, give us the gardens of paradise of eternal life, that You will be pleased with all of us. O God, if our tears flow like a river, forgive us—our fate has been severe.

For now, though, right now, the one-two-three are happy to the heartbeat. And their father is happy to careen.

I'M REALIZING, as time goes by, that I've been looking high and low for signs of hope. Looking so hard for those signs that—if I am honest with myself—I see I am capable of whitewashing terrible situations.

One day, when I arrive in Le Chambon after months of being away, I hear that Larissa—the Rapunzel who sings Beyoncé to me—is gone. Having been refused refugee status by the French government, she and her husband have left Le Chambon. When I last said good-bye to her and she sent me off with a powerful hug and the words *"liubliu tebia,"* I love you, I gave her a kitchen towel with yellow chicks on it, and she gave me a gift that may well be typical only in the Caucasus—a pair of high-waisted underpants. I try to text her, but her number has changed, and no one seems to have it. I hear some vague reports that she and her husband are off near Le Puy, and that they are okay for now in a place where others, too, are staying temporarily while they figure out their next steps.

Meanwhile, in Le Chambon, I'm getting closer and closer to families who tell me more and more of what they have seen back home, what they have lived. One day, the Dagestani woman, Arubika, recounts the long, strange story of her violent father, his brutish rejection of her, and his abandonment of her and her mother. She gives me details of her cousin's murder in the woods, and details about his unwashable blood draining into the green of the forest floor, and how she tried to wash the blood anyway, so her grandmother wouldn't see. I have been learning more about rapes and other violations of the African women. Or, from a new Armenian woman who has fled her violent husband in Iran, leaving her two children behind, what it was like to see people hanging by the neck in the streets of Teheran.

I don't know what to do with all of this pain around me. All of this fear. All of this hope. All of the dizzying love that has begun to accumulate for some of the children in particular. I don't know what to do with the magnified three-dimensional views I'm getting of my own terrible limitations.

Do I really understand anything about how to be good in the world?

One day, I go mushroom hunting with Amélie. Ever since the murder of Agnès, it's always a little strange in the woods. We find bright orange chanterelles, purple and brown girolles and cèpes. Later, I return alone to my apartment at Val du Rio to clean my own plastic bagful. I put potatoes on to boil. The apartment is dark except for a bright light overhead in the kitchen. When I sit down and open the bag, it smells sweet with dirt. Fishing out the mushrooms, one by one, I go after them with a knife, and think about my long and painful conversations with Arubika, earlier in the day. And about the shots Amélie and I heard fired in the forest—hunters, probably, but who knows. And how there were loud planes overhead. I think about Agnès, and her murder at that one tree.

Deep in the plastic bag—among the mushrooms and the bits of woody detritus—I notice that there is one tiny spider, and then one tiny inchworm, that have traveled back from the forest with me. I carefully transport the two out of the bag, using my knife, and place them on the table under the light. I think about how these little creatures, too, eat the cèpes and the chanterelles. I find I am crying—because of Arubika's tale of blood on the forest floor; because, to the spider and the inchworm, a mushroom is a mountain; because if I hadn't noticed anything just now—and why would I have, except by chance?—these tiny creatures would be in my frying pan, dead and gone already.

Hope comes here in the Plateau, but at a cost. Love comes, but at a cost. And what powers do I have to pay any of that debt? What gifts do I have to offer that are worth anything, really? I haven't made children, I can't fix a broken arm or a broken heart, and I don't know how to plant potatoes on my own or even how to drive. I can't do anything useful in the world, really. I am a lapsed anthropologist who thought she could figure out something about peace, but now my nights are haunted by faces of the living and faces of the dead. I find comfort when the children paw at my ukulele, or when they career down the road, singing and kicking. But . . . how am I anything more than a ghost myself? What can I fix?

ONE DAY WHILE I am with Rovzan, something new happens. She and baby Sulim and I are sitting together in their apartment playing and talking while the kids are at school and Akhmad is off somewhere. At one point, Rovzan tells me she needs to do something for a couple of minutes. Is that okay?

It is time for *namaz*. Would I like to watch television while she prays? Whatever is best for you, I say, I will do. I just don't want to get in the way. She says, you don't get in the way.

Rovzan goes into her bedroom. "Here are some family pictures, if you want to see," she says, handing me her phone. In the first is her mother, in Chechnya, with a heavy brow. Then her sister, who told Rovzan, "We should use money and love people. But so many love money and use people." Here are the children on their last visit to family in Chechnya before fleeing. And then, pictures of Akhmad with Dzhamal. Were they already on the road then? Akhmad's face is bloated and the children have red eyes with black circles under them. Zezag still looks like the wonderful horrible princess. And then there is a picture of them going to Paris for their first court date, with the train schedule in the background, flashing its orange letters. And then, a few more of the children: children playing; children dressing up for prayer; children hands on hips and dancing and upside-down, three headstands in a row.

Rovzan comes back quietly into the living room now, carrying some clothing folded in her arms. She carefully covers herself with a long brown and black dress over her skirt and T-shirt, she covers her head in a scarf, she puts a rug down in a clean place. The television is still on as she faces the holy qiblah, which happens to be in the direction of the toy corner where Dzhamal has taken to sitting in a cardboard box.

On the television, some neon-orange drumsticks flash to an electric baseline, then: *". . . That's the way you do it, you play the guitar on the MTV. . . ."*

Rovzan is silent. She bows gracefully, gently, and she comes up. She bows again and mouths holy words. She holds her palms up and her face looks up. She bows again, praying.

And I am a witness.

THE TRUTH IS, I've been hiding. Rovzan, in her praying, is not hiding, but I am. I have been for as long as I can remember.

And this, for me, is what hiding looks like:

IN PRECISELY THE SAME YEAR that Daniel Trocmé was born, 1912, something revolutionary happened in the social sciences. Émile Durkheim, a Jewish sociologist teaching at the Sorbonne, published a work, *The Elementary Forms of Religious Life*, which would lay the foundations for seeing all religions—every last one of them, from the most leafy and animist to the most velveteen and papal—as social institutions actively working out social problems. All religions shared the focus on something he generally called the sacred—that number of material or immaterial objects somehow connected to other, unseen worlds. And these sacred things were, each in their own way and in their own context, understood to be capable of heralding in life-altering power, a kind of huge, shimmering feeling of group coherence and belonging that Durkheim called "effervescence."

Why was this revolutionary? Because it was, in effect, a theft. In it, Durkheim managed to snatch, for science, a domain that had been considered essentially unamenable to scientific law—namely, things of the spirit.

European science—in contrast to the rich scientific traditions that had flourished in the Far East, India, and during the Golden Age of

Islam—had a whole history of just saying no to spirit. When René Descartes wrote his *Discourse on Method* way back at the dawn of the European scientific revolution, in the seventeenth century, he showed how, if you carefully chose your domain of inquiry in the physical world, you could examine things in close, orderly, and cumulatively enriching ways. And if you used that method well and rightly, your eventual prize would be the determination of physical law. Which is quite a prize. You'd get to figure out things like how to fly to the moon, or the big bang, or genetics, or evolution, or any of those stately, long-term miracles of understanding.

But like every single scientific model, this mind-body dichotomy—as it was called in shorthand—created its own bulwarks against the free imagination: As susceptible as stars and bugs and bodies and marbles were to law, it was deeply argued and consequently felt that we shouldn't even think of using the scientific method on the world of spirit, mind, emotion, love, poetry. No, those things were untouchable. Exalted. Somehow whole and complete and mysterious within their own terms. So if we wanted to ask questions about them, we should—who knows?— go into a trance and ask God our questions. But we shouldn't even try to apply science in their direction.

Now, in 1912, Durkheim—and some others who were struggling with the same rift in that dichotomy—had stolen spirit (here, religion) for science. Religion wasn't a marble or a worm or a corpse or a star. But it was a social thing, and it did social things. Because of that, *ta-da*, it could be analyzed like other social things. One act at a time.

In light of that monumental shift, religion became a social, analyzable thing that provides you and your community with ineffable spaces and objects and beings on which you can pin your hopes, that can usher in the power to veer life away from its obvious course. I am sick! Heal me! I can't bear children! Give them to me! My enemy is at the gates! Protect me! I'll never see my parents again! Bring them to me! Religion can turn the world upside down. Give you hope. It can promise you that you are eternal and will know your loved ones again after you die. It connects you with things you can't see, but things you know and feel to be true. Shimmery, big, awesome things you know to be true.

But it wasn't just the smashing of the mind-body dichotomy and the like that made Durkheim's ideas and assertions revolutionary. There was also the question of power. This science of religion made all religions analytically even and level. Which was in itself subversive. Putting it bluntly: Here, Christians didn't get to be the highest and truest and best, even if they happened to be running huge chunks of the world in 1912, and were used to being comfortably at the top of the ideological order in the West. No. Here, communities of people who called themselves, among other things, Jews, Christians, Muslims, Zoroastrians, Buddhists, Hindus, Bahá'ís, were all interacting with the sacred. They were all solving problems in the course of their religious lives vis-à-vis that sacred. All of them were figuring out how things were ordered, how to live, how to face chaotic times, how to survive catastrophe. They were, in that way, level, equal, the same.

I rediscovered Durkheim in the middle of my fieldwork in Russia. One day I found myself at a yearly spring ritual in the graveyard, where everyone was talking with their dead parents and grandparents and children and ancestors—a baby was born; someone got married; the green cabbage won't grow; the bees are dying, we don't know why—steadily drinking, getting drunk and drunker, and singing and crying and drinking some more. I couldn't believe my eyes. Effervescence! As everything blurred and drooped and the tears and the laughter mixed in equal measure, I saw how these lonely people with their thick hard lives, so far from any kind of institutional protection, were using every tool they had—their words, their drink, their soil, their dead—to feel something higher, something more. Their religion—with its icons and sorcery and incantations and invocations—was made up of that act of grabbing any tool at hand and reaching together upward, to fix themselves. There is dignity in that.

And here on the Plateau? The sacred here feels quiet, steadfast. It lacks rituals with big images or colors or words, except for, perhaps, the best ones. It lacks objects. It is too large to be contained by the word "Protestant." It is, rather, like Rilke's God, who is "dark, and like a webbing made / of a hundred roots, that drink in silence."

Durkheim's work was a small miracle, one that reinforced the idea then newly developing in world thought—an idea that newly reached even our own Daniel Trocmé—that there is not one civilization but many. That no one people is higher or lower than any other people—even, and perhaps especially, in their most sacred spaces.

It was a miracle that had a method: just study. Look hard. You can see how any people interacts with things that they can't see. Things that are, for them, higher, better, awesome, eternal. With this science, everyone, everyone, gets to hold up their own two hands and face their divine. And no one is degraded by it.

When Durkheim first wrote about all this, the world was choked and thirsty for his insights. It still is. But as good and right and miraculous as these insights were, this is why I started hiding: I was myself religious, and that made literally no sense to the social science that was built up all around me.

The logic, such as I have experienced it, goes like this: The revolutionary ability to level all the sacred systems depends on nothing being really, truly sacred. You can study this sacredness stuff, in other words, but you can't responsibly believe it. How can you? First of all, it will throw you off course if you go around secretly believing that the "natives" you study are full of nonsense and only your very own priests or rabbis or imams are right. No. It would be better for each and every one of these sacred worlds—the ones you come from and the ones you study—to be made of their own set of metaphysical propositions that you can then summarily dismiss.

As a researcher, it is better to clear the slate, and live sacred-free. You can delight, say, in the complex myths you learn up in the Himalayan mountains, and marvel at how the human mind can come up with possession rituals or speak in tongues. Maybe you will also get that tattoo on your penis (if you've got one) when you set out on a coming-of-age ritual, as some anthropologists have done in extreme feats of participant observation. But delighting in these things—the xenophile option—is the most you might let yourself feel about it all. You will not, if you're serious, be overtaken by things. You will not cry at night at the spiders who crawl in your mushrooms. You will not start talking with Daniel and wondering if he can hear you, wherever he is.

I don't know how graduate school was for everyone, but I know that I, Jewish-born Bahá'í from the sadder side of Rochester, New York, quickly sensed that to most others around me, having a religion meant also having a kind of epistemological handicap. I was living in a newly secular, giddily nationalist, and stridently atheist Quebec: So far as I could tell, none of my professors in anthropology, and none but very few of my friends, had any religious beliefs at all. To most of them, religion was a ridiculous artifact of an unjust and ludicrous world of the past—and frankly, how could anyone blame them for thinking that?

So I hid my beliefs in plain sight. People knew I had an unusual religious background (Jewish wasn't so out of the ordinary by now, but Bahá'í still was) and I laughed along with friends when they made jokes about how religious people believed in heaven or whatever else. Yes, ha-ha, it's sure pretty silly, put that way. They got used to my fasting or teetotaling without much notice or curiosity; and, for my part, I didn't share that every single day I would orient my prayers around the rising and setting of the sun. At the same time, I admit that I loved letting all those master narratives go—the ones about social ascendency, race, gender, thought, and faith that dominated in society, if not in my own beliefs—feeling free and clean of them all. And I loved how, later, when I taught a course on culture and history, not even a Trotskyite student of mine—whose day job was mailman—could tell whether I was a Marxist or not. Well, was I?

All religions give people a chance to raise their arms toward some ineffable sacred, which is sometimes beautiful, sometimes terrifying, sometimes both. All religions give people a chance to hope for release or rescue, for a transcendent something. In my own Bahá'í religion, I learned to believe that each and every religion is, in fact, equally sacred, equally endowed with divine light. And I have been required to figure out how to love "all religions and all races with a love that is true and sincere," knowing that they were all, really, in the deepest sense, the same. So I learned to understand that when you pray toward a tree or an icon or, sensing some Great Presence, within a church or in a quiet carpeted hall or at the Western Wall of the Temple, those prayers, sooner or later, will reach their divine home. Because our Creator loves us, and is generous toward us all—not just some of us—and wants us to spend our lives figuring out how to love back.

Through my religion, I also internalized the idea that God is absolutely unknowable. That tenet struck in a deep place inside me even early on, I think, because I recall how once, when I was about six, I picked up some crayons and drew a picture of God. When I did, God looked like a big yellow scribble of a ball overtaking the limits of the paper. God was just light. Just a huge, uncontained, too-big-for-crayons kind of brilliant light. One of my parents—it could as easily have been the Jew as the Bahá'í—saw this and informed me that We Do Not Draw God. And I never tried again. But still, I would live with this picture in my head— that blast of light that could never, ever be limited by a frame, much less by a kitschy figure with blue eyes and blond hair. That limitlessness always felt exhilarating, not sad, and kind of went with the fact that my faith also taught me that science and religion are both, equally, means of trying to approach that brilliant unknowable essence. Which meant that I, like those farmers in Russia, was free to pick up any tool I could find— from the Bible to the Quran and the Vedas; from Einstein to Whitman and Beethoven; from the spider to the eagle to the wild boar—to try to learn the reasons for my existence, and to try to feel—Is it there? Even in the darkest places?—the love of my Creator. And return that love.

But in most corners of my life, I never found a language with which to talk about the truly sacred. To this day, when I even say the word "prayer" out loud—or "blessed" or "grace"—I feel like an impostor, like I don't really know how to shape my lips around holy language. Those words, then, I have kept mostly silent, speaking them mostly just to myself.

Maybe, to be fair, there is no great epistemological mutation in me. Maybe mine is more like a social mutation. But, as I go through this journey in the Plateau, and meet with what feels like every single dimension of the human condition, I can't quite shake the fact that science shows me how to make all this beauty and all this terror and all this awe and all this devastation somehow smaller and flatter than it is. It shows me how to pat it all down nicely, and give it words and maybe numbers. And despite the seeker that lives inside me, hiding, I've grown a habit over the years of making big things small, and I've kept religion, in analytical ways, in a nice little box, like the stone that Rilke wrote about, the stone that can be lost.

The longer I think about all this now, and the more I learn of, say, Daniel's suffering in the Little Camp—or the suffering of George, Jacques, Leonidas, Herbert, and Charles in Auschwitz before him—the more I fall in love with Marie-Hélène or Muriel or Sandrine or the Vakhaevs or all the others, the more it seems to me that the sacred is actually like a mountain. When you first see it over the horizon, it is beautiful and clear, and seemingly somehow close enough to grasp with your hand. But with every step you take in its direction, the mountain grows larger, and you yourself grow smaller. By the time you are at its foothills, it towers over you, and by the time you try to climb it, its winds have begun to howl in your ears. And there you are, now suddenly in the heights, preposterously, wearing wooden clogs; and every step is a new chasm. And you are stopped, frozen, the first on the rope.

In the chasm below you is a man you have begun to love, now long gone, first sleeping in the bunkers of the Little Camp at Buchenwald. Or a girl, begging for her life in a forest, tied to a tree. Or the faces of *one-two-three* little children and their parents, who are crying at night, so far from their home.

Belief grows bigger with every step closer. It is large and perilous, beyond measure.

. . .

Rovzan finishes her prayer. She rolls up her little carpet. She looks at me, and smiles. She tells me she always feels better when she prays. She feels clean and clear. When she misses her prayer, for whatever reason, it's like something is off.

"What people don't realize," she says, her voice so lulling, "is that there is one God. It doesn't matter what color you are or where you come from or if you are rich or poor. There is just one God." She holds up her index finger and looks me right in the eye. "And there is one word, Amen—that's the same in all languages.

"You see," she adds, as if it were an afterthought, "to pray, you only need five minutes and one small clean place. And you pray even if the only place you can find is degraded in the world's eyes: on a train, in a bathroom. If you can't find water to wash with beforehand, you can use a little dirt." She mimes putting a small amount of dirt on one arm, then the other.

"You see life differently after you pray, after you've done what is written. Just because a person laughs and smiles doesn't mean that they have no troubles. But what is your choice? You have to hope."

She looks me in the eye again. You see?

———

Everything important I ever learned about social memory died at Buchenwald's Little Camp.

Émile Durkheim didn't just revolutionize the study of religion. He galvanized an entire generation of brilliant new social scientists in the early decades of the twentieth century who, using his insights about the social body and its sacredness, would go on to look deeply into the nooks and crannies of social thought.

One of Durkheim's students, another Frenchman, named Maurice Halbwachs, ended up providing the foundation of what would become, decades later, the rich and varied field of memory studies. In 1925,

Halbwachs published the field-defining *Les cadres sociaux de la mémoire* (The Social Frameworks of Memory). It was his insight, in fact, that groups remember together; his insight that they remember together for the sake of the present day. He was the one who saw that there is a sleight of hand in all this—that as the flags wave or the ritual is recited about some past moment of glory, we are inclining our hearts together because we need to or want to, now. Or because—and what an insight this was in 1925—someone else wants or needs us to. Because they want to use us. And with this kind of memory, they can.

The Nazis—like every participant in every single nationalist movement—were certainly using memory collectively whenever they did things like invoking the Great Germany of the heroic past, with its pure and ascendant race. Every time a Jewish person was called a degrader of humankind by Nazis, it was by means of collective memory that the public was stirred up into bloodthirsty forms of Durkheim's effervescence: "We, the pure; We the defenders of the boundaries; We the destroyers of all pollution." Halbwachs, born in 1877, had seen the full feverish rise of the age of nationalism and the power of these collective stories. From his vantage point, Nazi Germany would have been simply the latest version of this mad memory game.

Unlike Durkheim and many of his students, Halbwachs was not Jewish. But he was married to a Jewish woman. When he protested the arrest of his wife in France, Halbwachs, too, was sent to Buchenwald. He, too, was shaved and disinfected, and given a number, 77161, and a red triangle. He was also given clogs with no straps and sent down toward the Little Camp, where a wooden barracks first opened and he was first smacked with the stench of human rotting and disease.

I admit that, when I was first reading Halbwachs as a graduate student—self-importantly finding tiny flaws in his work while internalizing his big message—I didn't imagine that one day the man who wrote those words would be in an infirmary in Buchenwald, getting his bandages changed, as another prisoner, an artist named Boris Taslitzky, sketched a reedy portrait of him with single pencil lines—a picture titled simply: "Professor Halbwachs undergoes care, a few days before his death, Buchenwald Camp." But Halbwachs, that revolutionary ripple from Durkheim's revolutionary wave, was indeed there, just a frail old man in glasses, naked, with his chest caved in and his shoulders curved.

Nor did I comprehend that his ideas—which gave each people a level measure of dignity and showed the manifest dangers to humankind of nationalist obsessions—would also be the proximate cause of Halbwachs's deportation, his illness, his shriveling, his death.

And I did not know that he had died right there, in the place where Daniel was living at the time of the New Year, 1944.

There are no neat boxes where you can put science or the sacred. There never were. It's an illusion to think there could be.

AFTER DANIEL was officially registered into Buchenwald, he went quiet. Letters like the ones from Moulins and Compiègne were a thing of the past. There would be no more news sent home about seeing old friends or students or colleagues behind barbed wire, no recounting the lectures he gave to other prisoners about his life in the Middle East. No more comments about the deliciousness or aptness of packages his parents had sent, no more rejoicing at the birth of his niece and namesake, Danielle Trocmé. No more discussions of the books he'd read. No more worrying out loud that he was letting his own studies fall by the wayside. Not a single word, anywhere, about the nameless woman—the pretty box—whom, just a year and a half earlier, he had been agonizing about whether to marry or not. No more questions about the Little Crickets, no more fussing about them having received, or not, the money for their school badges that would say, "Act for all!" No more, in fact, of that image of him in a dark room or a light room, or at night or in the daytime, puzzling over those children, aching for them, trying to figure out what he might do at this imprisoned distance.

All that chatter, all those questions, all those vivid images, with the letters, they all disappear. What is left of Daniel, at Buchenwald, is mostly just a silhouette that we also have to imagine: a bald head, a pair of ears, some twisted wire glasses; a figure, sitting on the ground, knees up to his chin, arms wrapped around them. And walking by that figure, one, ten, a hundred, a thousand, skinny figures of a thousand different kinds—to each his own.

Having somehow survived almost four weeks in the pestilence of the Little Camp, Daniel was deemed fit to be transferred to work. And so, on January 12, 1944, he was sent to Buchenwald's subcamp at Dora. Dora had been set up to manufacture V-2 rockets—those black-and-white ballistic missiles that terrorized London and other cities from mid-1944 onward. The massive scale of this production effort required a great deal of free labor, and prisoners would be the main source of that labor. In all, around sixty thousand prisoners were said to have passed through the subcamp of Dora. Daniel was one of them.

And there, he was seen. Two eyewitness accounts exist.

The first was offered by a young man named Philippe Cambessédès, whose father was a doctor from Lyon and whose family was staying in a house on the Plateau during the war. The Cambessédès siblings were students at the Cévenol School and one of them, Philippe's sister, Catherine, was a brave and active member of the Resistance. Philippe saw Daniel at Dora and, after surviving the war, told the Trocmé family all he knew about Daniel's time there. He said that Daniel had been given a clerical job, and that he was "full of kindness." He said he saw that Daniel had some kind of abscess on his foot or leg and was staying, on and off, in an area for prisoners who weren't capable of working, called the *Schonung*. Later, Philippe added, he saw Daniel again. Daniel was walking badly, but was not yet emaciated, not in so much pain. One day, Philippe got a package from Le Chambon, which he was able to share with Daniel. "We spoke of Le Chambon," said Philippe. "It was delicious."

The brutality of life at Dora mirrored the brutality of its mother camp, Buchenwald. Prisoners lived and worked to construct the V-2 bombs mostly underground—no light, still air—in dangerous, unstable conditions. They were worked ragged and often to death. As in other camps, the labor was managed at the lowest level by other prisoners, most often hardened criminals. These men—called kapos—having been inside of this system of incarceration, often for years, could become merciless sadists. The *Schonung*, a place of recuperation, where Daniel was on and off allowed not to work, would have sounded like a kind of sanctuary, away from the underground labor and the kapos. But what we know of Dora, through testimonies, gives a different view. As one prisoner, named Michel Fliecx, wrote of his trip to the *Schonung*: "They had me take my clothes off, and sent me into the *Scheisserei* room," Fliecx wrote. *Scheisserei*, the shits, in other words—the dysenteric ward. "The first thing that hit me was the foul stench," he wrote, "then I moved a few steps forward. On all sides, lying on disgusting straw mattresses, were skeletons, their dirty gray skin hanging from them. . . . The next day . . . I, too, collapsed into the torpor that seemed to wipe out all the sick there."

In and out of the infirmary, in and out of the *Schonung*, Daniel was surrounded by people dying. He was surrounded by walking skeletons. Still, there was that one day when he got to imagine Le Chambon with an old friend. And he got to share a package. To be full of kindness. To hear, and to utter himself, delicious words.

And there is one more story.

One day in January 1944, a young man called 20021 was standing in one of the interminable roll calls at Dora. After the war, this young man would go on to write an entire memoir about life at Dora under the punishing command of his kapo—a green-triangle criminal named Georg Finkenzeller, who, in a sketch by another prisoner, looks like a small-headed, club-bearing, empty-eyed brute (and who, one presumes, first came into the world cherished and whole). But on that one day, in January 1944, as this young man stood waiting to hear the bark of his digits, 20021, something else happened.

"You," he heard a voice say. "You are Dominique Gaussen."

20021 was jarred to hear his name, the one his mother and father had given him, and jarred to recognize, in front of him, the figure of Daniel Trocmé, whom he'd known from the neat halls and velvety drawing rooms of École des Roches, growing up.

Years after the war, Dominique, like Philippe, also shared what he'd seen in Daniel that day. And this is how Daniel's brother Michel recalled that story:

> The two had a long conversation. Dominique talked about how many of the French had denounced the Jews, according to what he had heard from the police who had arrested them. Dani explained to him that this wasn't always the case, and that there was a whole band of people who had protected the Jews.

At that point, Daniel was in relatively good health. But a month later, Dominique saw Daniel again.

In Michel's words:

"[Dominique said] the change was incredible. Dani had been sent to the *revier*"—the sick ward—"he was being supported by two or three other men, who were seized [by camp authorities] right while Dani was talking with Dominique. The sick ward was maybe five hundred meters from them. Dani couldn't walk back alone. He and Dominque exchanged a few words. Their conversation was brief. Dani had a few kind words of encouragement for Dominique. 'He was detached,' Dominique told me. I asked him to specify what he meant by that.

"'Was he intellectually diminished?'

"'No, not at all. He was in the state that I saw many comrades reach who were in equally deplorable health.'

"'Resigned?'

"'No. He was above it. Death. It was all the same to him.'"

WHEN DANIEL ARRIVED at Buchenwald, he might have noticed that in the main square of the camp stood a single tree. All the other trees had been cleared to make way for the camp buildings, but not this one. In photographs of Buchenwald at the time, the tree—a barren, leafless oak in winter—shoots straight out of the ground and rises up to the height of the camp buildings before spreading out in three main branches, making it look like a man with his arms raised in threat. Like a man in the middle of a howl; like a man about to die. It's a terrible-looking tree, but it survived the mass clearing for the camp because under it, Goethe was said to have written a poem, nearly 170 years earlier. Even to Nazis building concentration camps, Goethe's poems were sacred. This one was called "Wanderer's Nightsong."

> Thou that from the heavens art,
> Every pain and sorrow stillest,
> And the doubly wretched heart
> Doubly with refreshment fillest,
> I am weary with contending!
> Why this pain and desire?
> Peace descending
> Come ah, come into my breast!

And here is where we must, despite our doubly wretched heart, watch as Daniel, too, grows weary with contending, grows thin, ever thinner and lighter. It is where we must face that face, as it ceases to be made even of the airiest lines of a bald man, with two large ears, and wire glasses.

And what? And pray?

On the way to the car, Zezag keeps dropping the little blue coin purse I brought her back from my travels. She drops it, Akhmad picks it up and gives it back; drops it, I pick it up and give it back. Drops it again. In the little patch of green hugging the road, she finds some forget-me-nots, and picks them, and runs back to me, puts them up into my hand.

It's summer now, finally, as one-two-three, the children pile into the red car again. Akhmad takes some time with Dzhamal's car seat. Dzhamal already knows how to buckle the front. We are heading down to the town to find out about children's activities for the summer. Fariza, Zezag, and Dzhamal have been in the house a lot and are full of energy the house can't contain: Dzhamal zooms his plastic car back and forth from the kitchen through the living area to his room; Fariza winds the arm of her brother around until he howls; Zezag—the wonderful horrible princess—her long hair all awry, looks grumpy as she draws in her book. It's time to go outside—today all the other CADA children are at the side of the river—and Akhmad has to go down to the recreation office to figure out how the kids can get signed up for camp. And I'll be there to translate.

We are heading down the hill now in the red car, when suddenly, Akhmad pulls off to the side of the road. Zezag is crying. What's wrong? She's pointing at her window. Akhmad opens his door and goes back to hers. It seems there is a spider on the window of the car. Zezag is afraid. Akhmad brushes her window, brushes the car all around, then looks at her and says look, no spider! Then closes her window and gets back into the car.

As he sits, fastening his seat belt, Zezag squeals again. There's another one! Another spider, crawling at the base of the window! She points and cries and cries more. Akhmad comes out his side of the car again, goes to the window, wipes the window with his hand, presses and presses invisible spiders with his index fingers. See? You are safe!

One-two-three, the children are packed in the back of the car again and we set off. Zezag, though, is still crying, looking out the window, bawling piteously, "Mama . . . Mama . . ." Her siblings are laughing at her.

We zoom down Route de Saint-Agrève, down toward the bridge, Akhmad careening in the red car, past everyone, zooming, turning with ease in the liquid logic of a well-known road. "My children are cowardly," he says to me. "She's afraid of a spider." For comfort, I think, he turns on the music again, and finds "Rolling in the Deep."

And there is the heartbeat again, and Adele, again: "We could have had it all! Rolling in the deep."

I look back at Zezag.

The children start to sing, One-and-two, but not three. Three looks out the window. In silhouette, I see tears are coming down still. I reach back and tap her leg with the beat, "There's a fire, burning in my heart."

And there it freezes, that picture this time. We are racing through Le Chambon in a red car. One-and-two are singing, mouthing the foreign words, tapping their feet to the beat, but not smiling.

Three is looking out the window with her private, tender desolation, where spiders and who knows what other terrors live.

Daniel. Help me. What do I do now?

Dear, sweet Zezag,

I have a story that I want to tell you, to make you feel better. But maybe it's not time for that, just yet. For now, I hope it will make me feel better.

It's a story about a spider.

Once upon a time, there was a very good and very kind man who lived in a desert city, where many people were thirsty for war. They say this man was also very beautiful, with black eyes and a dark brow just like your mother. And that he spoke, always, with sweetness in his voice.

One day, a magnificent angel named Gabriel visited this man, and told him that he was not a regular person at all, but someone who was destined to teach people great and wondrous lessons about peace and justice and goodness. The man was afraid, but he understood that the angel was from God, and he must obey.

Now, you would think that everyone would welcome this man's message with open arms, but only some did. Others began to hate the man and all his followers, and they were determined to kill them all. So, when things were at their worst, the man—now, the special teacher—decided that they would all need to find a new place to live. Kind of like your mother and father did a couple of years ago, when you all left your home in Chechnya.

First the man's followers fled. Once they were all safely out of the city, the man himself fled into the desert with his one last companion. The enemy followed close behind them. They needed to find a place to hide. But where?

Finally, by a mountain, they saw a cave. And they ran into the cave.

Surely, they would be seen! The enemy would find their tracks. They would be trapped!

But that's when the miracle happened. In the middle of all the commotion, a little spider was sitting right at the entry to the cave. That little spider began to weave a web. She worked so quickly, and so well, that soon her web covered the whole entrance to the cave.

You could barely see the web; it only just shimmered a little in the moonlight.

The enemies galloped up to the cave entrance. They were about to rush in when someone noticed the unbroken web. "No one could be inside the cave with a web like that!" the enemy said. "We'll have to keep looking!" And so, they galloped off, leaving behind the spider, and the man, and his companion, and a pair of doves that had nested at the cave entrance, too.

How had that little spider known that it was her work, and her destiny, to make that web? How could she have known?

Well, she didn't know! But she worked away at it, nevertheless, quickly, and steadily. She worked with no rest until her shimmery web was made in exactly the right dimensions. And though she never knew it, in making that web, she would become the spider who saved the life of a great teacher who would, in centuries to follow, be known as the Comforter, the Friend. Muhammad.

It was a great honor for such a small creature.

The spider's web was thinner than paper, softer than an eyelash, but it could defeat armies. Now, Zezag, you will learn to see some goodness in that little spider and her web, yes? And protect all of her many children and grandchildren and great-grandchildren, when you can, yes?

And try not to be afraid?

Chapter 14

MASHALLAH

━━━━━━━━━━

"Whoever it may be, the man who's at this moment
somewhere on the face of the Dru is one of us.
Let's pray for him, to our Lady of the Dru,
and of the Géant and of the Grépon."

—R. FRISON-ROCHE, *FIRST ON THE ROPE*

LAST NIGHT, my first night ever in Poland, the air was loud and electric. Thunder woke me up in my aerie-high hotel room in the lonely center of Warsaw; sleep was only ever fitful after that. Now, this morning on the train, the June skies over the Polish countryside are cool but moody still as I barrel south and east, trying to keep my balance.

I am in a compartment with two young women. The one sitting in front of me—we are knee-to-knee now—took my seat and wouldn't give it back. When I walked into the compartment, she was already in my place. I smiled with a question mark and pointed at my ticket—clearly marked *okno*, window—and then at my seat. The woman, who has piercing blue eyes and a broad swath of dark brown bangs, took one look at me and my ticket and my question-mark smile and waved me off with a frown and a flourish of the hand: "It doesn't matter." That *okno* ticket wasn't the easiest thing in the world to procure. I'd had to wait on a couple of ridiculously long lines at the train station, with several middle-aged women in a row dismissing me, one after the other, with *nie nie nie*, no no no, and the wave of a hand.

Now, on the train finally, the young woman sits in my place, her white, freckled arms folded across her chest, her mouth set in irritation. She looks out my window, icily. The thick green fields, the telephone poles, the abandoned buildings, the summer gardens, the swathes, here and there, of red poppies, all come rushing toward her in greeting. From me, they shrink away.

Where is my balance?

I'm not used to traveling like this, without a usable language of some kind. I feel oddly naked—like I have nowhere to hide. Before I came to Poland, friends who know the country well gave me a couple of pieces of important advice. First, they said, do not speak Russian to people, even if you are absolutely sure you'll be understood. Of course, both Russian and Polish are Slavic languages, and if you could somehow, *poof*, make hundreds of years of on-again-off-again hostilities disappear, it's clear the two do have intelligible overlaps. *Jeden bilet do Lublina*, in Polish, is, after all, pretty close to the Russian *Odin bilet do Lublina*. One ticket to Lublin. But no. No Russian. No risking an *odin* instead of *jeden*, even while holding up a single index finger and smiling. One. Poland and Russia share a past that is just too freighted with anger and pain. So, no bringing Russian into a train station, or a tea shop, or a museum. Better to wait for a half hour on the English line with its *nie nie nie nie*s. Better to pretend it is impossible to understand one another, even when it isn't.

The second counsel my friends gave me was even more important. Never, I was told, refer to "Polish concentration camps." An almost unforgivable error. Auschwitz-Birkenau, Bełżec, Chełmno, Majdanek, Sobibór, and Treblinka, these were all Nazi extermination camps in Occupied Poland. These camps were neither created nor maintained by Poles. Millions of Poles, after all—millions—were themselves victims of Nazi aggression and murder, including right in those very camps.

The combined lesson of my two warnings was this: Poland was not Nazi Germany and it was not the Soviet Union. It lived an epically tragic century of its own—caught in the overlapping maelstroms of two terrible regimes.

And yet, only the most nationalist of observers would claim that Poland—and Poles—were innocent of all crimes in that period. It's very hard to live as an innocent right in the eye of the storm—even harder when there is, say, a long and entrenched history of pogroms against vulnerable populations there.

I look over at the blue-eyed woman again. I notice now she has a thin layer of black liner drawn around each eye, like some of the meaner girls in my junior high school. She can't know that this is my first trip ever to Poland—the abandoned homeland of much of my mother's family. She can't know that Henry Herzog, my great-great-grandfather, had a shiny silk top hat, or that I was named after his daughter May, or that he had a grandson, Eddie Herzog, my first cousin twice removed, who would one day arrange music for Jimmy Dorsey and would compose a single hit song, "Love Is." She can't know that Henry left Kraków just in time.

And this woman—I see that she has pulled out a book that is marked up with notes and yellow highlighter—can't know that *nie nie nie nie* sounds like a taunt to me. Or that right now, I'm in the middle of reading Jan Gross's book *Fear*, about a murderous Polish pogrom against Jews in Kielce in the years after the end of the Second World War. She can't know that I'm sitting across from her right now not expressly to be irritating and foreign and petty about my place at the window, but to travel to Lublin, and then to Majdanek, for Daniel's sake. She can't know what it means to me to be on this very train, moving forward, watching the grasses and the trees and the red blotches of poppies in the fields come and then go.

At the town of Dęblin, just east of the Vistula River, the train stops. A top-heavy water tower, three stories high in peeling yellow paint, looms over crowds of people with suitcases, all waiting to get on the train. Seventy years ago, thousands were deported to their death right from this station, from under this water tower. They, too, had suitcases filled, hopefully, with the supplies of survival. Now, a young man enters our compartment. He looks at the blue-eyed woman knee-to-knee with me and smiles at her, maneuvering his bag into our small space. She looks up at him and says softly, prettily, *"Proszę."* You are welcome. He sits. The train strains with its first movements again. Two men, standing in a high window of the yellow water tower, turn to follow our departure. They grow smaller and smaller as we pick up speed. Then disappear into the infinite away.

Forward, we go. Backward again, for me. Southward.

My grandfather Sheldon Siskind smelled like cigarettes and felt like leather. He had a large, knee-slapping, room-sized laugh, like he was an extra in *Guys and Dolls*. He taught me to play poker and shuffle the cards in a fancy way; called me Toots. With only fully a high school education, he read every line of my big fat book about Russia, directing all queries to his rabbi. Whenever I got to dance with him—at weddings or in the kitchen, with the music up high—I would somehow, guided by his fluid ease, become improbably graceful myself.

She can't know—this blue-eyed woman in front of me—that my heart is aching today, with missing Grandpa's arms around me.

Or that today, as I travel backward toward the heart of darkness, I feel like a Jew.

THE YOUNG MAN EDUARD GALLAND, now 30482, cried all the way from Germany to Poland. André Rogerie, 31278, was a witness:

Tall and skinny, Galland started crying when, on February 5, 1944, a thousand prisoners were called to meet at the entrance of the Dora tunnel. He was feverish and needed help just to stand, so he cried as a blanket of snow fell on the camp that night and the thousand were sorted and stripped of all but one coat and one sweater, one shirt and one vest. And then he cried the next day when, in the already dirty snow, the thousand of them—all sick, all *vraies loques humaines*, true human wrecks—were loaded on a new train and the doors closed and locked behind them again. He cried in the wooden car, his bony legs intertwined with those of his dysenteric companions, and he cried when night came and the last glimmer of light left them alone in the rancid dark. Galland cried *comme un enfant*, like a child, as his friend André was beaten, blow after blow, by a brutish man who wanted André's spot at the wall of the car. And he cried as they stopped and started and stopped again under the dark sky.

And maybe, who knows, Galland was even crying right here, under the yellow water tower at Dęblin, from which thousands of local Jews had been deported to Treblinka in 1942, and thousands more to Sobibór in 1943.

I don't know if Daniel Trocmé shared that car with Galland, or heard his weeping, though he was certainly on that very train, traveling east, and then south. This was the second of three transports from Dora to Lublin in early 1944, designed to rid the camp of the sick and dying, to make more room for actual workers. I don't know if Daniel cried, too, though it would not seem quite like him to weep and weep, his face in his hands. But there's no way of knowing, is there?

My own train rocks south, still, on this ghost-heavy route. Out the window, twisted red pines rush by, backward. Clouds gather. So many faces, so many hands. So many tears under a single water tower.

If I am to be honest, faith first came into my life through fear. Fear of the night. Fear of the dark. Fear of dreams. I was that child who would lie in bed, eyes wide open in the dark, long after her big sister was already asleep. I was the one who, after stretches of waiting, would creak out of our little room, into the hallway, over to the staircase—feeling the cool corner of the wall at my cheek, and, after a pause, would finally say out loud, "I can't sleep." And then, louder, I would say it again, until my parents downstairs heard me. I was afraid of nightmares, which I felt with a shattering intensity. And I was afraid of what I might see hovering between life and shadow in the dark corners, because—who ever knew how thin that line might be. Ghosts.

Faith came when I looked up into the night, into the dark, still and small, and asked God—that big infinite yellow-crayon explosion—to protect me from bad dreams. Please. Please! It was how I learned my first Bahá'í prayer: "O God! Guide me! Protect me! Illumine the lamp of my heart, and make me a brilliant star. Thou art the Mighty and Powerful." Every night, I would say that prayer, sometimes crying as I said it. But still, the nightmares would come: The sky would rumble, the earth would tremble, monsters would climb out of dresser drawers, and I would stand, alone, small, and accused—"It's all your fault!"

It seems I've always been susceptible—for entirely nontheological reasons—to a feeling of awful cosmic judgment. I was just that kid. Night after night, I would keep asking for help, keep hoping for relief. And I would keep praying. Once in a while—rarely—I remember dreams of luminous beauty, dreams that floated in out of nowhere: a quiet lake, a peaceful forest, a loving smile. But still, nightly, I feared, and prayed, and feared some more.

And so, if I am to be honest, my faith was at least partly lizard-like in its origins. Primal, twitchy: Please, God. Take the monsters away.

But what does that kind of faith do in the world? Faith that is the fruit of fear?

Well. I suppose, if it never evolves further, it can do lots of things. Its prayers—recognizable in most of the religious traditions of the world—might look like this: O God. Protect me from the girls who are mean to me at school. Protect me from the drunk guys in the back of the bus. Protect me from nightmares. Protect me from this bad grade, or the fruits of a bad decision I myself made. Protect me, O God. From the Nazis. From the marauders. From the Bitch of Buchenwald. From bad health. From pain. Protect me from suffering, O God. Please, remove it. Wipe it away.

And, if you are on that train to Lublin, having now finally struggled past the yellow water tower onto the last leg of your journey, and you are with Daniel, 38221, who is already *une vraie loque humaine*, and André, 31278, who has been beaten by a brute for his seat at the wall, and the young Galland, 30482, weeping, ceaselessly . . . your prayers might be: God. Help me. Ease my pain. Take me from here. Send me a letter with news of the Little Crickets. Send me home.

And how could God not hear those prayers lovingly? Mercifully?

But if my faith was founded, to some degree, in fear—and never grew beyond that—that would mean that faith lived, for me, in the realm of the self . . . my very own self—a self that might in the end turn out to be sympathetic, or not. My faith would therefore be limited in its reach, propelled only by desires for my own protection, against my own monsters, my own dangers. My own ghosts.

That kind of faith doesn't bear up well under close scrutiny.

Because if faith lives in the realm of the self, then how is it not also a cousin of other lizard impulses? Like the ones that say, my pain must be relieved before your pain matters. The ones that say that my family's pain—or my clan's, or my people's, or my nation's—is more important than yours. Or that say that my holy book is holier than yours. Or that my heaven is higher, my eternity brighter.

About this self-bound faith, the anthropologist could ask: Who does what with whom? And the answer would be: God protects me and mine, while leaving you and yours out in the cold. God sends me to heaven, throws you in hell. To which the anthropologist might well respond: Wow. That's a small form of faith, indeed.

I sit on this train now, chugging farther into the heart of darkness. In that lizard form of faith, I can feel justified in looking at the blue-eyed girl across from me—who has caused me only the tiniest discomfort, really, on a day that probably is not so great for her, either—and decide that she is cruel, while I am kind. I can harden my own eyes toward her. Fix a frown onto my own countenance. Sniff with self-pity. And, abracadabra and *voilà*, I can decide that her people, her countrymen, her ancestors, are cruel. Dęblin, Jedwabne, Kielce. And mine—Sheldon Siskind with his big laugh and his liquid fox-trot, Eddie "Duke" Herzog with his hit song, "Love Is"—are sweet and dear and righteous. Fear—potent as it is—gets so quickly sidetracked into stiff-necked parochialism. If you're not careful, what begins as innocent and sympathetic in a stringy-haired child, creaking out of her room at night in tears, can become, in effect, the root of all evil.

My train speeds by the town of Puławy. There, on December 28, 1939, two and a half thousand Jews were forced to march out of town in minus-thirty-degree weather, surrounded by police. Those who couldn't march—mostly old people and children—were shut in a synagogue until they froze to death.

But on this day, there are twisted red pines and birches in the forests beyond the rail line. Barbed wire is strung between the train tracks and the trees. The dark clouds come in and out and in again.

I am afraid of ghosts. But what am I doing, if not seeking them out?

As the train lumbers on in its last leg from Dora to Lublin, the ghost of the man who is beating André for his seat at the wall might be praying, too. He was once a child. He, too, wanted to live, unmolested. Sick and starving, he, too, one might presume, longed for redemption and love. For his safe spot on the train.

When did I last raise a hand or a fist, righteously? How am I different from the brute?

Maybe I'm not.

The train stops. Rain begins, softly. Lublin.

———

It was a difficult technical problem, how to rid a whole continent—not to say the whole world—of a certain kind of person. The Final Solution, as static as the phrase sounds, kept having to evolve according to the exigencies of war and occupation. There were people's wills—born to decency—that had to be bent, in time, toward compliance and murderousness; and then whole lives that had to be extinguished; corpses—one; ten; a hundred; a thousand; ten thousand; a hundred thousand; a million; ten million—that had to be managed before they spread pestilence. Mountains of evidence—on paper, yes, but also in gray flesh and white bones—that had to be hidden. Various provisional solutions had been tried since the beginning of the war: chaotic street violence, roundups into prisons or ghettos, summary mass executions, mobile killing units that included gassing facilities, mass starvation, and then killing facilities located at concentration camps. By the time the Final Solution was explicitly drafted in January 1942, the actual work of genocide had been mostly exported out of Germany proper and into occupied lands—Poland in particular—where specialized killing centers were erected. In these centers—known also as extermination camps—lives could be ended quickly, on an industrial scale. With the famous use they made of gas chambers, fewer overseers had to deal directly with the last howls of the dying; corpses could be quickly turned to ash and dispersed on the winds above.

In September 1942—just as Daniel was writing to his parents, "I want to be part of the reconstruction of the world"—Majdanek, or Konzentrationslager Lublin, began operating as one of the small number of killing centers in Poland that were together responsible for the death of 2.7 million Jews. By November 1943, though—a year after the Allies landed in North Africa and ten months after the Soviets defeated the Germans in Stalingrad—the tactics of the Final Solution were in flux again, crackling with ever-increasing desperation. Armed resistance was springing up in the ghettos of Warsaw, Białystok, and Vilna; there were prisoner revolts in Treblinka and Sobibór. Konzentrationslager Lublin felt the reverberations of this tactical shift. It was decided that Jewish prisoners who remained as forced laborers at Majdanek and two smaller subcamps nearby would be summarily murdered. And so, on November 3, 1943, in three separate locations, forty-two thousand Jews were led, naked, by soldiers and barking dogs, to the top of specially dug ditches, where they were shot and fell, layer by layer, to their graves as crashing music played over loudspeakers. Erntefest, the mass killing was called, in code. Harvest Festival.

In all, historians estimate, at least 240,000 men, women, and children passed through Majdanek. Between 80,000 and 110,000 people perished there.

By the time Daniel arrived at the camp, virtually no Jews remained there, and its gas chambers—which had, unlike at Auschwitz, never been hidden from view—were defunct. Majdanek now had two main functions: First, it continued to serve as a depot for belongings that had been stolen from prisoners all over the Reich and other German-controlled lands; second, it would be a place where very sick prisoners from all over the camp system would come to stay. Daniel, together with André and Eduard and roughly a thousand others who arrived on February 9, 1944, were among those whose job was no longer to build a bomb, or fill in forms in an office, or make a road or a ditch, or bury the dead. Sick and useless now, they had just one job, and that was to die.

How strange it seems that Germany—with the massive war it was losing; the gray, shriveled bodies piling up day in and day out; the disease spreading anyway; the murderers going mad, one by one; all the country's wealth and resources stripped down to the bare bones—made an administrative point of herding all these skinny prisoners onto trains for new three-day journeys, weeping, howling, hungry, beating one another for space, just so that they could arrive at a new place, and fill out more forms, venture into a new kind of hell. And die there. In what currency was all the effort worth it? To have those boxes neatly checked?

Daniel arrived in Lublin among the living still. How he had survived this long is impossible to know. Maybe his heart had been strengthened by the months and months of climbing up and down the streets and forest paths of the Plateau. Maybe the air was so pure in that higher place that it had somehow infused his being with health. In any case, he lived to see Germany and then Poland. Lived to rumble on those train tracks for three days, east, and then south. And then stop.

André Rogerie, 31278, wrote a year later that their arrival in the industrial city was bitter cold and brutal. Once again, the group was pulled out of a cattle car to the shouts of soldiers, then sent off to march from the center of Lublin toward the camp. "With mathematical regularity," Rogerie recounted, "bodies fell, one after the other, the ranks lightened, corpses littered the road. A violent wind blew on the left, and froze us.

To add to this death scene, the SS soldiers killed with gunshot, whip lashes, kicks. I myself got a boot kick so solid that I shook in my wooden sabots, which were too large and filled with snow."

They marched for two kilometers before arriving at a new camp that was wrapped in barbed, electrified wire, with watchtowers and an incongruously square, high chimney that poured out black smoke. They were again sent into cold disinfection pools—Rogerie noted that he managed to plunge only to his waist—given a hot shower, then sent, naked, to rotten wooden barracks with three rows of bunks, water seeping through the boards.

"The smell of manure filled the atmosphere," wrote Rogerie. "There was no fire."

There would be no work here at Majdanek for them. "We were here just to croak." *Crever.* No long, agonizing lineup in the morning. No carrying heavy loads from here to there. No being beaten at any moment by kapos. Just life, day after day, as long as it lasted among the gray and dying, with the putrid smell of sickness, with camp hierarchies springing up, as they always did, over the control of food, or the passage through the barracks toward water or the facilities. Just life: among the corpses that would pile up each morning. Life, finding a scrap of cloth to wipe the filth off of other prisoners who could no longer use the toilet. Life, with the smell of the Polish prisoners' food filling your nostrils. Life, exchanging addresses, so that mothers might be contacted after the war. Life, saying "Hail Mary" the very last time with someone, and then finding a new bony figure to sleep next to. Life, under the constantly churning fires of a crematorium, under an ever-raining cloud of ashes, descending onto the frigid grounds.

It seems to me this is the life Camus wrote about: the life that rats made; the life of pestilence, under the Plague. These crematorial fires, bringing their "faint, sickly odor coming from the east," were the perfume of the new order; the freshest hell that we can, even now, imagine; the darkest corner of the darkest nightmare; the meanest legions of ghosts. And you didn't have to close your eyes to see them, then. You still don't.

TODAY, LUBLIN IS DARK. Outside the train station, it mists with rain. Cars zoom every which way. It's cold, and I can't find bus number 23—not at this corner, or that one, or that—which would take me to Majdanek. I'm supposed to be meeting with an archivist at the State Museum at Majdanek, and so time is of the essence. I take a deep breath and decide I will try for a cab at a stand across a busy street outside the station. In Russia, getting a cab—which is much more like hitchhiking there—can be a special kind of tricky.

I lean down toward the window of the first cab in line. *Do Majdaneka?* I ask. To Majdanek? The driver is a young woman. She smiles, and in English says yes. For sixteen to eighteen zloty—a really good, fair price. Okay! I open the door and pile into the car, and exhale. She is very pretty, the driver, with a thick twist of blond hair piled up on her head, capri-length tights circled in black lace, a big smile. She tells me her name is Ania.

Alert, cheerful, Ania is some kind of Polish urban cowboy Jim Jarmusch angel. It seems like she can fend for herself.

I look out the car window as Ania begins to wind us through the streets. No, it's not Russia here. But things do look familiarly Eastern European, a little like parts of Saint Petersburg. The yellow, red, rust-colored buildings from the last century and the beginning of this one are arranged on low, snaking streets.

"Is it very far to the museum?" I ask in English.

"Oh no, just three kilometers!" says the urban cowboy angel.

"Oh! I could have walked!"

"Ha. No, you don't walk. It's too dangerous."

"Why? Are the drivers bad?"

"No," she says. "It's the people around here. They are very poor." She points to a ramshackle store, the paint bleeding with years of chemical rain. "And they drink a lot"—she motions her index finger up to her neck and flicks it, like they do in Russia—"they drink and drink. And you wouldn't be safe."

"Not even in the daytime?" I ask.

"No, not even in the daytime."

Ania drives us quickly out of the center of town. We talk about her studies and what different passengers are like. We talk about being a woman cabdriver—doesn't it scare her? "Well, I have my mace"—she shows me where the can is, on the side of her door—"and I have my scream." She laughs. "But no, I don't work at night. Never at night."

Soon enough, we have turned out of the industrial center and ahead we see green fields made brilliant in the gray misty rain. Ania slows, and then stops at a sign made of barbed wire and bright red letters: MUZEUM MAJDANEK LUBLIN. She gives me her card and tells me I can call her when I'm ready to come back into town. It's better than the bus, she says.

I'm choking back tears, looking at the red letters of the sign. Not wanting Ania to leave. But soon enough, I walk through the camp gate, then to the information office—a rosebush has been planted outside it—and then over to the archives, where a mild-faced researcher named Robert Kuwałek tells me about the camp's history, and the "Harvest Festival," and the packages that might come for prisoners. And how Daniel, as a very sick prisoner, would have stayed up by the crematorium at block number five. Robert's desk is littered with faded index cards and Post-it notes. I am touched by how Robert clearly prepared for my visit, gathering all he could about Daniel: one prisoner of hundreds of thousands.

Just as I am about to leave, another researcher brings two objects into Robert's office. She tells me they were Daniel's. She is wearing gloves. She places two documents carefully on a white table. One looks like a social insurance card. *Click.* I take a picture. The other looks like a postcard written in the tiniest, blurriest hand. It would be impossible to read, just like that. *Click*, I take another picture. And *click*, another, for good measure.

Leaving the archives, I gird myself as I head out onto the grounds of the camp. I'm nearly alone. I need to be alone.

Now, the rain is finally loosed. Now, I cover my head with a hood.

I DIDN'T KNOW I would follow you all the way here, Daniel. I didn't mean to, when I set out on my journey to the Plateau. And yet, here I am, under dark heavy clouds, in front of a large field, barbed wire laced around the edges of the grounds—the city on one side, woods on the other. The grass is a luminous green under the rain, here; hay is bundled intermittently in tight, cream-colored discs. In the distance, there are buildings—wooden barracks, a watchtower, a crematorium—and a long pathway that leads to a saucer-shaped monument.

What is there to do but walk? Walk and listen to the crows, who perch and squawk on the wire, or the tower, or the fields themselves, where they dig for worms in the grass.

Daniel, it's me now. I wander into building after building, looking for you. I'm afraid.

The Germans evacuated this camp in mid-April 1944. They left the place with no time to hide their crimes. So these buildings—the gas chambers, the barracks, the crematorium—have been preserved better than at any other extermination camp. Their very existence was some of the most powerful early proof that the Holocaust had, in fact, taken place—a battle of acceptance that hasn't yet been won.

Rain, grass, hay, crows. The dank smell of wet wood.

In a first building, with an exhibit about camp leaders, there are photographs of men and women whose crimes were tried after the war. One man, SS Senior Squad Leader Erich Muhsfeldt—who once shot eighty prisoners in the back of the head before sending their bodies to the crematorium—looks like a cartoon demon with high pointy brows and pale blue eyes. A woman, Senior Overseer Elsa Ehrich, who'd gone from working in a slaughterhouse to running selection in extermination camps, looks like a lunch lady. In another building, there are photographs of the prisoners, and artifacts of objects that prisoners left behind: Here is a doll, its eyes gouged out.

Rain, grass, crows fly by. A priest walks the grounds, too, speaking Italian with a couple of companions.

I enter another building, a long dark barracks. Lying in heaps on either side of the wall, and in long high central lines of shelves, are row upon row upon row of shoes. Shoes by the thousands, all jammed together. Heavy walking shoes. Thin, flapping shoes. Shoes for ladies. Boots. Delicate, once-white sandals. Shoes that smell like shoes. Rotting shoes. Shoes, displayed behind glass, that go up to the ceiling. Walking the full turns of this long, dark room, I feel a pressure building on the back of my head.

Alone with all of the ghosts that may or may not hover here, I think: Skylark. Have you anything to say to me?

Daniel. It's me. Where are you?

By now the rain is pouring. I find my way to the gas chambers. The ceiling is very low. I see pictures in my head of fingers scratching at the ceiling to get out. I can't bear to stay long.

Grass. Rain. Dark, full rain. A crow lands on the top of an electric pole. One rough wind, and it flies off.

There is no mistaking now the function of that square chimney that juts up toward the sky. I walk into the crematorium, look at the long row of red brick ovens, with their black metal doors. I spend time in front of them, trying to make my thoughts clearer, cleaner. It's no use.

Turning a corner away from the ovens, I find myself in front of a separate room, a space lit by a small window, with only gray rain-light now seeping in. In this room stands a large table; the base is made of concrete; the surface, metal. This is the table where bodies—how many?—would have been laid out; where the last of the bodies' fluids would have flowed down the sides, toward the ground. Where remains would be ransacked for gold or other final possessions, before being conveyed into the fiery furnace.

Daniel survived until April 4, 1944. On that day, he was not yet thirty-three years old. Infirmary records from Majdanek place his death at 4:40 in the morning. Cause: Tuberculosis and enteritis.

This table is, I suppose, where Daniel's body was placed, too.

I think of Daniel's gray flesh. I think of him going into the fire. Think of his ashes, floating up out of the chimney. Into the skies, over the roof-tops, onto the fields, into the soil, into the hay, into the birds. Forever.

And this is what is left of you, Daniel: the boy with the curls and the big ears, the boy who said, "Don't cry Mam'selle, Dani is here." The man who didn't fly out the window into the forest to save himself; who crouched in trucks, and busses, and cars, on the way to prisons; who was hungry, who was sick, who was shorn. Who begged for news of every Little Cricket. Who, finally, was gray and dying. And then dead.

I leave the crematorium, nearly blinded with tears.

Daniel. I want to find a stone for you. And I want a holy place where I can put the stone.

I didn't mean to follow you all the way here when I began. This was supposed to be a story about one Plateau and its clean, clear air. And how that Plateau surprised the world of averages in that terrible, murderous time; how it beat the law of rational choice, there on the rainbow end of a bell curve. It was supposed to be about some social bond—who does what with whom?—that comes to life in the fields, in the hearths, in the schools, a bond that might teach me how to be good, or better at least. It was supposed to smell like fragrant grasses, and sound like an open melody. It was supposed to be about the people of the Plateau. About them.

And now here I am, looking for a stone for you, and a spot where I can put it. But I find no stone, and no spot.

I think of the holy words: "Were it not for the cold, how would the heat of Thy words prevail. . . . Were it not for calamity, how would the sun of Thy patience shine?"

I find a bench in the rain. I see a small bird land on a wire above. I say a prayer. The bird sings one sweet long note. And flies off.

I sit a little longer—the priest walks by again—and then finally head back to the road.

I dig into my bag, and find Ania's card; I touch my camera, inside it the postcard with the tiny handwriting.

I am haunted by this: I know I have left something undone.

———————

Caroline's house stands stone sturdy in a hamlet called Les Tavas, four forested kilometers from the center of Le Chambon. I'm staying with Caroline, her husband, Yves, and their children on this visit, a couple of weeks now since my trip to Majdanek. It's my first time as a houseguest here on the Plateau. I always worry that I'll be a bad guest, spending long days with the CADA folks and otherwise needing to be alone with the swirl of my thoughts, so I've regretfully refused several very kind offers. But I knew the house in Les Tavas was big and strong—it used to be a country school—and I've felt so heartsick ever since Poland, I long for real company. So when Caroline invited me again, assuring me it was okay for me to be away during the days, and then to be alone with my thoughts as much as I needed, I was most grateful to accept.

Caroline is universally loved around here, with her big laugh and her mane of brown hair, and her ability to mimic the sounds of animals and people—not to mention her ability to somehow always lead with her big, open heart. She has become a real friend. I can tell Caroline what Daniel has meant to me as the months and now years pass by. Or the CADA families. Or what the flood of stars at night means to me right here and now.

And it is a special bit of our friendship that Caroline, like everyone else in her family, sings. She can herself perform a driving solo rendition of Jacques Brel's "Dans le Port d'Amsterdam," and a fittingly theatrical one of Édith Piaf's "Milord," throwing an invisible scarf—*votre foulard de soie, flottant sur vos épaules*—around her neck. Sometimes her whole extended family, everyone looking nice and brown and cheery, travels great distances to eat and then sing together—the brother who is a doctor, the brother who is a nurse, the brother who is a priest, the sister who lives far away, their wives and husbands, their children—with their large and gorgeous matriarch in the coziest chair, closing her eyes, folding her hands in her lap, and listening as they do. A melody, a harmony, another harmony. A hymn.

The nights now are so quiet—with only birds and bugs and the occasional dog bark to disturb the silence. And this particular family is a balm to my tired heart. Even when the summer storms come—as they do in the mountains, the rain beating, the lightning flashing, the thunder roaring, sending the lights into an uncertain flicker—I am safe here, and clear again.

To set me up for work, Caroline has shown me how to walk from her house, through side roads and forest pathways, directly to the CADA residences. I've done it a few times now on my own, without getting lost, which is good, because my cell phone doesn't work much past the center of Le Chambon, and certainly not in the forest. But today, after spending some time with the Vakhaevs, I'm thinking I'll try something different. I know you can get from Le Chambon to Les Tavas if you just follow the train tracks, which pass through the valley just under Caroline's house. It's true the old-timey tourist train runs in the summer, so I'll need to check the schedule. And I know there are a couple of places, high up in the forest—not far from La Maison des Roches, in fact—where the tracks are perched up on a bridge. You wouldn't want to get stuck there.

Still. I feel I need that view, from above.

IT'S THE FIRST DAY of Ramadan today, and Akhmad is already going a little nuts with not being able to smoke. Still, I think he's about the happiest I've ever seen him. He just got back from the Resto du Coeur, with bags and bags of food. He's even been able to get some halal meat, and is now singing the lyric praises of its pink-purple-ness, and its lines of white fat.

Little Dzhamal takes a bag of groceries nearly as big as his own frame, and huffs and puffs it into the kitchen. The girls bounce around. Sulim, the baby, gurgles in their direction.

Mashallah, I hear Akhmad say. *Mashallah.* I ask him what it means.

"*Mashallah*, it's to be thankful. Something wonderful."

It means, literally, "God wills it." And yet it seems, there's a kind of joy inside the word, too. Some large, cosmic gratitude. I realize I've never seen Akhmad smile like he is smiling right now; an extra special accomplishment, given his cotton mouth ("During the fast, you can't drink, either!").

Rovzan serves me soup with meat and light broth and potatoes. Her head is uncovered now and she has a stuffy nose. She is fasting, too, a first time after her pregnancy and then the birth of Sulim. She teaches me how to say "I am fasting" in Chechen: *Sa markha du.* I have a fast. Ha-ha, the children laugh as I try to get the syllables right.

In my head, I try to get the meaning of words right, as the afternoon winds down: *Mashallah,* there is real pink-purple meat you can eat. *Mashallah,* Akhmad hired a lawyer for their immigration case. *Mashallah,* their car cost only 350 euros—and so Akhmad tells me the story again, one that has become a trope for him—of the lady who didn't need her car anymore because it was taking up a parking space that cost her money, and how she saw him counting his twenty-euro bills down to all the money he had, and gave him back the last one. Ah. *Mashallah. Mashallah,* the car, plus the meat, plus a new friend, who helped Akhmad figure out how he can get to a mosque during this holy season.

Mashallah, that I am able to see Akhmad's face turn from gray to pink.

It's getting late, I realize, and I'd told Caroline and Yves this morning that I'd be back in time for dinner. Out the window, there is a rumbling in the distance. It's sunny, but the storm that smashed the side of the mountains yesterday seems to be threatening some kind of return. Akhmad says he can take me to Les Tavas by car—it might rain—but the truth is, I really want to walk. It's only about forty-five minutes—even quicker if the train tracks are the shortcut I think they are. And when will I have another chance?

I get ready to leave and Dzhamal takes my bag from the chair where it was lying, puts it over his shoulder, and says, again, *"Tu ne sors pas."* I look at his brown eyes and triangle chin again. *Mashallah*. I leave, and set out down the road.

The train has just passed by—I can hear the blast of its steam whistle receding farther and farther away—so there is no danger there. I start walking, first down the street, and then onto the rails, passing the houses that line the train tracks near the center of the town. And then the path begins to turn, slowly, into woods.

This is the forest that spans broadly up and beyond both Les Grillons and La Maison des Roches, where the children looked for their mushrooms during the German raids, and where the Resistance fighters, for their part, slept at night among the mosses and tree roots. It's the forest that Daniel walked through, day after day, thinking, maybe, about his decision to leave his "pretty box," or, maybe just replaying in his mind the small moments in the life of every Little Cricket. It is where Amélie and I hunt for mushrooms now, and where the Chechens sigh for their *cheremsha*. It is, more or less, the forest where Agnès was tied up and killed.

Poland felt like a wound. Walking in holy places, like this forest, might be a cure. But I don't know.

MAJDANEK WAS ONE of the strangest of the strange fruits of the age of modern nationalism. But we are not now innocent of the perversities that caused it. With all of our chances—and all of the moral tools we've derived from any number of spiritual, religious, and philosophical orientations—we haven't learned. It's like we still don't even recognize the moral hazard of deciding we are anything—any nation, any race, any religion, any gender—before we are a human being. Even when we must know, in our deepest places, that the oneness of humanity is an absolute truth, we behave as though we don't.

Earlier this summer, I spent a few weeks in Istanbul; Charles had work in that city and it was easy to travel to Poland and then to France from there. It's been a summer of massive—and sometimes rather dangerous—antigovernment protests in the city. During the days while I was there, throngs of protesters were periodically sprayed down with tear gas—once, I inadvertently got a face full of it. Then, every night at nine, you could hear the clattering of pots and pans on the streets of the city core, people whooping along with the clattering, and cars would beep their horns, and flags would wave. In the more genteel neighborhoods of old Istanbul, by late dusk, under the leaves of linden trees, under the crescent moon—you could hear a flat *ting-ting-ting* as forks hit glass or knife hit plate. *Ting-ting-ting* to the clanging outside. Genteel people would smile at the consonance of it all.

I have felt this giddy effervescence—or some cousin of it—before. In the Palace Square of Saint Petersburg, with a quarter of a million people, in 1991, when the fate of the Soviet Union hung in the balance and tanks waited for orders to shoot; in the freezing streets of Kiev in 2005; at a distance, among the Kabardians in the Caucasus; or, even, in Quebec—where I danced some ridiculous jig on the Jour de Saint-Jean-Baptiste. And there was the time Nelson Mandela came to Montreal after his long imprisonment and I found myself in another giddy crowd, raising my fist with thousands of others. I remember how I looked at my own fist, then, held high in the air.

This summer, in Istanbul, everyone, on all sides, has been righteous and indignant. They throw tear gas at each other; they throw rocks. Their poison seeps into the air; dogs and cats and birds lie motionless in the yellow din.

What are we first when we wake up in the morning? In Istanbul. In Kiev. In the streets of Baghdad, the streets of Cairo. In Paris.

Or in the streets of Boston, where two young brothers—their roots in the North Caucasus of Russia—killed three and injured 364 innocents because when they woke up in the morning they decided they were Chechen.

We act like we're wandering through an identity grocery store, squeezing here and there for the ripest fruit: I am an American. A Jew. A Bahá'í. I am the granddaughter of a ballerina, the granddaughter of a card-counter. A woman, an anthropologist, a singer. I come from a decaying city. I lean left.

It's no use, this business of raising fists and pinging glasses or clattering pots and pans, however genteel it all may feel, however lofty the object, however sweet-seeming the fruit. It's all the same rough beast.

"We know only men," said the people of the Plateau during the Holocaust, when other people were becoming the Bitch of Buchenwald, or rounding up their neighbors in barns and then burning them alive. "We don't know Jews. We know only men," they said in the Plateau when they woke up in the morning.

Is that so hard?

My heart is sick, and for what? Daniel—who only knew men—is dead. And there was nowhere to put the stone for him. . . .

I'VE BEEN WALKING for a while on the train tracks. Walking and thinking, leaving the town behind, leaving the sounds of cars and conversations behind.

As I pace forward into the woods, lost in my thoughts, a ping of rain surprises me. Hits my face. The clouds—far off only a few minutes ago—must have caught up with me. I keep walking.

Ping. Ping. Ping-ping-ping. More rain.

On my left are stony, mossy cliffs topped by pines. On my right, farther and farther below, I can still see the road—Route de Saint-Agrève. The rocks on the rails cut into the soles of my thin cotton sneakers, so I do my best to avoid them.

Looking down, I see little fir saplings—like the ones Daniel described in his letter to the Little Crickets from Compiègne—tucked into the spaces between the tracks. The tiny trees were, he said, fragile like their young family: "And each one of us must take care, each day, many times, not to break [them]."

Ping. Ping. Ping. Ping. A curl of wind pulls my hair up away from my face.

I walk and walk, a little faster now, still trying to avoid the sharper rocks in my path. But now I notice that the sky is getting much darker. I turn around. The clouds are nearly blue-black behind me. I'm an idiot. I should have known this might happen. Without willing it, I pick up my pace again as the path pitches higher and higher away from the road. There's no way down, now, except through the woods, which are a messy tangle of large and small trees, bushes and brambles.

Down below, La Maison des Roches is within sight on my right. And I can just make out a man in an elegant pose just outside the door, all in black.

The rumble above is louder, closer. I walk faster still.

A little farther, a little faster, and it now arrives in earnest: a full-on, drenching rain. Full upsweeps of wind. And, here they come: clear thunderous crashes. Lines of light break open the slate-gray sky. The sky cracks; I flinch from my stomach to my chin. It cracks again. I twist, jerk forward. Lightning. Lightning! My one great earthbound fear. A bolt; a gut jolt: Now, I'm the girl clambering through the night forest at camp again; the girl in that dream, being blamed for everything under the roiling earth and skies.

It was lightning that killed a little girl in Rochester when I was a kid, as she hid under a metal turtle in a playground; lightning that felled the father of Pierre—hero of *First on the Rope*—on the peaks of Les Drus; lightning that lit up the skies of Warsaw, and my first night in the Caucasus. Lightning that turns me back into a frightened lizard time and again, in spite of every civilizing veil.

I start hopping from plank to plank, quicker and quicker, wilder and wilder, the stones piercing my shoes. And then I start to run. And run. And run.

In the din, thoughts rush forward: Electricity has laws! It seeks out high open lines like this one. I see my own body lying between metal and wood, alone among the trees, motionless. Lawless.

Running, I start to cry, and I say, up to the sky: I don't want to die yet. Please. I'm not ready.

I picture my body, again, now dead on the tracks. I picture Charles's face when he learns I am gone. I picture myself after the storm, surviving, and I picture myself forgetting how terrified I was today.

I don't want to die.

It feels somehow truer than almost anything I've ever said to myself: I don't want to die.

I ask God to forgive me.

I ask God that, if I live, not to let me forget what this felt like.

Then, as if by way of response, there is a crash and a blinding blaze of white that lands right next to me. And I, now, myself, first on the rope, scream at the top of my lungs, like the little girl I once was, scream with all of my breath, all of my lungs, alone, up high. Just me, alone, in the holy forest, on the holy tracks, with my picture of Daniel lingering in my heart from Majdanek . . . and, in a flash, that singular image of a brilliant, yellow-crayoned, infinite-sized God.

It is a steep, steep drop to the road below where trucks barrel by in the driving rain. I throw myself away from the tracks now, and down, down, down, grabbing small trees and branches and roots to hold me as I go, falling on my seat, sliding. I hear the roots crack and tug at the loose soil, and I grab another one and on I go, plummeting forward, down and down and down, until I find myself on solid ground.

I land; I stand. I am shaking. I'm safe. Or safe enough . . . I have to figure out where I am.

I start to walk down the road, in the direction of Caroline and Yves's place. I'm still at least a half hour away if I take the Route de Saint-Agrève. I try to get my phone to work. It's dead. The rain is still driving, sideways, but I'm shaking and oblivious. A truck tears by, too close.

There is a house on my left, oddly tucked into the side of the hill. I see something stirring there. A blond woman with hair pulled in a ponytail leans out of a large window. She tells me to come over to her. I'm soaked with rain and sweat. I tell her my phone doesn't work, that I'm staying with friends out past the Genest woods. Her big black dog leans out the window, too. He sniffs at me and starts to bark, with the sides of his cheeks. Her husband has a tattoo on his bare arm. He doesn't talk, doesn't look at me. *Quand même,* she tells me. "Anyway, come on in while I call—so you don't have to stand in the rain."

My hands are still unsteady. I step through their little front garden, enter the small house. It is full of little souvenir Native American figurines on a shelf—a dozen of them, maybe, all in the same browns and ocher reds. I say I'm from America, but have never been to the place where these Native Americans live. The woman says her husband likes the figurines. It's his kind of decor.

And then she gives me her phone so I can call Yves, who says he'll be there right away.

I tell the woman about the lightning, how it came so close and how I screamed and ran down the hill. She says she was outside, too, and was also scared, running right inside.

I notice the dark of her house on its uphill side, and her open window that brings all light in, on the side of the road. I notice that the dog is calm now, lying near my feet.

"Well, now I can say I welcomed an American in my house," says the woman. She has a soft face.

Yves arrives. I thank the woman and her husband. I thank Yves. And I thank God. *Mashallah.* Among other things, for answering my prayer to live, and my prayer to remember.

And for answering the prayer that I didn't even know to say: the prayer for the open door.

THE LIGHTNING STILL streaks across the sky tonight. You can see the whole line of its pathway, its electric bolts through the atmosphere along the hills in the distance. Caroline and Yves's house is stone, though, and from the very first time I walked into it, it has felt clean and clear.

Not long ago, I learned it was a schoolhouse during the war. Refugee children were sheltered here. Maybe the teacher stood and lectured about mathematics or history where the kitchen is—where Caroline now cooks, licking her fingers, and where her sister-in-law, Nathalie, once demonstrated the cancan to me. Maybe the children looked out that high window onto the road above, toward the forest, and thought of their families back in Poland or wherever else. Maybe, once in a while, they slept upstairs, where I sleep. Maybe they dreamed there, too, as I do. Maybe some traces of them remain.

Maybe they are not so frightening, as ghosts go.

Sandrine and Rémi and their children have come for dinner, and we are now sitting, all together, at the long wooden table, eating beautiful food. Bill and Boule, the black cats, curl up in various corners, aloof. Caroline asks me to sing something—to sing "Dona Dona" again—and I think about how I sang it last time with her whole family, and how they added magnificent layers of harmonies. So I sing "Dona Dona," this time with a full voice. "How the winds are laughing, they laugh with all their might . . ." Caroline sings, too.

And now I lay me down to sleep. *Mashallah*, I'm in this house. This house, here, in stone, with the electric cracking and cracking outside, and into the smallest hours of the night.

Seventy years ago, Daniel left two things behind at Majdanek.

The first was a social insurance card, as thin as onion skin and bearing his name, TROCMÉ DANIEL, the number, 1264950284, and the stamp ASSURANCES SOCIALES SERVICE RÉGIONAL—TOULOUSE.

The second was a postcard. It is, by now, a faded, creamy yellow. It is also frail, its edges torn. There is no image on the card, no photograph or anything, just the declaration CARTE POSTALE, with the sender and recipient on the front, and then crowded lines of fuzzy blue letters on the back. Addressed to Monsieur D. Trocmé at École des Roches in Maslacq, Basses-Pyrénées, it is from Madame Trocmé, at École des Roches up north, in Verneuil-sur-Avre.

From a discolored line that runs through its center, it is clear that the postcard was folded for a long period. Into a pocket, perhaps. For safekeeping.

By the date, I know it was written just as Daniel was weighing whether or not to take up André Trocmé's offer to come to the Plateau and help at Les Grillons. Daniel's job in Barcelona had fallen through, but there was also the chance to go to Paris and work on his doctorate or—his parents' clear preference—to continue teaching at the second campus of École des Roches, now located in as yet "unoccupied" Vichy France.

It is a letter from a mother to a son. And that son kept the letter from the moment he received it, in late summer 1942, until he died seventeen months later.

It begins:

My darling, where can we look for you soon?

What will you do next? the mother asks the son.

For the time being, it's simple. You are working hard preparing
the students for their exams and that means you can forget some
of your worries. We were very happy to see François. And now, it
is for you to choose.

You must choose yourself, the mother tells the son. *You must weigh everything.*

You know Papa will subsidize you if necessary. But François
would have told you all of that, along with everything else.
Monsieur Volode left us, and he will tell you some of the present
perplexities. However, the boys are no longer sleeping in the
lobby, which has resumed its normal appearance. We found a
room up high for three of them . . . three very nice boys.

The school back up north in Verneuil is chaotic, but settling into some normalcy. His parents are doing okay. The letter then turns to Daniel's other brothers and sisters:

> Michel is, happily, with us again. Marianne will come back in three days. . . . Suzi had thirty-five pneumothorax patients to insufflate for Delafontaine today.

There she is, in the smallest blue handwriting. Suzie Trocmé, who brought kindness to the last years of my great-grandfather's stern life. Who made my Jewish mother feel welcome among all the midwestern in-laws. Suzie, working away, filling sick lungs with air. Suzie, whose name sat folded somewhere in a pocket.

> We were determined to send something through you to the family. . . . We wanted to send 500 [francs]. Have we already? We can't remember. Send us word right away. You can say that it comes from the friends of Roches.

The letter gets fuzzier. I can't read it all, even with help. I can't figure out who each and every person was. But this sentence, near the end, stands out:

> My darling, what worries [are] still in your head and your heart. . . .

The message is signed with kisses. Then, wound up the corner of the card, in even tinier writing, is a postscript: "I am finishing the pull-over and the socks."

The *carte postale* was written on September 5, 1942. Daniel took a few days, clearly, to think about all of it. To choose. And then, on September 11, he wrote his response, full of resolve, about how the die was now cast, how Le Chambon represented an adventure for him, an almost religious calling, how he wanted to be part of the reconstruction of the world. And how he didn't want to be ashamed of himself.

Now I realize: It was not the answer that remained with Daniel, folded in his pocket, for the seventeen months until his death. His beautiful reply, after all, had been thrown out to the winds long before. It was the question that stayed with him through it all—the Plateau, the Little Crickets, the long walks, the arrest, Moulins Prison, Compiègne, Buchenwald, Majdanek. It was the question, written lovingly, trustingly, with the words "my darling," and "now it is for you to decide." It was the question that stayed with him perhaps all the way to that metal table in front of the ovens.

Darling, now it is for you to decide. Where can we look for you, soon?

ONCE, when I was around eight years old, I saw something in the dark.

It was the middle of the night. I was asleep in the little room I shared with my sister. But I don't remember the sleeping part—how could I? I only remember this:

In one violent surge, I sat, bolt upright, with my eyes wide open. At the foot of my sister's bed I saw, in the dark, a figure. It was a young man. He was sitting, wiry, with his legs folded up at his chest, and his arms wrapped around his legs. He was looking straight at me; he seemed deep in his thoughts. Then, in an instant, he was gone. Absolutely gone.

Almost since this journey began, I've been seeing Daniel in that same posture, over and over again, in my mind's eye. I see him like that in the hallways of Les Grillons as the children sleep—"Was he afraid that there would be a Gestapo raid at night?" I see him like that in a truck or a train, or under a water tower, or in a barrack. I see him thinking, thinking, lost in his thoughts. I see him watching me, too.

Sometimes, I see him that way when I talk with him, in secret.

Darling. Where can I look for you soon?

Chapter 15

THE FRUIT OF
THE TREE

Go thy way, Daniel: for the words are closed up
and sealed till the time of the end.

—DANIEL 12:9

BEFORE SHE SENT THEM OFF, my aunt Barbara wrapped the letters together with a pink ribbon, and tied the ribbon into a sweet little bow. The bow didn't surprise me. Barbara is an artist of meticulous and otherworldly predilections. The letters would never have arrived just like that.

Barbara called me a few days ago to tell me that, by chance, she'd found piles of correspondence among my grandmother Dorothy's things. Grandma died a few years ago now, but her belongings—still loaded with unreleased memory—continue to be sorted. Barbara thought some of the correspondence might be related to Suzie Trocmé. So, today, a package arrived, addressed in careful handwriting. And here I am, in front of a small stack of letters, tied like a miracle in a pink ribbon.

I loose the bow.

Together, the envelopes have the sweet, moldy smell of my grand-mother's house. I close my eyes, breathe them in deeply, and picture that house, stuffed full with my grandfather Gordon's mournful oil paintings and Dorothy's lyrical watercolors, and Barbara's African masks and Mami Wata dolls. Even decades after he died in a plane crash, the house that Gordon built was jammed with art, and jammed with light, which would come rushing in from a long line of windows that opened to a forest drop-ping down, down, down toward the Saint Joseph River. I remember sit-ting on my grandmother's rug in that light, cutting origami paper, sewing stuffed animals, drawing and drawing, fashioning villages' worth of clothespin dolls, and playing dress-up with my sister in old ballerina cos-tumes. And then, outside, climbing up the trees, and swinging on thick vines out over the drop and back. Over the drop, and back.

Dorothy's home—and her genteel poverty—smelled like sweet mold and beauty. And now, Suzie's letters do, too.

I disassemble the pile. Most of the letters are labeled with the same return address in Montpellier. These must have been written after my great-grandfather died, in 1973, and after Suzie returned to France, where most of her original family remained.

In recent months, I've learned some things about Suzie. She first came to the United States in 1947, just two years after the war ended. By that time, there had been a *rat-a-tat-tat* string of tragedies in her family. In the winter of 1943–1944, her older brother François had lost both of his hands when he instinctively grabbed a bomb that was about to ex-plode in his factory. By spring, her beloved Daniel had died in Majdanek. Late that summer, her mother, Eve Trocmé, was struck in the head and killed by shrapnel during an Allied bombardment of Verneuil-sur-Avre. Just a few months after that, her father, Henri, was struck and killed by an American jeep. So when, in 1947, with fresh memories of all that loss and, no doubt, fresh images, still, of the faces and bodies of the countless tubercular patients she had treated during the war, Suzie received a fel-lowship from the French government to visit hospitals across the United

States, she seized the chance. It was on that visit that she first met my great-grandfather, a medical researcher who also specialized on tuberculosis. He was, like Suzie's father, stern and stiff and bespectacled. And, like her father, he was named Henry.

So, somehow—who knows how—after embarking on that very voyage across the ocean in 1947, and arriving in New York on what would have been Daniel's thirty-fifth birthday, Suzie became someone to me, too.

The pile of envelopes in front of me has no order now. I reach for a thick one that I can tell is labeled in my grandmother's handwriting: "Dad's 2nd wedding." Inside are small snapshots in black and white and fading sepia. They are family scenes. Here is Henry, wearing a narrow necktie and sitting with folded hands and an uncharacteristically open smile next to Suzie. Suzie's arm is in turn wrapped around a child with a buzz cut, who is grinning as he slouches deep into a couch. In another photo, Suzie and Henry stand in front of one of my grandfather's paintings—a Madonna and Child in flat Cézanne-ish planes. In another, there is that buzz-cut kid again, now with a guitar in his arms. Suzie holds the neck of the guitar gently with both hands.

I see now that in the smoothness of the face, the roundness of the nose, the shape of the jaw, and the thick dark of the hair, Suzie looks like Daniel.

In several of the photos, there is a handsome face among the clusters of faces. This must be my great-uncle Bud, Dorothy's brother. He is wearing a bow tie and smiling. Dorothy lost him, too, just a short time after these photos were taken, to yet another plane crash. The Benton Harbor *Palladium* made her double loss its lead story on October 25, 1965: "[Saint Joseph] Teacher," referring to my grandmother in Saint Joseph, Michigan, "Is Hit by Air Tragedy—Again."

I hadn't realized that Uncle Bud's eyes were so dark and soulful. Or that he, like my grandfather, died in the manly prime of his forties. With the loss of her husband, and then her brother, Grandma's hair is brilliant white here, her brow still strong. I look closer: There is grace in the turn of her hips and arms. She smiles a pretty, dimpled smile. But her eyes, behind dark-rimmed glasses, are elsewhere.

Suzie, orphaned of her parents and her brother, is now sitting right there in that house I know, cutting a wedding cake, with Henry's hand on hers, tall tilted candles on the table next to them, still aflame. And Suzie, a refugee from her own country, in a strange new land of too much art and, truth be told, too much blurry sadness, now somehow coaxes Henry to a costume party: He is Maurice Chevalier, in a tilted straw hat; she is Simone de Beauvoir, *femme de lettres*, a braid on the top of her head, grinning, holding a book.

How far had Suzie come from her own family photograph in the velveteen drawing room of École des Roches—Suzie, in a chin-length bob, seated demurely, hands folded, on the far right; her brother Daniel, standing, gazing directly into the camera, on the far left, nine others between them? How many worlds from there to my grandmother's house? How many moments to decide whether or not to light the candle behind the eyes?

Before turning to the letters themselves, I notice one last picture: Henry on a couch with two little girls, one on his right and another on his left, one in bangs, one in pigtails. Me and my sister. I am holding my hands together, fingers twisted. I am smiling, looking right into the camera.

Suzie animated her letters—all of them—with questions. Remembered the names of children and friends and distant relatives. Asked about health and education, and sent constant encouragements. She knew about the job at the Smithsonian that Barb was a finalist for; knew about my aunt Liz's music and artwork and her darling new baby. She thanked my grandmother for the handmade Christmas cards: "I adore your six darling children around the table, looking up to the cheerful little blue angels." She wrote about her research, and the work she was doing for Amnesty International. She drew maps of France and genealogical charts of the Trocmé family. She sent little gifts of money. She wrote about how, after a long-awaited rain, the azaleas of her city were in full bloom.

Always, she asked for visitors to her little home in France. She asked Grandma and Barb. And she asked again.

And yes. It turned out that in these letters it is recorded, for posterity, that Suzie asked, once, specifically for me. "Dear Dorothy," she wrote to my grandmother, "I did get your birthday card in August with its many interesting news. I wrote immediately, exactly August 18, to Maggie c/o Kopecky, in Austria, with the address you had given me, hoping she could stop at my place before flying back to the U.S. But I imagine the time was too short or the address inaccurate, for I never received an answer."

No, I never answered. I got the letter—I did—but I never answered. Instead, in a daze of inattention, I let that chance float away.

Suzie wrote to my sister Laura, as well, when Laura lived in Sicily as an exchange student during her senior year of high school. And Suzie delightedly reported to my grandmother that the two began a lively correspondence about language and culture and all manner of other things. I see that Suzie, given a single chance at affection, returned it effusively. She would send special kisses to my sister, send her love. Years later, when Laura lived in Israel, Suzie wrote—"I looked up Haifa in my Atlas. But I am quite ignorant of what the Bahai believe. Are they closer to the Jews, or to the Christians? Or are they a sect among Jews? I remember that Florence, Laura's mother, is Jewish. Is that important to her, to Dana and to the children? Don't feel you have to answer all my questions; perhaps I shouldn't ask so many. . . ."

No, Suzie, please ask all the questions you can think of. Whatever they are. Keep asking, please. Keep trying, please.

She did.

Sept. 1 . . . I wrote to my nephew and his wife, who are now back in Montreal, that I had a step-great-granddaughter (that is what Maggie is to me!) studying at McGill university in Montreal.

Unfortunately, I could not give any precise address of Maggie neither at McGill, nor at her parents' (I wasn't sure they are still at 74 Salisbury Street in Rochester N.Y. and anyway I don't have Rochester zip code). So I gave [them] your address and you would forward a letter from [them] to Maggie. And here is [their] address. . . .

I HAD BEEN CLAIMED by Suzie. I had no idea.

I picture our green shag rug at 74 Salisbury Street, and our creaky stairs, and my little brother Michael and me fighting with our feet over who would get control over the heating vent in the living room. I picture static electricity and overcast milk-and-water gray skies, and the awkward blur of our teenage faces. I picture being numb to offers of love.

Sometimes things come in pink ribbons in our lives and we see them as such. Sometimes we don't.

And then, sometimes—because the world speaks its purpose in many tongues—we are claimed. And the pink ribbons come again, without our deserving them.

Montpellier, December 16, 1983

Dear Dorothy . . .

I was interested to read that you heard of Philip Hallie's Lest Innocent Blood Be Shed. Yes, André Trocmé (1901–1970) was closely related to me; he was my father's first cousin, but 28 years younger than he. . . . He and his wife organized shelter where Jews were protected until they could flee to Switzerland. The whole village of Le Chambon-sur-Lignon, in the Central Mountains of France, where André was a minister, participated in assuming dangerous responsibilities of hiding these Jews. My brother Daniel (just two years younger than I) was called by André to help him in 1942, which he did wholeheartedly, until he was

denounced to the Gestapo, arrested in 1943, deported to
successive concentration camps in Germany, and died in
Maidanek, Poland (April 2, 1944) . . . both André and Daniel have
been recognized by the Israeli as two of the "Justs (Righteous)
among the Nations." . . .

As a witness to that distinction, a diploma and a silver medal
in the name of Daniel were delivered to his brother Michel who
went to Israel with François for that special occasion (1977).

At the same time, and even more deeply symbolic, a young tree
(caroubier = locust tree) was planted, in memory of Daniel, on a
hill near Jerusalem, with Daniel's name, to be part of the "Forest
of the Righteous" . . . Michel planted [it] with his own hands.

AFTER KNOWING SUZIE for almost twenty years, my grandmother
finally learned the story of Daniel. But I didn't.

One pink ribbon. Two pink ribbons. Three pink ribbons . . .

One girl with twisted fingers, smiling into the camera. One girl with
stringy long hair, afraid of the dark. One girl with a blurry selfish teenage face.

One woman who rattles along snowy trains deep into the frozen
dark, a professional stranger. One woman, trained as a scientist, who is
missing something large and fundamental.

One woman who learns the story of Daniel on her own. One woman
who pictures, in scene after scene of her life now, the shadow of his
crouched figure, watching her.

Then, one woman, who screams on the train tracks when the lightning finally comes. *Mashallah.* Who has dreams where Rovzan is wading
in the ocean. Who sees, in little Dzhamal's face, the face of her own
child, never born.

Then, one woman, facing a pile of open letters, now fully in tears.
Crying at the letters with their teeming generosity, and at the image of
the static electric-green shag carpet, and the sad dazzling light of

Grandma's house. Crying at still not knowing how to be good in a precarious world where beauty is crushed. Crying that for some reason, her chances have kept coming, her whole life long, even if she didn't deserve them. Crying that she has, without knowing it, been claimed.

That woman reaches for another letter from May 1988. In this one, the news of Suzie's death is sent to my grandmother. Suzie herself had chosen the words for her death announcement: "Love thy neighbors as thyself."

Good-bye, says Suzie, with these hallowed words from the Torah, from the Bible, from the Quran, alike, now etched onto the stone of the church in Le Chambon-sur-Lignon: God's commandment to love. To love one another. To love your neighbor. To love . . .

Suzie's brother Charles apologizes to my grandmother for his English, and writes: "Suzie was for us indeed . . . a very dear sister. She owned a clear and genuine mind, a loving and uncompromising heart, [like] our brother Daniel, who lost his life in Maidanek for having defended miserable children in Le Chambon ([Suzie] wanted to follow his example). . . ."

One ribbon, two ribbons, three ribbons. Four.

Now unloosed.

I NEED TO GO and find a tree.

Paulina—a child refugee in the Plateau—tells how, before she was born in 1932, her father, Fejnel, fled Poland with no shoes. By the time he arrived in Brussels, he had thick skin on his feet, like leather. Paulina's mother, Riwka, when she first saw Fejnel, fell madly in love with him. The two were married. Fejnel would sing Yiddish songs to Paulina when she was a little girl. And Paulina would draw.

Paulina survived the Second World War because her mother stole carrots and milk and cherries for her to eat at Rivesaltes, and because she was smart enough to know how to avoid electrified barbed wire, and brave enough to know how to jump from a train when the time was right. Paulina survived the war because in very particular moments, a prison guard gave her bread, or a couple took care of her, only to be arrested and deported for that offense. And she survived because—instead of doing what any ten-year-old girl would most long to do when the world was made of dead bodies draped over barbed wire—she obediently separated herself from her parents and went up to the Plateau, without them. There, during the day, she could study and learn and play in the immense snows and, in special moments, she could go into the forest to observe Sukkot with the others. Paulina ended the war alive but doubly orphaned by Auschwitz, and brusquely separated from her beloved sister. And on a boat to Palestine.

And there, she was shocked to find that she was sent to live inside a tent, surrounded by barbed wire.

For Paulina's sake, here is a thought experiment:

The earth, a ball, is rotating around the sun, another ball. There is an axis—a black pole—thrust through the earth. That axis stands ramrod straight. The earth spins around that axis and then rotates around the sun in an erect mathematical fashion. *Chug-a-chug-a-chug-chug.* Johannes Kepler drew the arc of the orbit for me, so I know the path the earth chooses around the sun . . . and *poof,* I see it there, too.

But, like all metaphors-as-scientific-models, I know this one is wrong.

I animate the picture.

Now, the sun is fire-white. It is so bright, so hot an orb, you can't even look at it in your mind's eye. You have to figure a kind of derivative of it, even just to leave it there in your head. So you do that, and let it be yellow and bright. That's enough for now.

And the axis? The axis isn't straight up and down anymore. Like science says—glorious science!—it's 23.5 degrees tilted.

What of it?

Now, the earth rotates around the sun differently. It tilts. It tilts, so that during a portion of its rotation, the top half of the earth is closer to the sun, and during another portion of its rotation, the bottom half of the earth is closer to the sun.

And so: Because the sun is fire-white, because the axis is tilted, not straight, the earth now receives its light and warmth in the measures and rhythms of the arc of a year. It now has times of heat and times of cold, times of snow and times of rain. Times of verdancy and wind, times of aridity and stillness. It now has seasons.

Because of this, the earth is now blue and green and brown and swirling with white. That very tilt gives it time and gives it life and gives it change. It animates every mountain, every sea, and all the "creeping things beneath the earth."

The tilt, that glorious tilt, is life. It is the ever-churning seasons. It is the snow and the balm and everything between them. It is the life that comes out of the crusted soils of the dead.

And it is the life that could only ever be generated by movement, from places of paucity to places of plenty; from places of war to places of peace.

The earth tilts 23.5 degrees, and living things move and change and seek out the good. And so we are grateful for the tilt and for the seasons, and grateful to go from war to peace. And we move.

We move until our feet turn to leather. We move in order to forage for carrots and milk and cherries. We move up to a Plateau and down again. We move to avoid the ovens and find some promised land.

And sometimes, when we do, we are put in tents. With barbed wire all around.

When Paulina arrived on that far eastern shore of the Mediterranean and lived in her tent and surveyed the wire, the story of movement wasn't over for her. Palestine was, after that terrible war, in the midst of its own complex refugee crisis—between 1920 and 1948, a hundred thousand Jews had arrived in the contested territory, often hiding in old cargo ships to get there, and, when discovered, were forcibly sent to detention camps by British naval authorities. Paulina joined that crisis, too.

But she was not to be bound this time. Once, she snuck under the barbed wire out of the camp for an evening, and found her way to the top of Mount Carmel in Haifa. And there—in a land known by many names: Canaan, Eretz Yisrael, Judea, Yehud Medinata, Syria, Palestine—Paulina looked out over the city and above her were the heavens and beyond her was the sea. "In Israel," she later said, "you probably know, the skies are much lower, the stars are much closer." And on that mountain, about which Isaiah once cried, "The desert shall rejoice, and blossom as the rose. It shall blossom abundantly, and rejoice even with joy and singing," Paulina sighed. Ah. And said: "This will be marvelous."

I think, how mighty must be the Breath that blows the axis to a tilt. How mighty must be the Breath that, in causing the tilt, turns the earth over to the manifold, marvelous creeping things.

On my first day in Israel, the receptionist at the Dan Gardens hotel in Haifa let me sit on his stool at the front desk to order a pizza for delivery. On my second day in Israel, the Bahá'í Shrines were hushed and thick with the perfume of roses. On my third day, Avinoam, whom I knew from Washington, took me up a cable car to the top of Mount Carmel, where I, like Paulina before me, could see the skies above and the sea beyond. From that height, I pointed a little way north up the bay and asked, "Is that Akko?"—and Avinoam said, "No. That's Lebanon. And that"—he pointed to some hills up just a little higher and landward— "is Syria. So you see what we're talking about here?"

On my fourth day in Israel, in the gardens at Bahjí before sunset, I saw a hoopoe bird—the messenger of love from the Queen of Sheba to Solomon—fluttering off an olive branch in a tight blur of orange and black and white.

And on my fifth day, I was in Jerusalem.

Daniel Trocmé, as far as I know, never made it to Jerusalem in the 1930s. But he was close. He was so close you could point to where he was from a cable ride up Mount Carmel. He made it to the Levant, the land of milk and honey, to the lands of biblical and Quranic battles; he made it to the arid outpost that became the meeting place of many civilizations, many languages, and, after the mighty Breath exhaled its 23.5 degrees, the land of one-two-three-four great world religions. This was Beirut, where Daniel's contestations and dreams disappointed his parents. This was Beirut, which in mere decades would slip from one of the world's cosmopolitan gems into the darkness of civil war, and then more war again, producing refugees who would scatter its citizens to the corners of the earth. This was Beirut, which today—because the world is tilted—is taking in hundreds of thousands of other refugees of its own, most notably from Syria, just beyond a range of desert hills.

Daniel never made it, in his life, from Beirut to Jerusalem. Or at least I can't find where he did. But on March 18, 1976, Daniel Trocmé was named as one of the Righteous Among the Nations by the Holocaust Martyrs' and Heroes' Remembrance Authority at Yad Vashem, in Israel. This was done after years of careful research into Daniel's work at Les Grillons and La Maison des Roches. It required gathering all manner of police and concentration camp documents, but also lists of student refugees, and letters from witnesses to his work, and letters from young men who were arrested and deported with Daniel. Among the documentation, there was a most touching letter from Madame Orsi of Les Grillons: "All those who knew [Daniel] loved him, and his beautiful soul will remain forever in the heart of all those whom he approached; he lived a life of love for people, and he sacrificed his life for their well-being."

So, after years of research, Yad Vashem determined that Daniel had, in fact, saved Jews at the risk of his own life. And it was decided that his name would be recorded in that particular Book of Life, along with the names of more than fifty people who lived as farmers or teachers or merchants or pastors in the Plateau Vivarais-Lignon. For this honor, in the spring of 1977, Michel and François Trocmé, and their wives, Hellen and Hildegarde, prepared a voyage to Jerusalem. There, they would commune with the holy city of their own religious past, and, with their own hands, would plant a tree.

FOR THOUSANDS OF YEARS there has been plenty of communing going on for visitors to Jerusalem—the merchants, the builders, the prophets, the pilgrims. And there is plenty of communing going on today. There is communing in the dark, exhilarating passages of the Old City, where you can, if you want, buy a plastic crown of thorns, packed in a box with a crinkly cellophane window, or any manner of rosary, or any manner of religion-inspired trinket. You can talk with a whistling parrot there, or squeeze into a tiny shop for orange juice or pita stuffed with heart and spleen meat. In the Church of the Holy Sepulcher—built on the spot where Jesus Christ, in all meekness, is believed to have died on a cross— you can get huffed at and shoved by believers from any one of six separate churches, as they inch ever closer to their holiest threshold. In the Jewish Quarter, communing, you can pause under an olive tree, while black-clad young men rush by in *peyos* and stringy beards. In the Arab Quarter beyond, you can watch as a group of boys walk up and down the dark rabbit-warren streets hollering and pounding on a pizza box with wooden sticks. Or watch as an old man carefully folds a piece of paper into an airplane for a little boy who is standing below him, looking up.

You can walk past the Western Wall of the Temple, communing. You can walk past the Dome of the Rock, the Al-Aqsa Mosque—where Abraham prepared to sacrifice Isaac or Ishmael; where the First Temple was built, the place of the Holy of Holies, the place where Muhammad landed the mighty steed, Buraq, on his Night Journey with the angel Gabriel, and met with Moses and every other one of the Prophets and Messengers of old; and where today, a Palestinian policeman yells "SHORTS SHORTS SHORTS!!" when a tourist shows up at the entryway, not respectfully clothed.

And now, in this land of prophets and pilgrims and merchants and builders, and wave upon wave of refugees, wave upon wave of orphans and widows, I, too, am communing. And so I walk and walk in the Old City, winding and rewinding past the Via Dolorosa—and the ghost of that one crown of thorns, *Ecce Homo!* Past the Notre Dame de Sion Pilgrim House, where Daniel's brothers stayed in 1977; past my cousin's old yeshiva, which was bombed a couple of years ago; past the group of Russian tourists, lost and in need of directions; past a cheery cluster of African Catholics; past the gates of the city where, in times of conflict, certain people have been known to throw rocks at certain other people. Then, out of the gate, I commune on the walk toward my hotel, past the fire yellow of the broom flowers clinging to the roots of the city on the hill, into the dark streets at night, alone, under the stars, into the hotel room where all night, it seems, birds are whistling long melodies, even as young men brawl in the parking lot below.

I am communing with the thought of the hundreds of thousands who made their way here after surviving that war, made their way here with their waves upon waves upon waves of sorrow. I am communing with my grandfather Sheldon, who loved Israel, and would keep a little leather notebook in his pocket while he was here; and communing with what it means, and doesn't mean, to be a Jew.

In this land of orphans and widows and cocky soldiers, within this brash and beautiful cacophony, I am communing. In this promised land with its barbed wire, where so many arms and so many voices have been raised, under the one white hot sun, I am communing.

I think: This place. It will out any weakness in your orientations and your plans. If you think you are a Jew, a Christian, a Muslim, a Bahá'í, a socialist, a nationalist—and you know you are right—Israel will put you and your orientations and your plans to the test.

After three days of circling it, I go to the Western Wall. I feel the stones with my fingers, I feel the stones with my cheek. The woman standing next to me, her head covered, is weeping. I say my own prayer, up into this wall, where—who knows—maybe one of my ancestors once stood.

It was here that King David sang, line by line, to the measured strums of psaltery and harp, "My soul hath long dwelt with him that hateth peace. I am for peace: but when I speak, they are for war."

This city on a hill is built on prayer-drenched stones, and longing. Some prayers are for fear of the dark, or for the winning of trinkets in this life, and some are for higher things. But I feel sure that every pure-hearted prayer, sooner or later, must reach its holy destination.

At the front reception at Yad Vashem, I speak with a very old, ash-white man who looks into a dusty old book and tells me to write down the number 1754. And then he looks up at me with heavy-lidded eyes. This is the number of Daniel's tree. And this, the old man says, handing me a piece of paper, is the map of how you get there.

Yad Vashem, on the west side of Jerusalem, is flanked by a beautiful forest of Aleppo pines. It overlooks the ancient village of Ein Kerem, where John the Baptist is said to have been born, and out toward Mount Herzl. The sun is blazing hot today, the stones along the pathways burnt pale yellow. Outside, next to the library, is a bonfire-sized pile of black automatic weapons, lying in wait for the soldiers to come out from their Holocaust education classes. I look at the map the old man gave me. Here is the library. Here is the bookstore. Here is the museum—long and triangular. I walk, toward pathways lined with low, twisted trees. Here is the Avenue of the Righteous, and the Garden of the Righteous. Here are monuments and sculptures to people and ideas.

On my right, as I walk, I pass the Hall of Remembrance, where the ceremony for Daniel took place, where his brothers Michel and François were given a silver medal onto which had been inscribed: WHOSOEVER SAVES A SINGLE LIFE, SAVES AN ENTIRE UNIVERSE.

I walk on. Then, in the Garden of the Righteous, I see a bright stone that has been marked on my map. This is the monument that is dedicated, collectively, to the inhabitants of the Plateau during the war. Quoting Isaiah 60:21, it reads, in French: THEY ARE ALL RIGHTEOUS, THOSE OF YOUR PEOPLE.

I think how far I've come—from the time when I arrived in the Plateau and began to know the children and grandchildren and great-grandchildren of these righteous folk. When I learned not to ask about the past anymore, but to study with my eyes. When people first invited me over their thresholds and into their homes. When I first met the refugee families among them. When Larissa told me she loved me and hugged me good-bye; when Rovzan and the children wordlessly made a place for me at their table, as if it had always been mine. Then, when the students at Cévenol made me sing "You Go to My Head" to them before they would answer my questions. And when Agnès was tied to the tree and killed, and Sandrine tapped cigarette ashes into her fireplace and told me her secret—that you have to have faith not in men, but in this: that everything will be as it should.

I think about how sad I feel when I am far away from them, now. Because it is there that I have some small purpose. Because there, I am alive.

"The caroubier is a tree with evergreen leaves, [and] grows in the south of Europe, in Asia, and in Africa," wrote François, after returning home. Also known as the carob tree or the locust tree, it can grow up to twelve meters high, he noted. And then he added this detail: "Its fruit is a pod that can serve as animal food (the Prodigal Son in the Gospel, when he was hungry, would have liked to have eaten the carob pods that were used, then, as food for swine. But no one gave him any)."

Walking and walking, I see so many names on so many plaques—each name a person, each person a universe. Finally, at the far border of the Yad Vashem complex, just beyond a memorial to Jewish soldiers and partisans who fought the Nazis, I think I have found the spot. In photographs from 1977, the area is almost barren. Now there is a patch of hundreds of low green trees, standing at respectful distances from each other, on clay red soil.

There: 1754.

After thirty-seven years, the tree is still only about twenty feet high, with silver and black bark, a few solid central branches, and then long pairs of light green leaves on the lesser branches. It stands, steady, on a spot near the edge of a steep incline. Underneath the tree, the light of the day is softened and dappled. On the nearby ground, a black plaque reads, simply: DANIEL TROCMÉ, FRANCE.

Among the leaves, I see a few twisty carob pods—food for swine and Prodigal Sons.

The brothers planted this very *caroubier* for Daniel. And it has grown, as they wished it would. They had worried about Daniel's politics, his romantic life, his everlasting soul; but they loved him; they knew his heart to be generous and pure.

Their brother had, in his youth, tilted off the straight-up path—perhaps, who knows, by precisely 23.5 degrees. But, on that prodigal tilt, when forced to choose between love and fear, he had chosen love. And love led to prison, and love led to starvation, and love led to being half naked and barefoot in the snow, and love led to the fiery furnace.

In the blazing heat, I walk up to Daniel's tree, a few yards from the drop down toward Ein Kerem. I stand under it, now protected from the sun by its shade. I touch its silvery bark. Put my head on one of its branches. I close my eyes.

My shoulders sink downward, and I feel myself exhale, loosed.

Daniel, I have come so far. What do I want from you?

All I hear are birds, sweetly singing. And a car horn or two, now and then. And birds. And birds. And birds.

There is a difference between ashes and trees, a difference between bones and souls.

I find a clay-colored stone, finally. And place it in a spot where two branches meet.

On the flight from Tel Aviv to Frankfurt, I drift off to sleep.

When I open my eyes, my seatmate is looking right at me. It's a little disconcerting. This man, who introduced himself as Gaby, has wanted to talk ever since he saw me struggling to pop my ears after we took off—plugging my nose with one hand and an ear with the other, my face contorted (an unlovely ritual I had to learn after that operation when I was a kid). "That's not how you do it," Gaby had said, somehow brightly and solemnly at the same time. Gaby, it seems, is kind of an expert at ear popping. He learned all about it when he served in the Israeli navy, living for long stretches in submarines, underwater.

"Look," he says to me, "I'm popping my ears right now, you can't even tell." No hands. Frankly, Gaby looks a little odd while he demonstrates this skill—like a baby who might or might not be relieving himself into a diaper. But bravo to him, anyway.

I've liked talking with Gaby. He has animated, eager eyes; a *kippah* perched miraculously on his bald head; a comfortable round belly ("My wife is an excellent cook"); and tales to tell about how his family landed in Israel from Yemen in 1940; and how he used to be a dancer ("Not just a hobby, either!"). He puts on his glasses to make sure his kosher meal is kosher enough before he eats—reading the label, with its credentials, out loud. He rolls his *r*'s thickly in his throat.

Gaby is proud of his full name—Gavri'el, or Gabriel—one of his selling points, he says, when he first started wooing his future wife. "I told her, 'With me you get an angel, and a sailor!'" That's because he was named for the angel Gabriel—the one who talked to Daniel the Prophet and told of the time of the end, and, incidentally, the same one who rode with Muhammad to Jerusalem on the great steed Buraq. In Hebrew, "angel" is *mal'ach*. But our Gaby here, former navy man, is a sailor, too—in Hebrew *malach*. The two words are just the same, except for a glottal stop between the two syllables. I can see how Gaby's wife might have thought she would be getting a bargain. And he dances, too! Not just a hobby!

So yes, I've enjoyed talking with Gaby; still, it's a little strange to see someone looking right at you when you wake up from an airplane doze.

He asks why I was in Israel. I tell him about Daniel, but also about the refugees in France. I tell him, on purpose, about Akhmad and

Rovzan and their children, one-two-three-four. He asks if I am Jewish, if my mother is Jewish, if my husband is Jewish. Do I know any Hebrew? He puts his hand on his chest. "The world is so big," he says, after I answer him, "and there are so few Jews," he adds, holding up one finger and indicating just a fraction of it. "Intermarriage hurts my heart," he says.

"But how can I not be grateful for it?" I ask, by way of response.

Then Gaby tells me a joke about the Dead Sea.

A man who is very sick goes to his doctor and the doctor recommends that he take a trip to the Dead Sea, where people smear the black clay of its ancient floor onto the whole of their bodies, and then bask in the sun in the hopes for beauty and healing.

"So, is there a chance that the Dead Sea will heal me?" the man asks the doctor.

"No," says the doctor. "But at least you'll have a sense of where you'll be, soon enough!"

Ha. Mud and bones and my future in the dirt. I don't know if there's anything real about culture anymore. Or about blood. Or kinship, or what it means to be connected as kith or kin or kind. But maybe I'm Jewish enough to know to laugh at the eternal spa treatment of my own bones . . . at my future home in the blackest mud of the very lowest place on earth.

We are now almost in Frankfurt, and as the pressure grows in the cabin, I find I'm needing to pop my ears again. Gaby then says to me, as if it's urgent, that the Torah has five books, the Five Books of Moses. The third of these, he says, is called *My Laws*. "This is a very important book." And in it, toward the end, he says, you see a description of terrible times.

Ah, this is where we're going.

Gaby holds up one finger and looks at me. "There are those who say that the reason the Holocaust happened was that Jews didn't follow these laws in the Torah. There are those who say that such are the consequences, these terrible things." He adds, after a pause, "You should look at this book of the Torah and then write and tell me what you think of it."

I look back at him and, after my own pause, say, "I think it means I'm in big trouble." And I laugh looking at him.

He laughs, looking back at me. And then wags his finger in my direction and says, "You are very smart."

And I say, "It's okay, I'm used to feeling like I am in big trouble."

Once, when I was a small child, I lied to my mother. She asked if I'd climbed up on the bathroom sink, and I said I hadn't, when of course I had. I was always climbing up onto things. Later, I dreamed I was in a field and the earth started rumbling and the sky started rumbling and I heard a voice speaking a language that I didn't know but could understand. The voice told me that Noah's Ark was my fault. I had no idea what that meant. Maybe I'd heard something about Noah in Hebrew Sunday School, or seen something about him in *The Children's Illustrated Bible* at the dentist's office? Still, I felt the blame in my legs, my stomach, my very bones. It was my fault: live with it. And, who knows, in a way, maybe cosmically it was, and is—I have certainly been guilty of the very sins that, spun out into their darkest forms, make the world collapse: selfishness, forgetfulness, hubris, vanity, willful blindness; raising a fist, now and then, for this or that reason.

So now—says Gaby the sailor, Gaby the angel—the Holocaust is my fault. Not the fault of every impulse of division and hatred that are allowed to fester in men's hearts, not the fault of the urge to wake up in the morning and think that you are something besides a human being, first, but the fault of those Jews who don't live by the laws of Moses. My fault. The fault of my grandfather Sheldon, who probably loved his bacon and who, when he died, was called a "sweet man" by his rabbi.

Well. I won't argue with Gaby. I like him. And anyway, it's clear he believes that what he is saying is meritorious in the sight of God.

But this I know:

The God I ache for is the Creator of the sun, the Light the likes of which causes the creeping things beneath the earth to stir. The God I ache for is the Clement one, the Beauteous one, the Just one. That God is Singularity itself.

I know I live in the muddy waters, among the bones. Gaby; sailor. Gaby; angel. I; creeping thing. I know I can live my life in fear and debasement, if I choose. But there is more my heart aches for. More my heart knows. And I choose that.

I know the answer. And you do, too, Gaby. Your Book tells you the answer, in its truest places, like the Books of the Christians and the Muslims and the Hindus and the Buddhists and the Zoroastrians, and the Bahá'ís . . . and the hearts and souls of men without Books but who know, who *know*, who are sure. Who lift their hands and *know*.

I know you know, Gaby.

Look at Dzhamal's little face.

I arrive in Le Chambon, alone. In the dark, the bus creaks its way up and up the normal route from Saint-Étienne, and stops, finally, at the spot where Route de Saint-Agrève almost meets the train tracks. I thank the driver, gather my luggage—my suitcase and my ukulele—and the bus rumbles off again.

The night air is sweet and tangy. A streetlamp casts a solitary circle of orange light from above. A few moments later, Marie-Hélène pulls up in her car. What a quiet face she has. She drives me down the hill, past the church—AIMEZ-VOUS LES UNS LES AUTRES—over the river, around the bend, and to my apartment by the woods at Val du Rio. Marie-Hélène always saves the same apartment for me—IKEA-fresh and tidy. She and her mother-in-law and Muriel have left little things for me to eat tomorrow morning: tea and homemade jam and sweet dried bread. I put down my bags, turn on the lights in the little apartment, and take some time to let the piney air sink in.

France is different this trip. A couple of months ago, gunmen who claimed to be part of Al-Qaeda in Yemen began a shooting spree that started in the offices of the magazine *Charlie Hebdo* in Paris, where cartoonists had been publishing images of the Prophet Muhammad—images that sickened some hearts, and maddened others. Seventeen people were killed. In the days that followed, millions demonstrated all over France: *Je suis Charlie.* I am Charlie. Fists were raised. In the week after the massacre, scores of Muslims were attacked all over the country. Now police are everywhere—on the street, in the markets, in the train stations—where they march up and down the halls in balletic processions, loaded weapons cradled in their arms. There is simmering anger in the air, and a brooding suspicion. In the metro last week, a man walked by me, squinting darkly, and said one word under his breath, and out into the world: *Sauvage.* Savage.

Even beyond the situation in France, it's impossible not to sense a cracking and breaking in the wider world order: civil wars, uprisings, and crackdowns in Turkey and the Middle East; ever-evolving war zones in Afghanistan and Iraq; escalating clashes on the Russian borders; and then, in the frightful assertions of the natural world—upsurges of hurricanes and earthquakes and once-toppled diseases. All over Europe and the United States, you can feel the rumblings of nationalism and populism, in perilous cocktail forms. So many places where peoples go from being friends to antagonists to shape-shifting enemies, as regions snap into semi-states subsisting on semi-economies, and warrior bands turn into warrior states, and on and on and on it goes.

As the earth tilts and we move, again, from places of peace to places of war, a man, a woman, a family, a village, a people—whole rough bands of thousands upon thousands of souls—are now finding their way into flight. Again.

Most especially, eyes are on Syria today, where millions have been pushed out of their homelands into whatever territory will have them. In Lebanon alone, over a million Syrian refugees are living however they can. Soon, they say, the center will no longer hold, and refugees from that part of the world will be reaching European borders en masse. A tidal wave. Then, from North Africa, another heartbreaking crisis is in motion. Many thousands have been fleeing the continent on flimsy rubber boats, across the Mediterranean Sea. And though distances are short, the sea is still rough and mighty. By now, thousands have drowned in that sea, in the hopes of reaching solid new ground.

If you strain, you can almost hear the tocsin sound, you can almost see the danger sign light up the sky: "Beware! These are now—right now—terrible times!"

I sit down at a bench in the CADA courtyard in Le Chambon on a bright March day. Since I was last here, the composition of the CADA community has changed again. Some of the families I know have been granted asylum and moved on. Others have been refused asylum and have been given official notice that they must leave the territory of France. These have gathered their things tearfully and said good-bye. Larissa is gone; Arubika is gone; Rosine's family is gone. The police— who move back and forth through public spaces, their automatic weapons cradled in their arms—could arrest and deport them and their families at any moment, sending them off to goodness knows what, goodness knows where.

But for now, at least, these families at CADA are still safe. And as I sit here at the bench in their courtyard, it seems like the whole tilted world walks by: the gentle-faced man from Kosovo who now lives in Larissa's old apartment, with his little family; the engineer from Yemen, whose wife is still stuck in the civil war back home; the tall young man from Sierra Leone who tightens his lips when he says that his parents have both died, and his sister back home is in danger of Ebola. And then, in the form of a young woman with a black scarf surrounding a round and milky-white face, Chechnya walks by, anew.

She is holding a little brown bird in her hands; it is small like a sparrow, with eyes like a hawk. See, she says, it would have died if she'd left it in the road where it had fallen.

One morning—a thick and foggy Sunday—I finally decide to go to a service at the Protestant church in Le Chambon. *Aimez-vous les uns les autres.* Muriel texted me in the morning to say that Esther would be there, and I've been longing to see her again. The church inside is simple and modest. The pastor, at the same pulpit where André Trocmé stood during the war, speaks about love and purity, about releasing oneself from vanity. His voice rings out in a singsong, while a small light at his lectern casts a great, winglike shadow behind him on the wall every time he raises his arms.

I've been hearing through the grapevine that folks in the Plateau—with no particular connection to CADA—have taken in a family from Syria. They've also been finding places for African refugees who made the perilous journey to France over the Mediterranean, and who have been staying temporarily in the basement of a church in Saint-Étienne. Without my paying attention, a whole new season of shelter—commensurate with the tilt of the world out there—has begun in the Plateau.

There is so much to think about, and the air, though hazy and damp, is so sweet on this spring day. And yet, I've been having nightmares again. I decide to try again for a long walk on the train tracks, thinking maybe it will help to clear my head and heart a little. It's my first time back since the lightning storm. I head out on the rails, on the stones, higher and deeper again, around one bend, and then another.

When I reach the spot over La Maison des Roches, I stop. I sit down on the tracks. There's no danger of a train today. No barking dogs. No lightning. No rush. Just a gentle blanketing silvery gray fog, and the vision down below of a stone house where a young man once worked, and from which he went from prodigality to having saved, in a moment, a life or two or three or more—and from saving those lives, to having saved the universe.

Not long ago, I was able to read the eulogy that Pastor Poivre offered for Daniel, after news of Daniel's death finally reached the Plateau. "Daniel was good," he wrote. "Fundamentally good, of a goodness I judged excessive, even. It was, to my eyes, his greatest flaw. Because this scientist, trained in analysis, adept at creating a rational argument and avoiding rash hypotheses and constructions, from the moment he passed from the abstract to the real, from science to life, revealed an ironclad optimism. This optimism prevented him not only from seeing malice in others, but from even suspecting it, and this was certainly not someone who would have known how to unmask the emissaries of Satan, disguised as angels of light."

Daniel was excessively good, whatever that means. Okay. Daniel was rational—a scientist!—until life intervened, and he fell into an irrational optimism, no longer to see malice.

But from you, Daniel, I want to know:

How does your argument go?

I suppose if you want to know what an answer looks like in a given field of inquiry, you have to first know what matters to that field—the component parts, in other words, of the question. So, an answer in physics depends on how it delimits what matters to it. Things like: Mass. Speed. Force. Direction. Time. In physics, you can ask: How fast will this marble roll down this hill? How much destruction will it create when I drop it off the top of the Empire State Building? If it were rotating around the sun, what path would it take? If it were traveling close to the speed of light, what would its dimensions be? Physics is a marvel partly because its curiosity is, in fact, very narrow. By narrowing and limiting its scope, by knowing very precisely what questions matter to it, physics and math merge toward their common vernacular. So, an answer in physics might be something like "24 miles" or "23.5 degrees," or it might be an equation that demonstrates some kind of truth about relationships between things, in elegant ciphers: Energy equals mass times the speed of light, squared. And the bomb goes off.

An answer in biology would be different. Biology cares about many more things than physics does. It cares about growth and death and change—already far larger concepts than mass, speed, direction, spin, and the like. Can you make a variable and a formula in biology? For certain things that merge well with probabilities, yes. You can ask: How big will a community of starfish grow? How long will these starfish live, here? How quickly might a species evolve? An answer in biology, when carefully framed, might still look like a formula, with a specific unit attached, like, say, x number of years until global warming causes the destruction of a marine ecosystem. Or a community of polar bears. But an answer in biology—its questions so much larger and fuller than in physics—might also look like a lot of description and a lot of broad concerns about living things that can't be stuffed into narrow variables.

The more things you care about—the more things you think are important when you ask questions—the harder it is to make an elegant little equation your answer. When sciences act as if it is possible—or falsely narrow their variables into equations, as in much of economics or political science—they fail us. Goodness knows, they can't reliably predict the rise and fall of power and fortune in the world as they claim to be able to do. Goodness knows, there are consequences to that sort of hubris.

Even sociocultural anthropology has dabbled with the equation-as-answer now and then, though generally it throws the door open unapologetically wide for every kind of question, every imaginable variable: What do we think, feel, work at, dream at, fight for, make wealth from, make poetry from? Answers in anthropology go to other, non-equation places—toward the acknowledgment, say, of patterns and relationships, toward an insistence on how relevance works within a certain context, all while throwing the kinds of things you might stuff into an equation right into the winds.

So what is an answer, really?

Even if you could define every single variable—everything that mattered—to a human being, it doesn't take a math genius to understand that a system made of five variables is complex. But a system made of twenty variables? Of fifty?

All that to say: As complex and miraculous as a star is, even I, a poor lapsed anthropologist, know that a starfish is—in its growth, its movement, its spark of sentience—mathematically speaking, orders of magnitude more complex, more miraculous than a star.

And a human being, wandering through the tilted world with her questions and her imperatives and her hands upraised under the sun, is, for all intents and purposes, infinitely more complex and more miraculous than even that.

So if someone were making a science of . . . you or your people, which five or twenty or fifty variables would you chose as relevant? Would you say your faith matters? Or your kith or clan or country? Or your social position? Which variables would you leave out? Would your dreams count? Or the smell of your grandmother's house? What it was like to be crouched and starving in a train? Or to raise a fist, righteously?

What is an answer?

DANIEL LOVED THE LITTLE CRICKETS. He loved his fellow prisoners. He loved to distraction. Loved to excess. Villagers in the Plateau—though they didn't know who or what lay behind their door at night when they heard banging—loved, when they opened the door. Now, Sandrine loves her students, even if loving them means that someday one might come in and kill another.

Love is a lodestar. Love sits there—containing its ten, hundred, immeasurable thousands of variables—waiting to be solved once, twice, three times, a hundred times, a thousand times until there is some kind of mastery of the practice of loving. Love, about which Martin Luther King, Jr., said, "Jesus wasn't playing," is a lodestar—with variables yet undiscovered. Still, it must be sought, it still has to be tried out, lived in each moment, for it to become habit. For it to become part of the warp and weft of a character to such a degree that someday, when the winds blow and the tocsin sounds, that character will do the right thing.

Every religion tells you that you must love your neighbor. That you must love strangers. That you must love one another, *Aimez-vous les uns les autres*, "with a love that is true and sincere." Every religion I know guides with that lodestar.

Jesus asked, "Do men gather grapes of thorns, or figs of thistles?"

Who really lives by love? "Ye shall know them by their fruits." Not by their family, or their country, or their religion, or their philosophy, or their race, or their vocation. Not by their color, or their caste, or their intelligence, or their bloodline, or even by their glowing self-assurance that they are right. But by their fruits.

At any given moment of this life, you can fear or you can love—you can gather grapes or thorns. You can gather carob pods, too, for your time wandering in the desert. In this big wide world of pain and flight and suffering and drowning and barbed wire and guns going off, love is a guiding star. But it is also a cipher, a variable-crammed mystery.

You start in the regular logic of the rational world and you seek and you seek—and, if you are good, you use the gorgeous organ that you were given, your analytical mind—but somewhere along the way, as you seek . . . your heart skips. And then you love. You really love. The kind of love where you forget your own smallness, your own limitations, your own fear. And then, that day, you are different. And then, lo and behold, you've lived things that are real. And, more than a stone, more than a bone, more than an ash or a seed or a tree, those things you have become—the content of those loving acts—turn out to be eternal.

Every moment, in such a life, is a question. Every moment, every smallest thing, is vivid, electric, a variable-crammed mystery to solve. And then solve again.

Muriel brings me three wild pansies as a gift, for no reason. Tells me she knows—she is sure—that Daniel is with us right now. My neighbor, birdlike, sits with me on my stair now and talks with me about things of the spirit, and pats my leg and, when we take our leave, gives me kisses on the cheek, firmer than ever. Rovzan opens a space for me at her table with her children *one-two-three*, as if that space were always mine; out of the quiet, her children begin humming to themselves, each their own song.

Who does what with whom?

There is no holy man, it seems—not for us, the earthbound, anyway. No man of any particular philosophy or idea or religion. There is only a man, made holy by having loved.

And there is no holy place—no country, no village, no hamlet, no desert, no island, nor even any Plateau—that is, in itself, holy by the borders that delimit it. There is only a place, made holy by the aggregate acts of love within. Then, the desert blooms like a rose.

That's the science of it.

I take Muriel's three pansies. I touch my hand to the cheek my neighbor has kissed. I close my eyes and I see myself on a tightrope wire, between the two needle peaks of the Drus.

I have been a creature of so many fears. What would it mean to just let them go?

I open a book again, in my mind's eyes. It is the book my teacher gave me back when I was in the hospital, that one night, afraid. The book I so learned to cherish. My *Little Prince*.

ANTOINE DE SAINT-EXUPÉRY died in a plane crash, perhaps over the Rhône Valley, in July 1944, just three months after Daniel. It was the last flight for a man who, before the start of the war, had spent years working as a pilot with the mail service, flying for exhilarating stretches over the mountains and plains and deserts of Europe, South America, and Africa, alone under the millions and millions of stars.

That crash was not his first. Once, he and a partner had been attempting to break a speed record over the Sahara. The two survived the impact, but were alone in a long desolate stretch of great sand dunes, with minimal supplies. First, food was gone—the orange, the grapes, the crackers. Then water was gone. Then they began to see vivid mirages. Then they could no longer spit. Their teeth chattered with the killing cold at night. Their bodies, after several days and nights and many miles of trudging on and on, were about to fail. Their throats were closing. They would die very soon.

The Little Prince began where that story ended—after a plane crash, with a figure approaching a pilot in the lonely desert. That figure, in real life, was a Bedouin wearing a great turban. The man put his hands on their shoulders. He had water to give them. They drank like cows, their faces inside a basin on the ground.

Saint-Exupéry had this to say about the episode:

You, Bedouin of Libya who saved our lives, though you will dwell forever in my memory, yet I shall never be able to recapture your features. You are Humanity and your face comes to my mind simply as man incarnate. You, our beloved fellowman, did not know who we might be, and yet you recognized us without fail. And I, in my turn, shall recognize you in the faces of all mankind. . . . All my friends and all my enemies marched towards me in your person. It did not seem to me that you were rescuing me; rather did it seem that you were forgiving me. And I felt I had no enemy left in all the world.

It is a verdant land, the land where one sees well. With the heart.

＊

It is now autumn in the Plateau. I'm back in the little apartment near the woods. My cell phone rings.

It is Marie-Hélène of the quiet face, of the beautiful hands. How are you? I ask. Well, in fact, she says, it's been an interesting day.

She and her husband had, in recent months, been housing an African family—a mother, father, and two children. Because the family spoke no French but some English, I translated for them a little while. The mother—who possesses a great gap-toothed smile, and wears brilliant greens and yellows—was pregnant when they all came over the Mediterranean Sea in a raft. The father told me the whole story of his work on the African trade routes, and of the Arabs who could lead you through the thousands of miles of roiling desert by reading the stars, and of how the real danger of their journey was the sea itself. We all held hands around the table before food was served. The children ate Marie-Hélène's cake with relish, then played in her well-lit living room.

The African family lived with Marie-Hélène's family for many months. They thrived in the Plateau. Marie-Hélène would send me photographs of them from time to time, with notes about their progress. Their massive paperwork was completed while I was away, and now they are living elsewhere, officially, hoping to gain some real status in France.

Now, on the other end of the phone, Marie-Hélène tells me about her interesting day. The church that had been offering emergency shelter to these African families in its basement in Saint-Étienne has now been ordered by the authorities to close operations. This means that tonight, with the first frost of the year, the African families will be out in the cold. Something must be done. Marie-Hélène and a group of volunteers are going to Saint-Étienne to see if anyone needs a place to stay.

Is there anything I can do?

So that is how I find myself now in the backseat of a little car this dark night, roaming through the streets of Saint-Étienne with Marie-Hélène, her husband, and their son, looking for a man named Clarence, who apparently speaks no French. With the help of some directions from his friends, and the apps on our phones, we are doing the best we can to find Clarence. The streets are narrow and almost empty at this hour. And on and on we go, with our phones insistently failing us—and no particular stars to guide us—into the corners of the dark.

We know nothing about Clarence, except his name.

Marie-Hélène prepared a room in her house earlier today, just in case it would be needed. And she asked if I could translate, when the time came. There will be some rules, she tells me, for their guest: no smoking in the house, leave your boots at the door, and the like. The room has a dresser in it, and there is a private bathroom next door. And, Marie-Hélène tells me, if I could stay for dinner, that might help—though she knows, from experience, the stranger might not be hungry right away.

We drive and drive through the streets of Saint-Étienne, searching. Finally, in the distance, a man with a little rolling suitcase and a backpack appears. Closer, we see that he is looking into the pin light of a flip phone, winding into the city alone.

We drive up to him. We stop.

The car door opens; we see a face, so tired, so sad.

Clarence sits down in the car in the back, right next to me. He closes his eyes.

Darling, says a silent voice, to Marie-Hélène; to the face, so sad; to me: Where can we look for you soon?

And with that question—the answer—out into the dark threaded night we drive again, still and small: outward, then upward, upward.

Upward.

Acknowledgments

I wish I could write a pen portrait of each and every person to whom I am indebted for this book—and include the signs and wonders of their gifts and their offerings. I can't do that—not now.

But some of you I simply must name here, because in the course of my long journey, I needed you so.

Thank you:

Diane Afoumado, Henry Aubin, Philip Barnard, Victoria Barnett, Véronique Belin, Gérard Bollon, Rivka Brot, Kate Brown, Cindy Buckley, Aline Chastagnier, Anne-Marie Chastagnier, Anne Chazot-Philibert, Ron Coleman, Darcy Courteau, Jo-Ellyn Decker, Gili Diamant, Kelly Doe, Ada Emmett, Becky Erbelding, Shirin Ershadi, Helen Faller, David Finkel, Sharon Fisher, Peggy Frankston, Nida Gelazis Johansson, Corry Guttstadt, Hope Harrison, Krista Hegburg, Karleen King, Katharine Kripke, Fanny Kyriakides, Steve Lagerfeld, Mirta Lopez, Sovaida Ma'ani-Ewing, Johanna Merritt Wu, Magali Micaelli, Roger Montel, Ali Nakhjavani, Shiraz Nerenberg, Eliot Nidam Orvieto, Anne Nivat, Danielle Olgiati-Trocmé, Marlaina Palmeri, Barbara Paxson, Dana Paxson and Fran Carlisi-Paxson, Elizabeth Paxson, Florence Paxson and Chuck Littman, Lucian Perkins and Sarah Tanguy, Kathy Powers, Bob and Debbie Rosenfeld, Claire Sauvignet, Doc and Chou Chou Scantlin (and the entire Imperial Palms Orchestra, especially Sugar, Moxie, Gigi, and Belle-Bright), Sharona Shuster, Mark and Paula Siskind, Vincent Slatt, Sabrina Tavernise, Nicolette van der Linden, Axel and the dear, late

Jacqueline van der Linden, Teryl Watson, Diana Wells, Georgina Wilson, Ken and Carolyn Wilson, and Sufian Zhemukhov.

And, in memoriam, thank you:

Àli-Akbar Furútan, Firuz Kazemzadeh, Dr. Peter Khan, Rabbi Allan Levine, Margaret Lindsay, Dorothy and Gordon Paxson, Cecile and Sheldon Siskind, Suzanne Trocmé-Sweany, and, ever, Daniel Trocmé.

Also: I am immensely grateful for a fellowship I received early on—the Miles Lerman Center for the Study of Jewish Resistance Research Fellowship—from the Jack, Joseph and Morton Mandel Center for Advanced Holocaust Studies at the United States Holocaust Memorial Museum. Aside from providing me with crucial material assistance, the Center welcomed me into a community of scholars who have, with exceeding generosity, enriched my life and my work. The Center is also home to the most knowledgeable, passionate, creative, large-hearted librarians and archivists a researcher could ever hope to know. I am grateful as well for the warm welcome given me by George Washington University's Elliott School of International Affairs—in particular by its directors Dr. Hope Harrison and Dr. Henry Hale—who offered me a landing spot when I first returned to research. Later, Dr. Tom Banchoff, the then director of the Berkley Center for Religion, Peace & World Affairs, gave me yet another institutional base at Georgetown University. Thanks to you all.

I am indebted, as well, to *Aeon* magazine and *The Wilson Quarterly*, where I first worked through some of the ideas that would form the core of this book.

And I am so grateful to the members of my Grand Jury 1 family here in Washington, D.C. You have no idea how you refreshed my spirit over these years, when I needed it most.

And to Riverhead Books, for the dazzling talents and energies the team put into the making of this book. I am especially indebted to my editor, Becky Saletan; Ashley Gardner, publicist; Amanda Dewey, interior designer; Lauren Peters-Collaer, jacket designer; and Muriel Jorgensen, copy editor.

And:

Thanks to every single person with whom I crossed paths in the Plateau—you taught me by example. Thanks to every single refugee of the Second World War who shared their terrible and remarkable stories with the world. Thanks to every single family of today's asylum seekers who invited me into their lives, and whose beautiful names, for the sake of privacy and safety, I was forced to leave out.

Please know that this book is my love letter to every one of you, and that I have tried—with the best efforts of my own imperfect mind and heart—to honor your stories.

Finally, there are three people without whom I could never have told this story:

Rob McQuilkin, my agent and a brilliant wonder: huge of heart, brimming with enthusiasm, encouragement, poetry, and wise counsel—my food and water in the hardest moments. Thank you, dear Rob.

Becky Saletan, my editor at Riverhead, who—pointing her keenest eye, and pen, and ear, and heart, down into this work—made it deeper and truer than it ever would have been without her. Thank you, dear Becky.

Charles King, my *bashert*, who saw it all. Who heard it all. Who listened. Who helped me; who saved me. Who knew how to offer the holy words when I needed them most. Who is my one rose, among the hundreds of millions of stars. Thank you, my darling.

A Note on Sources

This is a work of observation and interpretation that relies most heavily on my own travels to the Plateau Vivarais-Lignon, and the time I spent there doing the work of an anthropologist: listening, talking, working alongside people, accompanying them on their everyday tasks. The people of the Plateau—those who have lived there for generations and those who have only recently arrived—have grown dear to me and have given me more gifts of the mind and spirit than I can ever fully describe, let alone repay.

For the historical portions of this book, the stories and testimonies I recount are drawn from a variety of papers, letters, and other written and recorded evidence in publicly available archives and collections, often in digital or online formats, or in published collections noted below. My interpretation of a specific incident may differ from that of some historians in cases where I have found that the documentary evidence points in another direction.

Daniel Trocmé's letters have been excerpted in a number of published sources, but I also consulted the originals in the André Trocmé and Magda Trocmé Papers, Swarthmore College Peace Collection. Eyewitness accounts assembled in support of the award of Righteous Among the Nations to Daniel, André, and Magda Trocmé, as well as to other key individuals on the Plateau, are housed at Yad Vashem in Jerusalem. The stories of several Holocaust survivors who spent time in the Plateau come mainly from their video testimonies in the USC Shoah Foundation

Visual History Archive and interviews conducted by the United States
Holocaust Memorial Museum's Oral History Collection.

Other major repositories include the United States Holocaust Memorial Museum Archives (including the archive of the International Tracing Service), the Société d'Histoire de la Montagne, the Fondation pour
la Mémoire de la Déportation, the Comité Français pour Yad Vashem,
the Mémorial de la Shoah, the Anonymes, Justes et Persécutés Durant la
Période Nazie dans les Communes de France (ajpn.org), the French National Archives (Archives Nationales), and the Service Historique de la
Défense.

I am especially grateful to Danielle Olgiati-Trocmé, niece and namesake of Daniel Trocmé, who showed me a privately published family
memoir by her father, François, and let me see beautiful family photos,
hold Daniel's Medal of the Righteous in my own hands, and bask in her
marvelous presence for three days. Gérard Bollon shared his profound
understanding of the history of the Plateau Vivarais-Lignon and guided
me toward deeper conclusions than I might have ever come to on my
own. Pierre Sauvage and Patrick Henry, noted authorities on the Plateau, kindly connected me with people and resources early on. Like
many before me, I am also thankful to Nelly Trocmé—daughter of André and Magda—who has done so much to preserve the memory of some
of the extraordinary people whose lives I have been privileged to come
to know.

I am indebted to the research and writings of historians, archivists,
and other experts from whom I have drawn specific details in the unfolding of the wartime history of the Plateau Vivarais-Lignon, the village
of Le Chambon-sur-Lignon, and the Holocaust in France, or who have
republished original documents and other information. Works that I
found especially important include: Amir D. Aczel, *The Artist and the
Mathematician*; Serge Bernard, *Traces légendaires, mémoires et construction identitaire: Étude socio-historique d'une "presqu'île" cévenole en
Haute-Loire*; Serge Bernard et al., eds., *Les résistances sur le Plateau
Vivarais-Lignon, 1938–1945*; Philip Boegner, *"Ici, on a aimé les juifs"*;

Pierre Bolle, ed., *Le Plateau Vivarais-Lignon: Accueil et résistance 1939–1944*; Gérard Bollon, *Les villages sur la montagne: Entre Ardèche et Haute-Loire, le plateau, terre d'accueil et de refuge*; Roger Debiève, *Mémoires meurtries, mémoire trahie: Le Chambon-sur-Lignon*; Father Patrick Desbois, *The Holocaust by Bullets: A Priest's Journey to Uncover the Truth Behind the Murder of 1.5 Million Jews*; Deborah Durland DeSaix and Karen Gray Ruelle, *Hidden on the Mountain: Stories of Children Sheltered from the Nazis in Le Chambon*; Jean Durand, *Les contes de la Burle*; Nathalie Duval, *L'École des Roches*; Annick Flaud and Gérard Bollon, *Paroles de réfugiés, paroles de justes*; Eva Fogelman, *Conscience and Courage: Rescuers of the Jews During the Holocaust*; Gedenkstätte Buchenwald, ed. (compiled by Harry Stein), *Buchenwald Concentration Camp 1937–1945: A Guide to the Permanent Historical Exhibition*; Martin Gilbert, *The Righteous: The Unsung Heroes of the Holocaust* and *Atlas of the Holocaust*; Peter Grose, *A Good Place to Hide: How One French Community Saved Thousands of Lives During World War II*; Jan T. Gross, *Neighbors: The Destruction of the Jewish Community in Jedwabne, Poland* and *Fear: Anti-Semitism in Poland after Auschwitz: An Essay in Historical Interpretation*; Philip Hallie, *Lest Innocent Blood Be Shed: The Story of the Village of Le Chambon and How Goodness Happened There*; Patrick Henry, *We Only Know Men: The Rescue of Jews in France During the Holocaust*; Beate Husser et al., *Frontstalag 122, Compiègne-Royallieu: Un camp d'internement allemand dans l'Oise, 1941–1944*; Philippe Joutard et al., eds., *Cévennes: Terre de refuge 1940–1944*; Vjeran Katunarić, "On Relevance of the Peace Culture Concept in the Study of Ethnic Relations on Local Levels" (unpublished paper); Serge Klarsfeld, *La Shoah en France*; François Lecomte, *Jamais je n'aurai quatorze ans*; Jacques Lusseyran, *And There Was Light*; Michael R. Marrus and Robert O. Paxton, *Vichy France and the Jews*; Geoffrey P. Megargee, ed., *United States Holocaust Memorial Museum Encyclopedia of Camps and Ghettos, 1933–1945*; Pearl Oliner et al, eds., *Embracing the Other: Philosophical, Psychological, and Historical Perspectives on Altruism*; Samuel P. Oliner and Pearl M. Oliner, *The Altruistic Personality: Rescuers of Jews in Nazi Europe*; Charles

Rist, *Une saison gâtée: Journal de la guerre et de l'occupation 1939–1945*; Pierre Sauvage, *Weapons of the Spirit* (film); André Sellier, *A History of the Dora Camp: The Untold Story of the Nazi Slave Labor Camp That Secretly Manufactured V-2 Rockets*; Tracy Strong, Jr., *The Better Part of a Century*; Alice Resch Synnestvedt, *Over the Highest Mountains: A Memoir of Unexpected Heroism in France During World War II*; Nechama Tec, *When Light Pierced the Darkness*; Olivier Todd, *Albert Camus: A Life*; André Trocmé, *Jesus and the Nonviolent Revolution*; Richard P. Unsworth, *A Portrait of Pacifists: Le Chambon, the Holocaust, and the Lives of André and Magda Trocmé*; Christine van der Zanden, "The Plateau of Hospitality: Life on the Plateau Vivarais-Lignon" (dissertation); Maria Wiśnioch, *Majdanek: A Guide to the Historical Buildings*; Susan Zuccotti, *The Holocaust, the French, and the Jews*; as well as the writings of Albert Camus, Antoine de Saint-Exupéry, R. Frison-Roche, and Primo Levi, which inspired and devastated me throughout the writing of this book.

This book is also the record of a search. My faith orients me toward being a lifelong seeker, independently investigating truth. It has been my aim to show love and respect for the peoples of the world, the persons of the world, their homelands, and the holy texts and sacred Founders of their faith traditions.

The "holy words" referred to in Chapter 14 come from *The Fire Tablet* of Bahá'u'lláh. The "creeping things" quotation in Chapter 15 is from "Selections from the Writings of 'Abdu'l-Bahá."